BREAKING I1

A Ploughshares Anthology

BREAKING INTO PRINT

Early Stories and Insights
into Getting Published

Edited by DeWitt Henry

Beacon Press
BOSTON

Beacon Press
25 Beacon Street
Boston, Massachusetts 02108-2892
www.beacon.org

Beacon Press Books
are published under the auspices of the
Unitarian Universalist Association of Congregations.

05 04 03 02 01 00 8 7 6 5 4 3 2 1

This book is printed on acid-free paper that meets the uncoated paper
ANSI/NISO specifications for permanence as revised in 1992.

Text design by Wesley B. Tanner / Passim Editions
Composition by Wilsted & Taylor Publishing Services

Library of Congress Cataloging-in-Publication Data

Breaking into print : early stories and insights into getting published :
a Ploughshares anthology / edited by DeWitt Henry.
p. cm.
ISBN 0-8070-6235-9 (pbk.)
1. Short stories, American. 2. Short story—Authorship—Marketing.
3. Fiction—Authorship—Marketing. I. Henry, DeWitt.
PS648.S5 B73 2000
813'.0108—dc21   99-057070

For the memories of
Raymond Carver, Richard Yates,
Seymour Lawrence, Andre Dubus,
and Gina Berriault;
and for the past and present staff
and advisory editors of
Ploughshares

Contents

Introduction: Kept Promises
ix

Tim O'Brien: *Going After Cacciato*
1

Jayne Anne Phillips: *Gemcrack*
29

Sue Miller: *Expensive Gifts*
43

Carolyn Chute: *"Ollie, Oh . . ."*
54

Edward P. Jones: *A Dark Night*
74

Janet Desaulniers: *After Rosa Parks*
89

Mona Simpson: *Approximations*
115

Howard Norman: *Unicycle*
131

Melanie Rae Thon: *Little White Sister*
145

David Wong Louie: *Displacement*
164

Susan Straight: *Back*
184

Christopher Tilghman: *Mary in the Mountains*
192

David Gates: *A Wronged Husband*
209

Carolyn Ferrell: *Proper Library*
227

Gina Berriault: *The Infinite Passion of Expectation*
248

*Resources for Writers on Contemporary Writing Careers
and the Writing Life*
261

The Adventure: Recommended Literary Magazines for Short Fiction
272

Credits
283

Acknowledgments
285

Introduction: Kept Promises

Several of my graduate writing students were born thirty years ago, around the time that I cofounded *Ploughshares* (initially subtitled *A Literary Occasional*) with a handful of other young writers who felt exiled in the Cambridge-Boston of the time and whose sense of promise had been nurtured elsewhere and galvanized by the counterculture movements of the civil rights and Vietnam War years.

A few years earlier, while still an undergraduate at Amherst College and editor of the college literary magazine, I had felt discovered in the big world by Margaret Cousins, a romance writer and an editor at *McCall's,* who helped me find summer work at *Redbook* and took pains to recommend me to Robert Giroux, of Farrar, Straus and Giroux. Giroux looked at my novel in progress and took me out for lunch, where, as he may have done for many other young writers, he gave me a copy of Cyril Connelly's essay "The Enemies of Promise."

I still pass this essay on to my students. "Whom the gods wish to destroy," writes Connelly, "they first call promising. . . . Young writers if they are to mature require a period of between three and seven years in which to live down their promise." The enemies or hazards of maturing, as discussed by Connelly, include conversation, sloth ("that laziness which renders them incapable of doing the thing which they are most looking forward to"), sex, drugs, domesticity ("a writer who is not prepared to be lonely in his youth must if he is to succeed face loneliness in his middle age"), journalism, and success ("social, professional or popular"). Connelly quotes Van Wyck Brooks on the poison of success in America: "The chronic state of our literature is that of a youthful promise which is never redeemed." F. Scott Fitzgerald's "The Crack-Up" testifies with genius about "the failure to function," as does Tillie Olsen's *Silences.*

Ideally, the editor's role is that of recognizing and cultivating promise. In his 1985 essay "Writing in the Cold," Theodore Solotaroff wonders what has become of "all that bright promise" that he had discovered during a decade of editing the *New American Review,* since only about one-fourth of his discoveries have "gone on to have reasonably successful careers." Considering "why some gifted writers have careers and others don't," he cites *durability:* "For the gifted writer, durability seems to be directly connected to how one deals with uncertainty, rejection, and disappointment, from within as well as from without, and how effectively one incorporates them into the creative process itself, particularly in the prolonged first stage of a career."

Ploughshares functioned for the first few years as an editorial roundtable where each member of the group served as coordinating editor for a given issue. We saw enough in each other's work for mutual respect, solicited work from peers and established writers, responded to an ever increasing volume of unsolicited submissions, and sought collectively to attract an audience that we believed could and should exist. Later on, our policy of rotating editorship evolved into the practice of regularly having guest editors.

We were debating tastes, as many of us had already done in writing workshops and literature classes, both as students and as teachers. For instance, I recall arguing with other editors in favor of publishing Tim O'Brien's first fiction, "A Man of Melancholy Disposition," and his story "Going After Cacciato," and still later urging Tim himself as a coeditor to publish Jayne Anne Phillips's early story "El Paso" (her second in *Ploughshares*). We also had the help of more established, older writers, mentors who believed in us and in the integrity of our editorial passion and judgment, and, as issue by issue the magazine earned respect, we developed a wide network of writers, editors, and teachers who were dedicated to the discovery of new talent. Richard Yates, Richard Wilbur, George Garrett, Tillie Olsen, Seymour Lawrence, Donald Hall, and Frank Conroy—each of whom would suggest us to young writers, and young writers to us—deserve special mention.

In this anthology we are proud to collect stories that were remarkable as discoveries—"firsts" or early appearances in print by then unknown writers—and which now appear even more remarkable in hindsight as their authors have realized their early promise and made significant contributions to contemporary literature. Many of the writers represented in this volume have gone on to publish well-received collections and/or novels; most have earned wide readerships and won major fellowships and awards; and five have in turn come back to guest-edit issues of *Ploughshares*, and to discover and encourage the next generation of unknown, talented writers. Several have also published award-winning stories in *Ploughshares* at later stages in their careers, growing in mastery even as the magazine itself has grown. While celebrating fiction discoveries, I should mention that *Ploughshares* has never been exclusively a fiction magazine, and that a proud record exists for poets and nonfiction writers as well.

While in the 1970s we often viewed "the establishment" as repressive and indifferent to promise, *Ploughshares* and other literary magazines, largely funded by grants and volunteer zeal, helped writer after writer to attract attention from established agents, trade editors, and publishers.

The literary agent Maxine Groffsky, for instance, read Sue Miller's early work in *Ploughshares*, contacted her, and later sold her novel *The Good Mother* to Ted Solotaroff at Harper and Row. Sue Miller was astonished by the outcome. "Sales for paperback and movie rights radically altered Miller's income-tax bracket; the reviews were almost universally effusive in their praise; and the novel sold out and sold, and continues to sell—over 1.5 million copies to date. . . . She chose to look at the success . . . as a 'tenure' of sorts. She now had license to move on to different, more ambitious projects" (Don Lee, "About Sue Miller," *Ploughshares*, fall 1993).

In 1988, the novelist, teacher, and editor George Garrett edited a special issue of "Fiction Discoveries" for us, asking several established writers each to recommend and introduce a discovery. Andre Dubus introduced Christopher Tilghman's "Mary in the Mountains," an appearance that led to an agent and a sale a year later of *In a Father's Place* (the title story having just appeared in another *Ploughshares* issue) to Jonathan Galassi at Farrar, Straus and Giroux. Tilghman then guest-edited his own issue of *Ploughshares*, commenting that "honest practitioners of literary discovery operate from the work outwards, looking for the distinct voice, a promising mother lode of unusual material, or—quite a bit more rare—a natural gift for storytelling. One makes the selections, and then waits patiently to see what happens." To date, Tilghman's career includes two highly regarded collections of stories and a novel; he is now writer in residence at Emerson College and we share graduate students.

I have asked the writers whose works are included here for brief accounts of their early publication histories and used their responses as the basis for my headnotes to the selections, but the need to have work duly recognized and celebrated extends past the "discovery" stage of a writer's career. It seems fitting to reprint here our *re*discovery of Gina Berriault, whose early work appeared in *Stories for the Sixties,* edited by Richard Yates in 1963. Berriault went on to publish story collections and novels, but then went silent for nearly a decade. Her return to writing was marked by "The Infinite Passion of Expectation," published in a 1979 issue of *Ploughshares* along with an appreciation by Yates, who wrote, "Gina Berriault knows that ill-educated or inarticulate people are as sensitive as anyone else. She renders their speech with a fine and subtle ear for the shy or strident inaccuracies, for the bewilderment of missed points and for the dim, sad rhythms of cliches; but when she takes us into the silence of their minds, their thoughts and feelings come out in prose as graceful, as venturesome and as precise as she can make it. That's a rare ability, and reflects a rare degree of insight." Other Berriault stories soon followed, as did a new collection (bearing the title of the *Ploughshares* story) and a new novel, a reissue of her earlier books by North Point Press, a film script produced, a Guggenheim Fellowship, and other honors. Her most recent collection is *Women in Their Beds,* which in 1998 won both the National Book Critics Circle Award and the PEN Faulkner Award.

Keeping and fully realizing talent's promise—growing as a writer—is as much a personal as it is a cultural feat, depending on both persistence and luck in dilatory time. Many important writers are still out in the cold, winning awards and respected by their peers but supporting their writing with second jobs (primarily teaching). Their example should serve to inspire young writers as much as the example of writers who have "broken through," those who have reached large audiences while continuing to function with integrity and high art.

Approaching my sixties now, I have accomplished more as an editor and teacher than as a writer, but as a writer, whenever I feel discouraged by still incompleted or unpublished work, I invoke the figure of Andre Dubus, who survived debilitating physical trauma as well as divorces and the complications of a lived life and through it all continued to grow and to function fully as an artist while also sharing his deep vocation with others. I think of Tim O'Brien and James Alan McPherson, of Gina Berriault, of writers who will not be silenced by life or culture but remain dedicated to their talents and *write*. And then, always, there is the work itself, whoever the author, sometimes famous, sometimes unknown, sometimes even me. There is exhilaration in the art itself. As Tim O'Brien wrote in the 1996 issue of *Ploughshares* that he guest-edited, "I am now a cheerleader. . . . [Here] is a story that makes me do cartwheels and yell, 'Wow—read this!' . . . It's the woven *wow* that endures . . . stomach squeezes mind."

Since 1988, *Ploughshares* has been published at Emerson College, where it has flourished and has engaged yet another generation of writers and readers. The editor responsible for its second life is Don Lee, who graduated as Emerson's first master of fine arts in creative writing in 1986, served as managing editor and fiction editor, and, since 1991, as editor. Among the magazine's many discoveries during his tenure is Carolyn Ferrell, whose story "Proper Library" he found in the slush pile. The story was taken by guest editor Al Young for the spring of 1993 issue, then was selected for *Best American Short Stories, 1994,* and recently was included in *Best American Short Stories of the Century.* Ferrell's initial publication in *Ploughshares* also caught the attention of Houghton Mifflin's Janet Silver, who gave Ferrell a contract for her collection in progress, *Don't Erase Me;* the book came out in 1997 and won the

Los Angeles Times Award for First Fiction and *Ploughshares'* John C. Zacharis First Book Award.

Raymond Carver, whose best work, "A Small, Good Thing," appeared in *Ploughshares* in 1982, and who later guest-edited a fiction issue in which he introduced Mona Simpson, has written about his own background as an M.F.A. student of John Gardner's at Chico State: "[Gardner] introduced us to the 'little' or literary periodicals. . . . He told us that this was where most of the best fiction in the country just about all the poetry was appearing. I felt wild with discovery in those days" (Carver, "Creative Writing 101," from the foreword to John Gardner's *On Being a Novelist* [Knopf, 1983]).

We offer this anthology in hopes it might convey conviction in promise and in the adventure of literary discovery. We hope that it encourages experimentation on the part of young writers; that it offers a range of literary styles and forms that reflects not only the past thirty years but the future of American society; and that it offers a range of urgent subjects and voices and suggests various contexts in which to appreciate new works. The magazine is a living anthology, as dynamic as the writers themselves, who continue to persist, to grow, and to explore in time. Our purview is possibility and the process of discovery.

A Note on Shoptalk

From its earliest issues *Ploughshares* has included editorial keynotes and introductions, interviews with writers, essays of appreciation, and book reviews. The flavor of these discussions has been that of impassioned shoptalk between writers about writing, and is reflected in the excerpts from the magazine presented as "shoptalk" reflections interleaved throughout this collection.

—*DeWitt Henry*

TIM O'BRIEN

Going After Cacciato

In 1973, Boston publisher Seymour Lawrence suggested that I read Tim O'Brien's account of serving in Vietnam, If I Die in a Combat Zone, *and write to O'Brien asking for fiction for* Ploughshares. *At the time, O'Brien was working as a national affairs reporter for the* Washington Post. *I wrote a fan letter, impressed in literary terms by the Orwellian clarity of the book and in personal terms by our similar ages and the fact that O'Brien had been drafted and served in Vietnam while I had been granted prolonged draft deferments for graduate school: O'Brien had, in fact, lived my worst nightmare. I also wrote that I was editing a "special realism issue" of* Ploughshares *in response to the prevailing fashion of the times for "innovative writing," summed up best by John Barth's proclamation that realism was an "aberration in the history of literature."*

In return, O'Brien sent me "A Man of Melancholy Disposition," intended as a chapter in his first novel, then under contract to Seymour Lawrence. This story appeared in Ploughshares *in 1974, along with stories by Richard Yates, Brian Moore, Andre Dubus, and James Alan McPherson; it was left out of the novel* Northern Lights, *which was published in 1976. O'Brien meanwhile had moved to Cambridge to pursue graduate study at Harvard, and that same year we coedited* Ploughshares *3, no. 1 (with Henry Bromell), to which Tim contributed another story, "Going After Cacciato." After "Cacciato" appeared, a commercial magazine offered Tim several thousand dollars*

1

*for it, but then withdrew the offer, to his agent's consternation, when
they discovered it had already been published in* Ploughshares. *Subsequently it was reprinted in* Best American Short Stories, 1977 *and*
The Pushcart Prize II. *I had no idea at the time that it would prove
to be the first chapter of another novel still to come.*

*O'Brien coedited fiction with me again for James Randall's 1977
issue, acquiring a story from John Irving, whom he had met as a fellow
staff member at the Bread Loaf Writers' Conference, just before Irving
published* The World According to Garp *(this story, in fact, was included as one of Garp's own four stories within the novel). Tim had also
become friends with John Gardner at Bread Loaf, and perhaps that
encounter prompted some of Tim's explorations of magical realism in*
Going After Cacciato *the novel.* Going After Cacciato *was published
in 1978 and won the 1979 National Book Award (prevailing over* The
World According to Garp).

*O'Brien taught briefly in 1980 as writer in residence at Emerson
College, but has written full-time for a living throughout his career. His
generosity to younger writers has taken the form of his staff role at
Bread Loaf and, later, at the Joiner Institute and at other writers' conferences. His next contribution to* Ploughshares *appeared in the issue
edited by Raymond Carver in 1983; "Quantum Jumps," which also
won a Pushcart Prize, was adapted from his then upcoming novel*
The Nuclear Age *(1985). Most recently, O'Brien edited fiction for*
Ploughshares 21, no. 4, *in 1995 (with Mark Strand editing poetry).*

Tim O'Brien's story cycle (spiral might be a more apt term) The
Things They Carried *appeared in 1990, was immediately hailed as a
masterpiece, and has since held up as an influential classic, which I am
privileged to discuss semester after semester with graduate students. It
was followed by the 1994 novel* In the Lake of the Woods *and by
O'Brien's disturbing confession of depression in the essay "The Vietnam
in Me" (*New York Times Magazine, *October 4, 1994), which in turn*

was followed by a public announcement of his decision to stop writing. The witty and timely Tomcat in Love *is his most recent novel (1998) and was a Book of the Month Club selection. A dedicated O'Brien fan manages a web page worth visiting at* http://www.illyria.com/ tobhp.html; *in addition to full bibliographical and biographical information, the homepage currently has one link to O'Brien reading from* Tomcat in Love, *and another to a letter of commiseration from the protagonist, Thomas Chippering, to President Clinton over the Lewinsky scandal. Tobey C. Herzog has published a full-length study,* Tim O'Brien, *in Twayne's United States Authors Series (1997).*

It was a bad time. Billy Boy Watkins was dead, and so was Frenchie Tucker. Billy Boy had died of fright, scared to death on the field of battle, and Frenchie Tucker had been shot through the neck. Lieutenants Sidney Martin and Walter Gleason had died in tunnels. Pederson was dead and Bernie Lynn was dead. Buff was dead. They were all among the dead. The war was always the same, and the rain was part of the war. The rain fed fungus that grew in the men's socks and boots, and their socks rotted, and their feet turned white and soft so that the skin could be scrapped off with a fingernail, and Stink Harris woke up screaming one night with a leech on his tongue. When it was not raining, a low mist moved like sleep across the paddies, blending the elements into a single gray element, and the war was cold and pasty and rotten. Lieutenant Corson, who came to replace Lieutenant Martin, contracted the dysentery. The tripflares were useless. The ammunition corroded and the foxholes filled with mud and water during the nights, and in the mornings there was always the next village and the war was always the same. In early September Vaught caught an infection. He'd been showing Oscar Johnson the sharp edge on his bayonet, drawing it swiftly along his forearm and peeling off a layer of mushy skin. "Like a Gillette blueblade," Vaught had grinned. It did not bleed, but in a few days the bacteria soaked in and the arm turned yellow, and Vaught was carried aboard a Huey that dipped perpendicular, blades clutching at granite air, rising in its own wet wind and taking Vaught away. He never returned to the war. Later they had a letter from him that described Japan as smoky and full of bedbugs, but in the enclosed snapshot Vaught looked happy enough, posing with two sightly nurses, a long-stemmed bottle of wine rising from between his thighs. It was a shock to learn that he'd lost the arm. Soon afterward Ben Nystrom shot himself in the foot, but he did not die, and he wrote no letters. These were all things to talk about. The rain, too. Oscar said it made him think of Detroit in the month of May. "Not the rain," he liked to say. "Just the dark and gloom. It's Number One weather for rape and looting. The fact is, I do ninety-eight percent of my total rape and looting in weather just like this." Then somebody would say that Oscar had a pretty decent imagination for a nigger.

That was one of the jokes. There was a joke about Oscar. There were many jokes about Billy Boy Watkins, the way he'd collapsed in fright on the field of glorious battle. Another joke was about the lieutenant's dysentery, and another was about Paul Berlin's purple biles. Some of the jokes were about Cacciato, who was a dumb, Stink said, as a bullet, or, Harol Murphy said, as an oyster fart.

In October, at the end of the month, in the rain, Cacciato left the war.

"He's gone away," said Doc Peret. "Split for parts unknown."

The lieutenant didn't seem to hear. He was too old to be a lieutenant, anyway. The veins in his nose and cheeks were shattered by booze. Once he had been a captain on the way to being a major, but whiskey and the fourteen dull years between Korea and Vietnam had ended all that, and now he was just an old lieutenant with the dysentery. He lay on his back in the pagoda, naked except for green socks and green undershorts.

"Cacciato," Doc Peret repeated. "He's gone away. Split, departed."

The lieutenant did not sit up. He held his belly with both hands as if no contain the disease.

"He's gone to Paris," Dock sid. "That's what he tells Paul Berlin, anyhow, and Paul Berlin tells me, so I'm telling you. He's gone, packed up and gone."

"Paree," the lieutenant said softly. "In France, Paree? *Gay* Paree?"

"Yes, sir. That's what he says. That's what he told Paul Berlin, and that's what I'm telling you. You ought to cover up, sir."

The lieutenant sighed. He pushed himself up, breathing loud, then sat stiffly before a can of Sterno. He lit the Sterno and cupped his hands around the flame and bent down, drawing in the heat. Outside, the rain was steady. "Paree," he said wearily. "You're saying Cacciato's left for gay Paree, is that right?"

"That's what he said, sir. I'm just relaying what he told to Paul Berlin. Hey, really, you better cover yourself up."

"Who's Paul Berlin?"

"Right here, sir. This is Paul Berlin."

The lieutenant looked up. His eyes were bright blue, oddly out of place in the sallow face. "You Paul Berlin?"

"Yes, sir," said Paul Berlin. He pretended to smile.

"Geez, I thought you were Vaught."

"Vaught's the one who cut himself, sir."

"I thought that was you. How do you like that?"

"Fine, sir."

The lieutenant sighed and shook his head sadly. He held a boot to dry over the burning Sterno. Behind him in the shadows sat the crosslegged, roundfaced Buddha, smiling benignly from its elevated perch. The pagoda was cold. Dank and soggy from a month of rain, the place smelled of clays and silicates and old incense. It was a single square room, built like a pillbox with a flat ceiling that forced the soldiers to stoop and kneel. Once it might have been an elegant house of worship, neatly tiled and painted and clean, candles burning in holders at the Buddha's feet, but now it was bombed-out junk. Sandbags blocked the windows. Bits of broken pottery lay under chipped pedestals. The Buddha's right arm was missing and his fat groin was gouged with shrapnel. Still, the smile was intact. Head cocked, he seemed interested in the lieutenant's long sigh. "So. Cacciato's gone away, is that it?"

"There it is," Doc Peret said. "You've got it now."

Paul Berlin smiled and nodded.

"To gay Paree," the lieutenant said. "Old Cacciato's going to Paree in France." He giggled, then shook his head gravely. "Still raining?"

"A bitch, sir."

"You ever seen rain like this? I mean, ever?"

"No, sir," Paul Berlin said.

"You Cacciato's buddy, I suppose?"

"No, sir," Paul Berlin said. "Sometimes he'd tag along, but not really."

"Who's his buddy?"

"Vaught, sir. I guess Vaught was, sometime."

"Well," the lieutenant said, dropping his nose inside the boot to smell the sweaty leather, "well, I guess we should just get Mister Vaught in here."

"Vaught's gone, sir. He's the one who cut himself—gangrene, remember?"

"Mother of Mercy."

Doc Peret draped a poncho over the lieutenant's shoulders. The rain was steady and thunderless and undramatic. Though it was mid-morning, the feeling was of endless dusk.

"Paree," the lieutenant murmured. "Cacciato's going to gay Paree—pretty girls and bare ass and Frogs everywhere. What's wrong with him?"

"Just dumb, sir. He's just awful dumb, that's all."

"And he's walking? He says he's walking to gay Paree?"

"That's what he says, sir, but you know how Cacciato can be."

"Does he know how far it is?"

"Six thousand eight hundred statute miles, sir. That's what he told me—six thousand eight hundred miles on the nose. He had it down pretty well. He had a compass and fresh water and maps and stuff."

"Maps," the lieutenant said. "Maps, flaps, schnaps. I guess those maps will help him cross the oceans, right? I guess he can just rig up a canoe out of those maps, no problem."

"Well, no," said Paul Berlin. He looked at Doc Peret, who shrugged. "No, sir. He showed me on the maps. See, he says he's going through Laos, then into Thailand and Burma, and then India, and then some other country, I forget, and then into Iran and Iraq, and then Turkey, and then Greece, and the rest is easy. That's exactly what he said. The rest is easy, he said. He had it all doped out."

"In other words," the lieutenant said, lying back, "in other words, fuckin AWOL."

"There it is," said Doc Peret. "There it is."

The lieutenant rubbed his eyes. His face was sallow and he needed a shave. For a time he lay very still, listening to the rain, hands on his belly, then he giggled and shook his head and laughed. "What's for? Tell me—what the fuck for?"

"Easy," Dock said. "Really, you got to stay covered up, sir, I told you that."

"What for? I mean, what for?"

"Shhhhhhh, he's just dumb, that's all."

The lieutenant's face was yellow. He laughed, rolling onto his side and dropping the boot. "I mean, why? What sort of shit is this—walking to fucking gay Paree? What kind of bloody war is this, tell me, what's wrong with you people? Tell me—what's *wrong* with you?"

"Shhhhhh," Doc purred, covering him up and putting a hand on his forehead. "Easy does it."

"Angel of Mercy, Mother of Virgins, what's wrong with you guys? Walking to gay Paree, what's *wrong?*"

"Nothing, sir. It's just Cacciato. You know how Cacciato can be when he puts his head to it. Relax now and it'll be all fine. Fine. It's just that rockhead, Cacciato."

The lieutenant giggled. Without rising, he pulled on his pants and boots and a shirt, then rocked miserably before the blue Sterno flame. The pagoda smelled like the earth, and the rain was unending. "Shoot," the lieutenant sighed. He kept shaking his head, grinning, then looked at Paul Berlin. "What squad you in?"

"Third, sir."

"That's Cacciato's squad?"

"Yes, sir."

"Who else?"

"Me and Doc and Eddie Lazzutti and Stink and Oscar Johnson and Harold Murphy. That's all, except for Cacciato."

"What about Pederson and Buff?"

"They're the dead ones, sir."

"Shoot." The lieutenant rocked before the flame. He did not look well. "Okay," he sighed, getting up. "Third Squad goes after Cacciato."

Leading to the mountains were four clicks of level paddy. The mountains jerked straight out of the rice, and beyond those mountains and other mountains was Paris.

The tops of the mountains could not be seen for the mist and clouds. The rain was glue that stuck the sky to the land.

The squad spent the night camped at the base of the first mountain, then in the morning they began the ascent. At mid-day Paul Berlin spotted Cacciato. He was half a mile up, bent low and moving patiently, steadily. He was not wearing a helmet—surprising, because Cacciato always took great care to cover the pink bald spot at the crown of his skull. Paul Berlin spotted him, but it was Stink Harris who spoke up.

Lieutenant Corson took out the binoculars.

"Him, sir?"

The lieutenant watched while Cacciato climbed toward the clouds.

"That him?"

"It's him. Bald as an eagle's ass."

Stink giggled. "Bald as Friar Tuck—it's Cacciato, all right. Dumb as a dink."

They watched until Cacciato was swallowed in the rain and clouds.

"Dumb-dumb," Stink giggled.

They walked fast, staying in a loose column. First the lieutenant, then Oscar Johnson, then Stink, then Eddie Lazzutti, then

Harold Murphy, then Doc, then, at the rear, Paul Berlin. Who walked slowly, head down. He had nothing against Cacciato. The whole episode was silly, of course, a dumb and immature thing typical of Cacciato, but even so he had nothing special against him. It was just too bad. A waste of time in the midst of infinitely wider waste.

Climbing, he tried to picture Cacciato's face. The image came out fuzzed and amorphous and bland—entirely compatible with the boy's personality. Doc Peret, an acute observer of such things, hypothesized that Cacciato had missed Mongolian idiocy by the breadth of a single, wispy genetic hair. "Could have gone either way," Doc had said confidentially. "You see the slanting eyes? The pasty flesh, just like jelly, right? The odd-shaped head? I mean, hey, let's face it—the guy's fuckin ugly. It's only a theory, mind you, but I'd wager big money that old Cacciato has more than a smidgen of the Mongol in him."

There may have been truth to it. Cacciato looked curiously unfinished, as though nature had struggled long and heroically but finally jettisoned him as a hopeless cause, not worth the diminishing returns. Open-faced, round, naive, plump, tender-complected and boyish, Cacciato lacked the fine detail, the refinements and final touches that maturity ordinarily marks on a boy of seventeen years. All this, the men concluded, added up to a case of simple gross stupidity. He wasn't positively disliked—except perhaps by Stink Harris, who took instant displeasure with anything vaguely his inferior—but at the same time Cacciato was no one's friend. Vaught, maybe. But Vaught was dumb, too, and he was gone from the war. At best, Cacciato was tolerated. The way men will sometimes tolerate a pesky dog.

It was just too bad. Walking to Paris, it was one of those ridiculous things Cacciato would do. Like winning the Bronze Star for shooting a dink in the face. Dumb. The way he was forever whistling. Too blunt-headed to know better, blind to the bodily and spiritual dangers of human combat. In some ways this made him a good soldier. He walked point like a boy at his first county fair. He didn't mind the tunnel work. And his smile, more decoration than an expression of emotion, stayed with him in the most lethal of moments—when Billy Boy turned his last card, when Pederson floated face-up in a summer day's paddy, when Buff's helmet overflowed with an excess of red and gray fluids.

It was sad, a real pity.

Climbing the mountain, Paul Berlin felt an odd affection for the kid. Not friendship, exactly, but—real pity.

Not friendship. Not exactly. Pity, pity plus wonder. It was all silly, walking away in the rain, but it was something to think about.

They did not reach the summit of the mountain until mid-afternoon. The climb was hard, the rain sweeping down, the mountain oozing from beneath their feet. Below, the clouds were expansive, hiding the paddies and the war. Above, in more clouds, were more mountains.

Oscar Johnson found where Cacciato had spent the first night, a rock formation with an outcropping ledge as a roof, a can of burnt-out Sterno, a chocolate wrapper, and a partly burned map. On the map, traced in red ink, was a dotted line that ran through the paddyland and up the first small mountain of the Annamese Cordillera. The dotted line ended there, apparently to be continued on another map.

"He's serious," the lieutenant said softly. "The blockhead's serious." He held the map as if it had a bad smell.

Stink and Oscar and Eddie Lazzutti nodded.

They rested in Cacciato's snug rock nest. Tucked away, looking out on the slate rain toward the next mountain, the men were quiet. Paul Berlin laid out a game of solitaire. Harold Murphy rolled a joint, inhaled, then passed it along, and they smoked and watched the rain and clouds and wilderness. It was peaceful. The rain was nice.

No one spoke until the ritual was complete.

Then, in a hush, all the lieutenant could say was, "Mercy."

"Shit," was what Stink Harris said.

The rain was unending.

"We could just go back," Doc Peret finally said. "You know, sir? Just head on back and forget him."

Stink Harris giggled.

"Seriously," Doc kept on, "we could just let the poor kid go. Make him MIA, strayed in battle, the lost lamb. Sooner or later he'll wake up, you know, and he'll see how insane it is and he'll come back."

The lieutenant stared into the rain. His face was yellow except for the network of broken veins.

"So what say you, sir? Let him go?"

"Dumber than a rock," Stink giggled.

"And smarter than Stink Harris."

"You know *what*, Doc."

"Pickle it."

"Who's saying to pickle it?"

"Just pickle it," said Doc Peret. "That's what."

Stink giggled but he shut up.

"What do you say, sir? Turn back?"

The lieutenant was quiet. At last he shivered and went into the rain with a wad of toilet paper. Paul Berlin sat alone, playing solitaire in the style of Las Vegas. Pretending, of course. Pretending to pay thirty thousand dollars for the deck, pretending ways to spend his earnings.

When the lieutenant returned he told the men to saddle up.

"We turning back?" Doc asked.

The lieutenant shook his head. He looked sick.

"I knew it!" Stink crowed. "Damn straight, I knew it! Can't hump away from a war, isn't that right, sir? The dummy has got to learn you can't just hump your way out of a war." Stink grinned and flicked his eyebrows at Doc Peret. "I knew it. By golly, I knew it!"

Cacciato had reached the top of the second mountain. Standing bareheaded, hands loosely at his sides, he was looking down on them through a blur of rain. Lieutenant Corson had the binoculars on him.

"Maybe he don't see us," Oscar said. "Maybe he's lost."

"Oh, he sees us. He sees us fine. Sees us real fine. And he's not lost. Believe me, he's not."

"Throw out smoke, sir?"

"Why not?" the lieutenant said. "Sure, why not throw out pretty smoke, why not?" He watched Cacciato through the glasses while Oscar threw out the smoke. It fizzled for a time and then puffed up in a heavy cloud of lavender. "Oh, he sees us," the lieutenant whispered. "He sees us fine."

"The bastard's *waving!*"

"I can see that, thank you. Mother of Saints."

As if stricken, the lieutenant suddenly sat down in a puddle, put his head in his hands and began to rock as the lavender smoke drifted up the face of the mountain. Cacciato was waving both arms. Not quite waving. The arms were flapping. Paul Berlin watched through the glasses. Cacciato's head was huge, floating

like a balloon in the high fog, and he did not look at all frightened.
He looked young and stupid. His face was shiny. He was smiling,
and he looked happy.

"I'm sick," the lieutenant said. He kept rocking. "I tell you, I'm
a sick, sick man."

"Should I shout up to him?"

"Sick," the lieutenant moaned. "Sick, sick. It wasn't this way
on Pusan, I'll tell you that. Sure, call up to him—I'm sick."

Oscar Johnson cupped his hands and hollered, and Paul Berlin
watched through the glasses. For a moment Cacciato stopped waving. He spread his arms wide, as if to show them empty, slowly
spreading them out like wings, palms up. Then his mouth opened
wide, and in the mountains there was thunder.

"What'd he say?" The lieutenant rocked on his haunches. He
was clutching himself and shivering. "Tell me what he said."

"Can't hear, sir. Oscar—?"

There was more thunder, long lasting thunder that came in
waves from deep in the mountains. It rolled down and moved the
trees and grasses.

"Shut the shit up!" The lieutenant was rocking and shouting at
the rain and wind and thunder. "What'd the dumb fucker say?"

Paul Berlin watched through the glasses, and Cacciato's mouth
opened and closed and opened, but there was only more thunder.
Then his arms began flapping again. Flying, Paul Berlin suddenly
realized. The poor kid was perched up there, arms flapping, trying
to fly. Fly! Incredibly, the flapping motion was smooth and practiced and graceful.

"A chicken!" Stink squealed. "Look it! A squawking chicken!"

"Mother of Children."

"Look it!"

"A miserable chicken, you see that? A chicken!"

The thunder came again, breaking like Elephant Feet across the mountains, and the lieutenant rocked and held himself.

"For Christ sake," he moaned, "what'd he say? Tell me."

Paul Berlin could not hear. But he saw Cacciato's lips move, and the happy smile.

"Tell me."

So Paul Berlin, watching Cacciato fly, repeated it. "He said goodbye."

In the night the rain hardened into fog, and the fog was cold. They camped in the fog, near the top of the mountain, and the thunder stayed through the night. The lieutenant vomited. Then he radioed that he was in pursuit of the enemy.

"Gunships, Papa Two-Niner?" came the answer from far away.

"Negative," said the old lieutenant.

"Arty? Tell you what. You got a real sweet voice, Papa Two-Niner. No shit, a lovely voice." The radio-voice paused. "So, here's what I'll do, I'll give you a bargain on the arty—two for the price of one, no strings and a warranty to boot. How's that? See, we got this terrific batch of new 155 in, first class ordinance, I promise you, and what we do, what we do is this. What we do is we go heavy on volume here, you know? Keeps the prices low."

"Negative," the lieutenant said.

"Well, geez. Hard to please, right? Maybe some nice illum, then? Willie Peter, real boomers with some genuine sparkles mixed in. We're having this close-out sale, one time only."

"Negative. Negative, negative, negative."

"You'll be missing out on some fine shit."

"Negative, you monster."

"Okay," the radio-voice said, disappointed-sounding, "but you'll wish . . . No offense, Papa Two-Niner. Have some happy hunting."

"Mercy," said the lieutenant into a blaze of static.

The night fog was worse than the rain, colder and more saddening. They lay under a sagging lean-to that seemed to catch and hold the fog like a net. Oscar and Harold Murphy and Stink and Eddie Lazzutti slept anyway, curled around one another like lovers. They could sleep and sleep.

"I hope he's moving," Paul Berlin whispered to Doc Peret. "I just hope he keeps moving. He does that, we'll never get him."

"Then they'll chase him with choppers. Or planes or something."

"Not if he gets himself lost," Paul Berlin said. "Not if he hides."

"What time is it?"

"Don't know."

"What time you got, sir?"

"Very lousy late," said the lieutenant from the bushes.

"Come on."

"Four o'clock. O-four-hundred, which is to say a.m. Got it?"

"Thanks."

"Charmed." His ass, hanging six inches from the earth, made a soft warm glow in the dark.

"You okay, sir?"

"I'm wonderful. Can't you see how wonderful I am?"

"I just hope Cacciato keeps moving," Paul Berlin whispered. "That's all I hope—I hope he uses his head and keeps moving."

"It won't get him anywhere."

"Get him to Paris maybe."

"Maybe," Doc sighed, turning onto his side, "and where is he then?"

"In Paris."

"No way. I like adventure, too, but, see, you can't walk to Paris from here. You just can't."

"He's smarter than you think," Paul Berlin said, not quite believing it. "He's not all that dumb."

"I know," the lieutenant said. He came from the bushes. "I know all about that."

"Impossible. None of the roads go to Paris."

"Can we light a Sterno, sir?"

"No," the lieutenant said, crawling under the lean-to and lying flat on his back. His breath came hard. "No, you can't light a fucking Sterno, and no, you can't go out to play without your mufflers and galoshes, and no, kiddies and combatants, no, you can't have chocolate sauce on your broccoli. No."

"All right."

"No!"

"You saying no, sir?"

"No," the lieutenant sighed with doom. "It's still a war, isn't it?"

"I guess."

"There you have it. It's still a war."

The rain resumed. It started with thunder, then lightning lighted the valley deep below in green and mystery, then more thunder, then it was just the rain. They lay quietly and listened. Paul Berlin, who considered himself abnormally sane, uncluttered by high ideas or lofty ambitions or philosophy, was suddenly struck between the eyes by a vision of murder. Butchery, no less. Cacciato's right temple caving inward, a moment of black silence, then the enormous explosion of outward-going brains. It was no meta-

phor; he didn't think in metaphors. No, it was a simple scary vision. He tried to reconstruct the thoughts that had led to it, but
there was nothing to be found—the rain, the discomfort of mushy
flesh. Nothing to justify such a bloody image, no origins. Just Cacciato's round head suddenly exploding like a pricked bag of he-
lium: boom.

Where, he thought, was all this taking him, and where would
it end? Murder was the logical circuit-stopper, of course; it was
Cacciato's rightful, maybe inevitable due. Nobody can get away
with stupidity forever, and in war the final price for it is always paid
in purely biological currency, hunks of toe or pieces of femur or
bits of exploded brain. And it *was* still a war, wasn't it?

Pitying Cacciato with wee-hour tenderness, and pitying himself for the affliction that produced such visions, Paul Berlin hoped
for a miracle. He was tired of murder. Not scared by it—not at that
particular moment—and not awed by it, just fatigued.

"He did some awfully brave things," he whispered. Then realized that Doc was listening. "He did. The time he dragged that
dink out of his bunker, remember that."

"Yeah."

"The time he shot the kid in the kisser."

"I remember."

"At least you can't call him a coward, can you? You can't say he
ran away because he was scared."

"You can say a lot of other shit, though."

"True. But you can't say he wasn't brave. You can't say that."

"Fair enough," Doc said. He sounded sleepy.

"I wonder if he talks French."

"You kidding, partner?"

"Just wondering. You think it's hard to learn French, Doc?"

"Cacciato?"

"Yeah, I guess not. It's a neat thing to think about, though, old Cacciato walking to Paris."

"Go to sleep," Doc Peret advised. "Remember, pal, you got your own health to think of."

They were in the high country.

It was country far from the war, high and peaceful country with trees and thick grass, no people and no dogs and no lowland drudgery. Real wilderness, through which a single trail, liquid and shiny, kept taking them up.

The men walked with their heads down. Stink at point, then Eddie Lazzutti and Oscar, next Harold Murphy with the machine gun, then Doc, then the lieutenant, and last Paul Berlin.

They were tired and did not talk. Their thoughts were in their legs and feet, and their legs and feet were heavy with blood, for they'd been on the march many hours and the day was soggy with the endless rain. There was nothing symbolic, or melancholy, about the rain. It was simple rain, everywhere.

They camped that night beside the trail, then in the morning continued the climb. Though there were no signs of Cacciato, the mountain had only one trail and they were on it, the only way west.

Paul Berlin marched mechanically. At his sides, balancing him evenly and keeping him upright, two canteens of Kool-Aid lifted and fell with his hips, and the hips rolled in their ball-and-socket joints. He respired and sweated. His heart hard, his back strong, up the high country.

They did not see Cacciato, and for a time Paul Berlin thought they might have lost him forever. It made him feel better, and he climbed the trail and enjoyed the scenery and the sensations of being high and far from the real war, and then Oscar found the second map.

The red dotted line crossed the border into Laos.

Farther ahead they found Cacciato's helmet and armored vest, then his dogtags, then his entrenching tool and knife.

"Dummy just keeps to the trail," the lieutenant moaned. "Tell me why? Why doesn't he leave the trail?"

"It's the only way to Paris," Paul Berlin said.

"A rockhead," said Stink Harris. "That's why."

Liquid and shiny, a mix of rain and red clay, the trail took them higher.

Cacciato eluded them but he left behind the wastes of his march—empty tins, bits of bread, a belt of golden ammo dangling from a dwarf pine, a leaking canteen, candy wrappers and worn rope. Clues that kept them going. Tantalizing them on, one step then the next—a glimpse of his bald head, the hot ash of a breakfast fire, a handkerchief dropped coyly along the path.

So they kept after him, following the trails that linked one to the next westward in a simple linear direction without deception. It was deep, jagged, complex country, dark with the elements of the season, and ahead was the frontier.

"He makes it that far," Doc Peret said, pointing to the next line of mountains, "and we can't touch him."

"How now?"

"The border," Doc said. The trail had leveled out and the march was easier. "He makes it to the border and it's bye-bye Cacciato."

"How far?"

"Two clicks maybe. Not far."

"Then he's made it," whispered Paul Berlin.

"Maybe so."

"By God!"

"Maybe so," Doc said.

"Boy, lunch at Tour d'Argent! A night at the old opera!"

"Maybe so."

The trail narrowed, then climbed, and a half-hour later they saw him.

He stood at the top of a small grassy hill, two hundred meters ahead. Loose and at ease, smiling, Cacciato already looked like a civilian. His hands were in his pockets and he was not trying to hide himself. He might have been waiting for a bus, patient and serene and not at all frightened.

"Got him!" Stink yelped. "I knew it! Now we got him!"

The lieutenant came forward with the glasses.

"I knew it," Stink crowed, pressing forward. "The blockhead's finally giving it up—giving up the old ghost, I knew it!"

"What do we do, sir?"

The lieutenant shrugged and stared through the glasses.

"Fire a shot?" Stink held his rifle up and before the lieutenant could speak he squeezed off two quick rounds, one a tracer that turned like a corkscrew through the mist. Cacciato smiled and waved.

"Look at him," Oscar Johnson said. "I do think we got ourselves a predicament. Truly a predicament."

"There it is," Eddie said, and they both laughed, and Cacciato kept smiling and waving.

"A true predicament."

Stink Harris took the point, walking fast and chattering, and Cacciato stopped waving and watched him come, arms folded and his big head cocked as if listening for something. He looked amused.

There was no avoiding it.

Stink saw the wire as he tripped it, but there was no avoiding it.

The first sound was that of a zipper suddenly yanked up; next, a popping noise, the spoon releasing and primer detonating; then the sound of the grenade dropping; then the fizzling sound. The sounds came separately but quickly.

Stink knew it as it happened. With the next step, in one fuzzed motion, he flung himself down and away, rolling, covering his skull, mouth open, yelping a funny, trivial little yelp.

They all knew it.

Eddie and Oscar and Doc Peret dropped flat, and Harold Murphy bent double and did an oddly graceful jackknife for a man of his size, and the lieutenant coughed and collapsed, and Paul Berlin, seeing purple, closed his eyes and fists and mouth, brought his knees to his belly, coiling, and let himself fall.

Count, he thought, but the numbers came in a tangle without sequence.

His belly hurt. That was where it started. First the belly, a release of fluids in the bowels next, a shitting feeling, a draining of all the pretensions and silly hopes for himself, and he was back where he started, writhing. The lieutenant was beside him. The air was windless—just the misty rain. His teeth hurt. Count, he thought, but his teeth hurt and no numbers came. I don't want to die, he thought lucidly, with hurting teeth.

There was no explosion. His teeth kept hurting and his belly was floating in funny ways.

He was ready, steeled. His lungs hurt now. He was ready, but there was no explosion. Then came a fragile pop. Smoke, he thought without thinking, smoke.

"Smoke," the lieutenant moaned, then repeated it, "fucking smoke."

Paul Berlin smelled it. He imagined its velvet color, purple, but he could not open his eyes. He tried, but he could not open his eyes or unclench his fists or uncoil his legs, and the heavy fluids in his stomach were holding him down, and he could not wiggle or run to escape. There was no explosion.

"Smoke," Doc said softly. "Just smoke."

It was red smoke, and the message seemed clear. It was all over them. Brilliant red, thick, acid-tasting. It spread out over the earth like paint, then began to climb against gravity in a lazy red spiral.

"Smoke," Doc said. "Smoke."

Stink Harris was crying. He was on his hands and knees, chin against his throat, bawling and bawling. Oscar and Eddie had not moved.

"He had us," the lieutenant whispered. His voice was hollowed out, senile sounding, almost a reminiscence. "He could've had all of us."

"Just smoke," Doc said. "Lousy smoke is all."

"The dumb fucker could've had us."

Paul Berlin could not move. He felt entirely conscious, a little embarrassed but not yet humiliated, and he heard their voices, heard Stink weeping and saw him beside the trail on his hands and knees, and he saw the red smoke everywhere, but he could not move.

"He won't come," said Oscar Johnson, returning under a white flag. "Believe me, I tried, but the dude just won't play her cool."

It was dusk and the seven soldiers sat in pow-wow.

"I told him all the right stuff, but he won't give it up. Told him it was crazy as shit and he'd probably end up dead, and I told him how he'd end up court-martialed at the best, and I told him how his old man would shit when he heard about it. Told him maybe things wouldn't go so hard if he just gave up and came back right now. I went through the whole spiel, top to bottom. The dude just don't listen."

The lieutenant was lying prone, Doc's thermometer in his mouth, sick-looking. It wasn't his war. The skin on his arms and neck was loose around deteriorating muscle.

"I told him—I told him all that good shit. Told him it's ridiculous, dig? I told him it won't work, no matter what, and I told him we're fed up. Fed up."

"You tell him we're out of rations?"

"Shit, yes, I told him that. And I told him he's gonna starve his own ass if he keeps going, and I told him we'd have to call in gunships if it came to it."

"You tell him he can't walk to France?"

Oscar grinned. He was black enough to be indistinct in the dusk. "Maybe I forgot to tell him that."

"You should've told him."

The lieutenant slid a hand behind his neck and pushed against it as if to relieve some spinal pressure. "What else?" he asked. "What else did he say?"

"Nothing, sir. He said he's doing okay. Said he was sorry to scare us with the smoke."

"The bastard." Stink kept rubbing his hands against the black stock of his rifle.

"What else?"

"Nothing. You know how he is, sir. Just a lot of smiles and stupid stuff. He asked how everybody was, so I said we're fine, except for the scare with the smoke boobytrap, and then he said he was sorry about that, so I told him it was okay. What can you say to a dude like that?"

The lieutenant nodded, pushing against his neck. He was quiet awhile. He seemed to be making up his mind. "All right," he finally sighed. "What'd he have with him?"

"Sir?"

"Musketry," the lieutenant said. "What kind of weapons?"

"His rifle. That's all, his rifle and some bullets. I didn't get much of a look."

"Claymores?"

Oscar shook his head. "I didn't see none. Maybe so."

"Grenades?"

"I don't know. Maybe a couple."

"Beautiful recon job, Oscar. Real pretty."

"Sorry, sir. He had his stuff tight, though."

"I'm sick."

"Yes, sir."

"Dysentery's going through me like coffee. What you got for me, Doc?"

Doc Peret shook his head. "Nothing, sir. Rest."

"That's it," the lieutenant said. "What I need is rest."

"Why not let him go, sir?"

"Rest," the lieutenant said, "is what I need."

Paul Berlin did not sleep. Instead he watched Cacciato's small hill and tried to imagine a proper ending.

There were only a few possibilities remaining, and after what had happened it was hard to see a happy end to it. Not impossible, of course. It could still be done. With skill and boldness, Cacciato might slip away and cross the frontier mountains and be gone. He tried to picture it. Many new places. Villages at night with barking dogs, people whose eyes and skins would change in slow evolution

and counterevolution as Cacciato moved westward with whole
continents before him and the war far behind him and all the trails
connecting and leading toward Paris. It could be done. He imagined the many dangers of Cacciato's march, treachery and deceit at
every turn, but he also imagined the many good times ahead, the
stinging feel of aloneness, and new leanness and knowledge of
strange places. The rains would end and the trails would go dry
and be baked to dust, and there would be changing foliage and
great expanses of silence and songs and pretty girls in straw huts
and, finally, Paris.

It could be done. The odds were like poison, but it could be
done.

Later, as if a mask had been peeled off, the rain ended and the
sky cleared and Paul Berlin woke to see the stars.

They were in their familiar places. It wasn't so cold. He lay on
his back and counted the stars and named those that he knew,
named the constellations and the valleys of the moon. It was just
too bad. Crazy, but still sad. He should've kept going—left the
trails and waded through streams to rinse away the scent, buried
his feces, swung from the trees branch to branch; he should've
slept through the days and ran through the nights. It might have
been done.

Toward dawn he saw Cacciato's breakfast fire. He heard Stink
playing with the safety catch on his M-16, a clicking noise like a
slow morning cricket. The sky lit itself in patches.

"Let's do it," the lieutenant whispered.

Eddie Lazzutti and Oscar and Harold Murphy crept away toward the south. Doc and the lieutenant waited a time then began
to circle west to block a retreat. Stink Harris and Paul Berlin were
to continue up the trail.

Waiting, trying to imagine a rightful and still happy ending, Paul Berlin found himself pretending, in a vague sort of way, that before long the war would reach a climax beyond which everything else would become completely commonplace. At that point he would stop being afraid. All the bad things, the painful and grotesque things, would be in the past, and the things ahead, if not lovely, would at least be tolerable. He pretended he had crossed that threshold.

When the sky was half-light, Doc and the lieutenant fired a red flare that streaked high over Cacciato's grassy hill, hung there, then exploded in a fanning starburst like the start of a celebration. Cacciato Day, it might have been called. October something, in the year 1968, the year of the Pig.

In the trees at the southern slope of the hill Oscar and Eddie and Harold Murphy each fired red flares to signal their advance.

Stink went into the weeds and hurried back, zipping up his trousers. He was very excited and happy. Deftly, he released the bolt on his weapon and it slammed hard into place.

"Fire the flare," he said, "and let's go."

Paul Berlin took a long time opening his pack.

But he found the flare, unscrewed its lid, laid the firing pin against the primer, then jammed it in.

The flare jumped away from him. It went high and fast, rocketing upward and taking a smooth arc that followed the course of the trail, leaving behind a dirty wake of smoke.

At its apex, with barely a sound, the flare exploded in a green dazzle over Cacciato's hill. It was a fine, brilliant shade of green.

"Go," whispered Paul Berlin. It did not seem enough. "Go," he said, and then he shouted, "Go."

Shoptalk #*1*
On Modality

I have heard strong, insistent, influential voices saying
for a long time that there should be, must be, value
judgments on the question of modality. I have heard it
said . . . that amost *any* other form is better suited to
our times than realistic fiction, and that those who write
and read realistic fiction are, somehow, second-class
citizens in the world of books. . . . I believe that non-
realistic fiction, at its best, has thrust into areas of imagination which give new and needed definition to contemporary human consciousness; but I also believe that
some of these experiments in form are masks for self-
indulgence and triviality. Equally I believe that much
realistic fiction has been—and is—a tiresome pander-
ing to whatever fashion in prurience or politics is going
at the moment; but I also believe that realistic fiction at
its best finds within the conventional areas of human
imagination enough contradictions to make the rational
mad and the humanistic murderous.

(Seymour Epstein, "Bread Loaf Address," vol. 3, no. 1, 1976)

JAYNE ANNE PHILLIPS

Gemcrack

Jayne Anne Phillips, having waitressed and traveled, entered the Iowa Writers' Workshop in 1976. Her earliest publications were poems and "short shorts" in Truck *magazine and a chapbook,* Sweethearts, *from* Truck Press, *edited by David Wilk and Jonas Agee. She was at Iowa when she sent "Gemcrack" to* Ploughshares *and her cover letter simply said that she had heard good things about the magazine.* Ploughshares *was operating out of my second bedroom at the time, without even file cabinets. Manuscripts were heaped in piles and I had to put up a barricade to keep my infant daughter from crawling in. One day I pulled out a desk drawer and found the manuscript of "Gemcrack" wedged behind it, glanced at the date, and guiltily read it through. The Son of Sam murders were recent news (now revived in Spike Lee's film), and I was startled by the writer's audacity in attempting the serial killer's point of view. I was also dazzled by the use of rhetoric and poetic metaphor. Was this show-off prose or was there imaginative depth and insight underneath the dazzle of lines such as "Love is the outlaw's duty" and "crack these gems and expose their light in the dark"? Second, third, and fourth readings deepened my conviction: the manner and the subject matter recalled Faulkner, and the story was especially impressive in its balance of feminist anger, dramatic perception, and perverse beauty. How long had it been lost behind my drawer?*

I wrote to Phillips immediately, apologizing for the delay, hoping that she hadn't sent "Gemcrack" elsewhere, and telling her I was forwarding it to Rosellen Brown for the special issue we were editing on

"Women Imagine Men / Men Imagine Women" (1978). Rosellen accepted it immediately. Meanwhile, Jayne Anne, invited to the St. Lawrence Writers' Conference as a Houghton Mifflin Fellow, met an actual Saint Lawrence: Boston publisher Seymour Lawrence, an early and avid supporter of Ploughshares. *She asked if he published short stories. "Not if I can help it," he replied, but he changed his mind after reading* Sweethearts. *He told her to "bring her stories to Boston" and signed her to a two-book contract. I recall Lawrence's comment to me that suddenly all the writers he trusted were aware of her. He suggested she call her collection* Black Tickets. *Shortly after that, Jayne Anne submitted her second story to* Ploughshares, *"El Paso," which appeared in a fiction issue that Tim O'Brien and I were coediting. I sent her the galleys and Jayne Anne returned them with remarkable, lapidary revisions that embodied fundamental principles of style. When* Black Tickets *was published in* 1979, *John Irving singled out "El Paso" as her best story in his review for the* New York Times Book Review. *Later still, having moved to Boston as a Bunting Institute Fellow at Radcliffe College, Jayne Anne agreed to coedit a* Ploughshares *issue with the poet Lorrie Goldensohn. By then* Ploughshares *had moved to a storefront office in Watertown that was furnished "off the street." I recall Jayne Anne in that office tilting back in my ratty swivel chair in front of yet another desk heaped with manuscripts as if contemplating for a second whether this was a life she wished to lead.*

As for "Gemcrack," in hindsight, Jayne Anne's exploration of criminal psychology and male violence toward women in this story (as well as the Faulknerian use of poetic metaphor to articulate complex, non-verbal emotion) was a prologue to the mature exploration of such characters as Carmody in her lyrical novel Shelter.

Jayne Anne Phillips's work to date includes Black Tickets *(1979),* Machine Dreams *(1984),* Fast Lanes *(1987), and* Shelter *(1994). Her new novel,* Mothercare, *will be published by Knopf.*

She is sitting in the car and I do my number. Looking down the sight I see an auriole fly to the right and left, all around in haloed flutters. Then it wavers like underwater noons, I have to split, my Uncle doesn't wait. He says be back, be quick, be reverant. We pray for these great states, for the Great State of the City of New York. We make em break em cart em away, Zing! like a silver cat scratch burning way down where you recognize your name. My lips make a sound: the letter S, snakes leaving skin to sun. Her head sinks down; I hear the sound and right away I'm fluttering. Gemstepping down the alley I turn, squeeze off a quick shot and the other girl half dazed on sidewalk falls over, lays down like she's home. And I'm running, rolling round like the eyes of Jesse James. Love is the outlaw's duty.

You see me everywhere. I spit on the surface of night, on the rattling backdrops of subway gutter art. I suck you up like erasers. I am that glittering drop of mercury spilled out a broken glass stick. Mark me in numbers and names of the dead. I take your temperature, your pulse. I have my fingers on your wrist and I will twist it. You suppose I fade as my women fade, buried or barricaded; my women with their swinging hair and their protectors. But no, I am with you though you walk through the lit-up noise of Mondays; I comfort you. I know the accountant's language of knuckles and swivel chairs, the jostling streets, the department store blues of floorwalkers and lyric radios, the sweat of the laundress scheming in powders and starch, the burger joints deemed blessed by girls in their thin white legs. I love my work. I crack these gems and expose their light in the dark Saturdays, the nights. My Uncle leads me astray into the paths of right thoughts. He holds my hand. Wait, he says, The time is not right—but we will yet have what we need. And surely, what we need comes in its time.

I read the papers. I save the stories in a box. They print my letters to the press, my exhortations to action. Get off your collective ass and rise to the occasion, rattle doors, knock on the deafened tombs. Haunt the alleys of the city which shine with slivered glass and clues to the underside. Inspect the eyes of winos. Inspect bellies in rotten shirts beached up on curbs, heads cradled stupid in a pasty arm. The whores, the Catholic girls, speak well of these whales of the streets. They sit on lumps of sleeping flesh to wait for a bus or a trick. They keep their jewels in trash cans and adorn themselves by the light of the moon. The drunks, the sleeping whales, have seen it pass. Ask these prophets where I lie in wait, where I sleep to evade your manhunters in their uniforms and carbolic faces. Ask the prophets whose shaggy heads slumber on newsprint fantasies of my face, on news of the latest sacrifice. I live in the gutters of dog manure, wine and urine; in the sewers which eat these melodies delivered by the sprays of the sweeper trucks.

Remember Babylon. I live in a swelter of bobbing heads navigating east and west far down in the streets. I ride the elevators up sixty floors; I stand at the windowed corner of a big hotel on a forgotten floor. Alone in a hallway while the rows of locked doors sleep, I watch the swelter break and sigh. The swelter rolls like waves; an ocean of passengers on foot. Watch it move. Beneath me, far down in the streets, the ocean wobbles in red shoes and three-piece suits. Those red shoes! Wooden heels stacked in layers of light and dark like a parquet floor dismantled and cut to fit. Ankles above the shoes are strung thin and tuned to recite. Though I see only tops of heads, female heads smaller than the metal caps of straight pins, I remember the ankles: their nylon sheen, the round bones rising up to glint like a covered eye.

Once I shot marbles. Glass and porcelain. Agates. Colors snaked in stripes through the centers, formed a wavered pupil of no determined expression. Handfuls of lovely eyes. I propelled one with my thumb to hit others, drive them out of a circle scratched on the ground. I crouched with the rest. I crouched in my scarred shoes and took aim. I dented my shoes on rocks and sticks. Those shoes were brown and tied with long ties which tangled or dragged in the dirt. Gouged scratches in the leather turned pale and tempered like scars on skin. I dug my fingernails into the dirt and aimed. We played marbles on the hard-packed ground, dust baked blond in the sun. I kept my prizes in a string bag. Scooping up the captive jewels, I rolled them in my hands and kept them warm. Later I would examine them by a light, sit home alone and stare into their centers. Now the boys crowded round with smears of dirt on their faces, silent, while the high-pitched screams of girls signaled they were sweating at their games of tag. Girls ran close and teased us with the sounds of their buckled sandals. Slaps on the ground. Quick. Flat. No one looked. The boys watched me, my cat's eye. Its chatoyant luster glimmered onto my skin: a stripe of shade burned in.

Shade falls on me as I walk among the faces. I walk east and west with my hands in my pockets. By day the discos are only the flat mutes of their doors and lightless signs. The crowd flows past them. Some of us walk in the black slant. A shadow falling from a long place is cast across us. Perhaps we will meet at night, in an alley beside a club. They sit in a parked car. They see me, some stand and sink. As they fall off their shoes I remember my own, those scarred leather ones with rounded toes. Was my Uncle watching me then, in my crouch? My cat's eye shot in its spinning roll across the dirt, rolled with its chosen celebrant beyond the scratched circle into no-man's land. Listen: I'll discuss my country; the playgrounds of the Bronx where buildings hedge their sooty roofs together and the dented rainpipes glitter. The ground was littered with smashed bottles. We ate Push-Ups, slender creamsicles frozen to a stick. We bought them across the street from the school for a dime. The sticks were saved, sharpened with pen-knives, used in games of pirates.

The girls and boys. We evaded each other. No one wanted the secrets yet, just the surging underskin like splinters. Some days it rained. They kept us inside. Ceilings of the classrooms were high and cracked. Above us in a heavy frame hung a portrait of George Washington in clouds, his patrician nose rouged and tipped with a ball of light. Each morning we recited the Pledge. Then the prayer about the hollow Father and the coming Kingdom, the heavenly will. My Uncle grinned in my mind but kept silent. He saved his commands and watched me. In the rain the old school building smelled of chalk and dirt. Dirt rubbed into the floor and packed itself firmly in cracks. We dug it up with pencil tips. Outside, the grounds were grey. Swings moved on chains. The teacher left us alone for recess. She snuck cigarettes in a lounge with a closed door; she thought of nothing. Noise in the classroom got louder and louder. The girls made games and diversions. Some wore full dresses with crinoline slips, ankle socks, patent leather shoes. They stood inside the reading circle and twirled to records of rhymes. Goosey Goosey Gander, whither shall I wander? Upstairs and downstairs and in my ladies chamber. There I met an old man who would not say his prayers. I took him by the left leg and threw him down the stairs . . . The girls twirled, seeing how big their skirts became. I lay on the floor inside the circle of chairs. Above me the skirts volumined like umbrellas. I saw the girls' legs, thin and colt-ish. Pale. The ankle socks chopped their calves above ankle and gave the illusion of hooves. I saw their odd white pants and their flatness. They were clean like dolls. They smelled of powder. They flashed and moved. I turned my face to the hard blond legs of the chairs.

At night I wake up. I put my hands across my face but the smell persists. My fingers smell of onions. I want to peel back the skin layer by layer, find the smell and wash it. I smell of something cut up, limp curls on boards, limp curled skins of onions.

My Uncle says, Come close. He stands in the shadows by the window. He stands behind the long curtains and ripples the dirty cloth. I see his shoes sticking out beneath, laced-up military boots and green woolen socks on his ankles. Come, he says. I see his head moving behind the cloth. He is unkind when he is angry. He is waiting for me to get on with the work. He comes at me out of everyone's mouth until I know he is the only one talking. He's inside the hippie across the hall with the moon poster tacked to his door, inside the Black girls I see in the elevator. They say Hi, they taunt me with their sloe-fizzed eyes and the pinkish palms of their hands. My Uncle waits at night in the dark bedroom until I wake up and listen. Come close to me, he says. And then he begins the giggling, long idiot sounds drawn out warbling and buckling, drawn out circling to choke me.

I have a job in the days. Always on time. Holding my computer card to the time clock, I hear its magic click writing numbers. The clock has a face of cats and rats; a black-ringed face with hands like whiskers. I like to check sizes, work in the stock shelves. I pull a folding ladder along the shelves, between the endless rows. Rows and rows of shoe boxes stacked to the ceiling, printed in size and swirled calligraphy; Spectator, Top O' The Town, Mr. Rocker. Mr.

Rocker shoes are spangled with mirrors on clear plastic heels, sewn in satin stripes, dappled with brass studs. Girls paint their toenails red and go dancing in Mr. Rockers. They sway on their transparent platforms while the music bleats. Mostly they don't move their feet; they bend at the waist, side-by-side, arch hips and slinky strut. They close their eyes. Smile. Others stamp their feet, beat time with Mr. Rockers, pound sequined heels the width of a peg-leg. I know because I go to watch them. My Uncle stands beside me; he whispers and points. He tells me what to do in his voice that whines and excites, his old voice that talks in the eyes of the reeling prophets and clattering cans in the streets. He knows languages with no letters. When he sees Mr. Rockers glitter under strobes, he grips my arm and buzzes like a bee.

But now I watch the escalators, shoes on the moving steps. They pass up and down, back and forth in front of our department. The manager rubs his hands and nods. I have a silver shoe horn in my pocket. When no one comes in, sits in our enclave of padded chairs, I dust shelves of Mr. Rockers with a feather duster. The salesgirls sit and saw their nails with emery boards embossed in the name of the franchise. They wear sensible shoes, beige wedgies and weejuns with pennies. They are required to wear stockings and shoes with covered toes. Their ankles are shy and crossed with a strap. I could show them places to go. My Uncle nods. He is serious about my work; only I can serve him in my way.

By late afternoon the store slows down. The empty escalators move. Women at the jewelry counters lean on the glass, looking closely at rows of pierced earrings. But they aren't really looking, only flicking at dangling golds with a fingernail. They're thinking of catching buses, eating dinner, locking their doors to sleep. And the accountants walk by, hurried, lace slips for wives tucked in a briefcase. The days get darker. The lawyers, deli owners, insurance salesmen, aging girls from publishing houses: they fill up subway cars and stare straight ahead. They remark on the newspapers. Some save clippings, fascinated. At the stalker, the legions of manhunters, the series of chosen faces innocent in those painful graduation pictures. I know which readers follow the stories. Their faces are looking for secrets. I'm pushing them. I could tell them light comes in one quick flash to the seeker.

The apartment was always dim. The Bronx was rows of tenements, metal fire escapes at spindled angles, thin grass strips by lengths of sidewalk. Junked cars in the street. Basketballs made their repetitive rubber slaps on pavement. My mother worked a factory in Brooklyn; she rode the trains home late. We were alone in the place. Every night I waited for her. We kept a wooden crate by the door, a steel door like the rest with a 2″ square window high up. I stood on the crate to watch for her, a short wire-haired woman lumbering in kerchief and shapeless dress up the stairs. She always carried groceries. She said she liked my eyes right there at the window after she'd climbed three flights with the heavy bag. So I pushed the crate to the door and watched. One rectangular light in the hall cast a yellow shape on the floor. I stood there for hours. I watched them all come and go.

Daughters of the Spanish family across the hall folded clothes at the laundromat. They were dark and brassy, gold hoops in their ears, wrinkled cigarettes. They came home after five and fumbled with keys, shifting big purses and bundles of towels bound with a paper strip. In the warm box of light their faces lost sharp expression, seemed rounder, tawny. They all had moles near their lips, dark little pigments ignored and sexual. The dark spots rose like tiny scarabs on their faces. The girls tossed their heavy black hair. They sighed, shifted hips, jingled their rings of gold keys. They were sleepwalkers slouched by the metal doors. I wanted to wake them up.

And there were others, all asleep, all waiting. Fat women who worked in the markets, cleaning women, women who did nothing. Men came back with their silver lunch pails. Most of them lived alone or transient. Their faces were putty in the light. Only the shamblers, the rocking drunks, didn't care. They yelled and pounded on doors, walked into walls and laughed. Their stubbled whiskers gleamed. They opened their mouths wide and threads of spit glistened like dewed web. I believed they had spiders inside them. They were the only ones: they saw my eyes at the window. They pointed at me. They bowed, doffed their lumpy hats, and fell down in a heap.

Mostly I'm invisible. I stay in my apartment. I go to work and come home. In summer I turn off the air conditioner and open windows. I like to feel it all heat up. The city gets hotter and hotter. Tar bubbles on roofs and tops of cars shine white. The air gets heavy and hums. Suddenly, when its hardest to breathe, sirens cut loose. The heat is punctured like a big bag; the awful weight leaks out and whines. Ambulances or fire trucks. Or cops. Long sirens blurring in and out, screaming to make things real. I sit still. After the sirens there will be sounds again; doors slammed, strays barking in the streets. Colors start in the sky and night comes on. I hear footsteps in the hall. My Uncle is walking around. His sounds are in my head like a voice in a radio.

My mother said to stay inside. She said those sleeping drunks in the halls would steal my clothes. I counted marbles I'd won and left the best ones out to show her. The Bronx smelled of garbage left in a heat, smelled of a whole city wasting. I watched the electric fans revolve their whirring heads. I turned off the lights and watched them in the dark; the glinting of circles they made.

When my mother got home we played cards. Crazy 8's or Slapjack. She was quick at slapping Jacks. Her hand came down hard on their faces, their jeweled capes, their little hatchets. She wore no rings; her nails were blunt-cut straight across. After she'd won all the cards she shuffled the deck and dealt us hands of eight. Sometimes she let me win. I changed suits to hearts or diamonds, neat red shapes: I still see them when I look at neon signs. My mother smoked Pall Malls and took the combs out of her hair. She was always old. She rolled down her heavy support stockings, rubbed lotion on her calves. She rubbed gingerly at places the dark blue veins were coming up, as if she were afraid of her insides. She told me once she never knew her mother. Other times she'd say how sick she'd been when I was born.

Once we heard a shuffling in the hall, snarls and squeaks. One of the alley dogs had got in and caught a rat. The dog had it by the throat and their eyes were wild, wide open, rolling. I called her to look and she grabbed me. She pulled me back from the door, from the window that fit my eyes. She held me to the opposite wall and stood shivering while the sounds went on. She kept her hands around my neck. I looked up from beneath her and saw her parted lips, the edges of her teeth. And her eyes had sharp edges to them, watching the metal door.

Each time, I do the same things. I come home and lock the locks. I have a mattress on the floor and a box of clippings. I read them over and over and listen for his voice. It starts coming every night; my Uncle is there all the time. I go for weeks and then it is time again. I take the gun out and look at it.

When I went in the army my mother cooked a big dinner. She fried chicken and mashed the potatoes. She stood cooking gravy, stirring it round and round with a fork. The skin of her arm was cracked and crossed with tiny lines. She thought the army would be good for me: I could go to school on the G. I. Bill. I watched her standing at the stove. She wore white waitress shoes with thick soles and she had a big safety pin fastened to the collar of her dress. She saved rubber bands, paper clips, thumb tacks, safety pins. When she found them in the apartment she put them in a pocket or fastened the pins to her clothes. She stirred the bubbling gravy and hummed hymns. By then her face was pasty and she wheezed. She hummed "We Gather Together." The army, she said, Maybe I'd be an engineer. Design machines and engines. I'd always been smart, she said, Why shouldn't I have the best.

At Fort Dix I was a typist. I hated the khaki uniforms. I hated the southern boys and their jokes. They only noticed me when they told their dirty stories. If I didn't laugh they said I needed a whore. They came close to my face and their little pig eyes glittered through slits.

I learned how to shoot. I practiced. I shot at clip-on targets printed in red and yellow rings. The black bull's eye spiraled deep. I hit it and dreamed of hitting it. In dreams I laced up my boots and walked in the dark to the target range. I saw each step and when I touched the gun I saw through the bones of my hands. I kept shooting into the eye of the black and a star burst up each time. At first I didn't notice the girls. Then, one by one, they started filtering out of the woods; slim girls in knee-length dresses whose bare arms stayed still as they walked. They walked slow, their hair billowed out. They stood dotting the meadow and gazed at me like waiting deer. I kept shooting. Stars in the black bull's eyes burst brighter and brighter. The girls stayed motionless, their faces toward me.

The sky grew lighter above their pale dresses. Their feet were hidden in grasses. Across the rolling field their arms gave off faint glows.

I wait for a weekend. Saturday night. All day I wait for the dark. My Uncle is with me though he is not present.

I look at the gun and I touch it. I turn it over and touch it everywhere. I have everything I need and his voice has stopped and I go where his voice said to go. I park the car and I walk a few blocks. I have the gun in my pocket and the note I have signed for his voice. I don't think about the girl or wonder; I'll read about her later, her parents, where she lived, what she did. Now she is dancing or she is getting smoke in her eyes from the cigarettes in the crowded room and she is getting ready to walk outside. I hear a buzzing and my vision flickers. In an alley by the side entrance of the club I have my hand ready; I see her hair and her red coat. Sometimes they don't see me but she does and that's good, it's very good; because she shakes me, I'm fluttering, she rushes in like electric shock in the instant she looks at me and knows—I never hear the gun—But after she falls there is a loud crack. Something big caves in. The whiteness comes up brilliant, sudden, stutters sparks and spreads its burning arms. Then a flash like imploding air. I pass through like flame. My shoes bleach concrete where I touch. Sometime, someone will see and follow me. I'll say they found me with special eyes; I'll say they have grown up in light.

Shoptalk #2
On Moral Fiction

Morality is a problem for a serious fiction writer first because the writer's own work consists essentially in an unfettered confrontation with his or her own *im*morality. The first freedom from censorship is the internal, personal freedom to plumb *that* forbidden depth. . . . What do we write about if not about falling short, limitation, fallenness, flaws, jealousy, greed, lust, worry, despair? . . . The writer is devoted in advance not to some respectable notion of "value" or of "the good" or of "morality," but to this process itself, wherever it leads. . . . Moral fiction enables readers to identify with—become one with—someone else's experience. That knack of identification is the simple antidote to the deadliest form of our moral malady, our inability to *feel* with others, to understand them, to stand-under the weight of what they carry.

(James Carroll, "The Virtue of Writing," vol. 15, nos. 2 & 3, 1989)

SUE MILLER

Expensive Gifts

Ploughshares was Sue Miller's first publisher. She writes that she had already sent "Expensive Gifts" around to other places that might have paid more, money being a pressing concern at that time in her life, and she was circulating several other stories at the same time; in fact, Robley Wilson Jr. at the North American Review *had accepted "Given Names," but "Expensive Gifts," accepted for* Ploughshares *by Jay Neugeboren, appeared in print first, in 1980. Miller had taken a course at Harvard's Extension School with novelist Anne Bernays, and "Expensive Gifts" had been written for this class. "I'd never attended a conference. I had read in literary magazines, and I usually bought the* Best American Short Stories. . . . *I was full of a probably foolish optimism about my possibilities for publication." As a result of publication in* Ploughshares, *she signed on with her literary agent, Maxine Groffsky. "I've always told other young writers, there are a lot of people out there reading [literary] magazines, people who care about fiction enormously, so that even though the circulation may not be as high as some more commercial magazines, the readership may be very important."*

A grant from Radcliffe's Bunting Institute in 1983–84 gave Miller the time to finish a large chunk of her first novel; otherwise she was supporting herself "by working in day care, and then by teaching writing anyplace in the Boston area that would have me." Groffsky submitted The Good Mother *to six or seven publishers and sold the book to Ted Solotaroff at Harper and Row. The novel was a surprise best-seller, touching a nerve at the time. On reflection, Miller now says, "I think the women's movement was supportive of my work in a general sense. Certainly I felt publishing was more open to women by the time I began to write, and more open to fiction about women's lives. Personally, I think age was a boon to me, and having a child, and working in the world for as long as I did." (Miller was thirty-five when she began writing, forty-two when* The Good Mother *appeared.)*

Inventing the Abbotts and Other Stories *appeared in 1987, including "Expensive Gifts" and two other stories that originally appeared in* Ploughshares, *"The Birds and the Bees" and "What Ernest Says." Hilma Woltizer commented on the collection, "She has a genius for understanding sexual behavior, and for transforming it into art." In addition to* The Good Mother, *Sue Miller's novels to date include* Family Pictures *(1990),* For Love *(1993), and* The Distinguished Guest *(1997). Her latest novel is* While I Was Gone *(1998), a Book of the Month Club main selection. She lives in Boston and is at work on a new novel.*

When it comes to encouraging new writers herself, Sue Miller comments that while serving as editor for Ploughshares *19, nos. 2 and 3 (1993), nine of the fourteen writers she included were previously unknown to her. Among a number of gifted writers she has taught over the years, the best known at this point is Elizabeth McCracken.*

Charlie Kelly was her eighth lover since the divorce. He was standing naked in silhouette, as slim as a stiletto in the light from the hall, rifling through the pockets in his jacket for his cigarettes. The sight of him gave Kate no pleasure. She hated the smell of cigarette smoke in her bedroom. She hated the horrible silence that fell between men and women who didn't know each other well after making love, but she hated even more for it to be filled with the rustling little rituals of the smoker.

"I'm afraid there are no ashtrays in here," she said. Her voice was pinched and proper. Five minutes before she had been expelling short, pleased grunts, like a bear rooting around in garbage.

"That's okay," he said, sitting on the bed again, and lighting up. "My wineglass is empty."

"Actually," she said, although she wasn't at all sure of it, "that was *my* wineglass. And I was going to get some more wine." She stood up on her side of the bed and smashed her head on the Swedish ivy. She usually occupied Charlie's side of the bed. She wasn't used to the pitfalls on the other side. He appeared not to have noticed her accident.

"Here," she said, reaching over for the glass. "I'll bring you a real ashtray." He handed her the expensive wineglass, one of her wedding presents. The cardboard match leaned at an angle within it, its charred head resting in a tiny pool of red liquid. Kate felt Charlie's eyes upon her as she walked away from him, her slender silhouette now harshly revealed in the glare of the hall light. Her gait felt unfamiliar to her, awkward.

In the kitchen she threw the match away and set her glass down. She wanted to check Neddie. He always kicked the covers off in the intense, private struggles that dominated his dreaming life, and he had a bad cold now. Kate dressed him for bed in a big sleeper that made a blanket unnecessary, but she still had a mystical belief in tucking him in, in pulling the covers right up to his chin.

The night light was on in his room, a tiny leering Mickey Mouse head that leaked excess light from a hole where its nose had been until Ned had knocked it off with a toy one day. The covers had slid sideways off the bed into a tangled heap on the floor, and Neddie lay on his stomach. His hands were curled into fists, and one thumb rested near his open mouth, connected to it by a slender, almost invisible thread of saliva. His breathing was labored, thick with mucus.

Kate bent over him to tuck the covers in on the far side. Her breasts swung down and brushed his back. He muttered in his sleep, and reinserted his thumb in his mouth. He sucked briefly, his throat working too, in the same thorough way he'd pulled at her breast when he was nursing; but he couldn't breathe. His mouth fell open after a moment, and his thumb slipped out. His face puckered slightly, but he slept on. Kate watched his face smooth out, and stroked his hair back.

She stopped in the kitchen and poured herself a new glass of wine. She looked briefly and half-heartedly for an ashtray for Charlie, and settled, finally, for a saucer. She didn't want to return to her bedroom and make polite conversation with him. She wanted to call Al, her ex-husband, and talk comfortably; to make a joke of Charlie's stylized flattery of her and her own dogged unresponsiveness. But she couldn't have called him. Al was getting married again soon. He'd fallen in love with his lab assistant, a dark, serious woman, and she would be sleeping there beside him.

She had called Al frequently in the two years since he had moved out. Usually it was late at night; often she was drunk. Almost always it was after she'd been with someone else for an evening. Though they had fought bitterly in the year before they separated, the year after Neddie's birth, they were kind and loving during these drunken phone calls; they commiserated on the difficulties of a single life.

"Jesus," he'd said to her. "I can't seem to get the hang of anything. All the goddam rules have changed. Either I'm a male chauvinist pig, or I'm being attacked by an omnivorous Amazon, and I'm always *totally* surprised. No wonder those statistical people remarry so fast."

There was a silence while she thought of Al attacking, being attacked. He was small and slender, with curly brown hair and thick, wire-rimmed glasses that he removed carefully before starting to make love. They left two purplish dents, like bruises, on the sides of his nose.

"Oh, I don't know. It seems to me the main thing to remember is that there just aren't any rules anymore. You just have to do what makes you feel comfortable and good about yourself."

"Oh, Katie. You've been taking those *wise* pills again." She didn't respond. He cleared his throat. "Well, how about you? You feeling good about what you're doing?"

Kate had thought about the evening she had just spent. Her voice rose to a dangerously high pitch as she said, "No," and started to cry.

Now she carried her wine and the saucer back to Charlie. In some previous life her bedroom had been a sunporch. Two of its walls were a parade of large drafty windows. As if to compensate, the landlord had installed huge radiators the entire length of one of these walls; they clanked and hissed all winter long, and made her room the warmest in the apartment. Kate had hung the lower halves of the windows with curtains that moved constantly in the free-flowing air currents. She liked to lie in bed and look out of the naked top panes at the sky. It had been a luminous soft gray earlier, and now thick flakes, a darker gray against its gentle glow, brushed silently against the panes.

"Look," she said to Charlie, handing him the saucer. He was lying on his back with the open Marlboro box on his chest, using the lid for an ashtray.

"Yeah, I saw. It's sticking too, and I don't have snow tires. I'm going to have to leave pretty soon."

She looked away so he wouldn't see relief leap into her eyes.

"It's so pretty, though. I almost feel like waking Neddie up to show him. He doesn't really remember it from last year. It's all new to him again. Can you imagine that?"

Charlie put out his cigarette in the saucer.

"You must be freezing your ass off." Kate was standing by the windows watching the snow's straight descent. "Slide in here, lady, I'll warm you up."

She turned obediently and got in, but she said, "My father had a dog named Lady once. A collie. Horrible barker. He finally had someone shoot her. She just wouldn't shut up." None of that was true, but Kate didn't like to be called *lady*.

Kate was, in fact, a reflexive liar. She hated to be unpleasant or contradictory, and when she felt that way, a lie, fully formed almost before she began to think about it, fell from her lips. Al had had a knack for recognizing them—he'd said it was as though her voice resonated differently—and he would simply repeat them slowly so she could hear them herself, and then tell him what it was that was making her angry. Once in a fight about whether Al should work less and help her more with Ned, she had cried out, "Ned is wonderful because I've given up my fucking *life* to him!" His patient echo had made her weep; her claim seemed at once the truth and a terrible lie.

Now Charlie tried to pull her over to him, but she said, "Ah, ah," and held up her full wineglass as an explanation. She took a sip. He turned away to get another cigarette.

"The kid all right?"

"What, Neddie?"

"Yeah, is that his name? Is he okay?" He leaned back with the cigarette in his mouth, and exhaled two long plumes of smoke from his nostrils. Kate thought about how the pillows would smell after he'd gone.

"He's sound asleep, but really stuffed up."

"How old is he?"

"He's just three."

"Cute age," Charlie said, tapping his cigarette on the saucer. "I've got two, you know."

"Two kids?" She was surprised. He nodded. "I would never have guessed that about you, Charlie. You're too much the gay blade, the town rake."

He grinned appreciatively. He worked at it, and liked to know his efforts were successful. "They're in Connecticut with my ex-wife."

"Do you see them often?"

"About once a month I guess. She's remarried, so they've got a whole family scene there, really." He shrugged. "It doesn't seem so important anymore. They're pretty much into their life, I'm pretty much into mine, *you* know."

"Yes," she said. They sat in what she imagined he thought was companionable silence. Two used parents. She had an old iron bed-stead with a large ornate grille for a headboard. Charlie's head had slipped into the space between two of the white painted rods. They pushed his ears forward slightly. He looked a little like the Mickey Mouse night light in Neddie's room. She smiled. She wondered why she had been so excited about going out with him tonight. When he'd finished his cigarette, he reached for her again. She set her wineglass down on the floor by her side of the bed and they made love. Charlie seemed interested in some variations on their earlier theme, but she shook her head no, no, and their lovemaking was short and somewhat neutral in character. Just as he pulled limply and stickily away from her to find another cigarette, Neddie's agonized shout floated back through the apartment to her. She leaped out of bed, upsetting her half-empty wineglass, but avoiding the plant this time, and sprinted into the light and down the long hallway, pushing her breasts flat onto her chest to keep them from bouncing painfully.

Neddie's eyes were still shut. He had turned over onto his back and tears ran down his cheeks into his ears. The covers were piled on the floor. "Nooo, monkey!" he moaned, and thrashed. Kate picked him up and cradled him close, his wet face pressing on her neck.

"Neddie, it's Mommy. Mommy's here now. *No* monkeys. The monkeys are all gone. You're in your room, Neddie, with Mommy, see?" She pulled her head back to look at him. His eyes were open now, but he looked blank. She walked around the room with him, talking slowly.

"We're at home, Neddie. You had a dream. That wasn't real. That silly monkey was a dream. See, here's Sleazy. He's real." She pointed to Ned's bear, sitting on a shelf. Ned reached for him. "Sleazy," he said, and tucked him in close under his chin, the way Kate held him. She shifted him to her hip now, and went around the room, showing him all his favorite things. Kate was tall and thin. She had down-drooping breasts and flat narrow hips. She looked like a carved white column in the dim light.

"And look, Ned. Look what's happening out here." she carried him to the window. Under the street light outside Ned's room the flakes danced thickly in a sudden gust of wind: a thousand suicidal moths. "Do you know what that is?"

"Dat's da snow!' he said. His mouth hung open and his breath was hot and damp on her breast.

"And it's all piling up on the ground, Neddie, see? And tomorrow we can find the sled that Daddy gave you in the basement, and put on boots and mittens . . ."

"And my hat?" Ned wore a baseball hat every day. He watched her face now to be sure that they were in agreement on this.

"Yeah, your hat, but you have to pull your hood up over it to keep your ears warm. And we can play all day because tomorrow's Sunday. Mommy doesn't have to work."

"Not day care?"

"No, tomorrow we can stay home *all* day. Okay?" They watched the snow together for a moment. Then she turned from the window. "I'm going to tuck you in now." She carried the child to his bed and started to lower him. His legs and arms gripped her tightly, a monkey's grip.

"Stay here, Mumma."

"Okay." He relaxed, and let her put him down on the bed. "But Mommy's cold. You move over and make room for me under these covers." He wiggled back against the wall and she slid in next to him and pulled the covers over them both. His face was inches from hers. He smiled at her and reached up to pat her face. His hands were sticky and warm. "Mumma," he said.

"Yes," she said tenderly, and shut her eyes to set a good example for him. Sometime later she woke to hear the front door shut gently, and footsteps going down the stairs. Then dimly, as if at a great distance, or as if it were all happening in some muffled, underwater world, a car started up in the street, there was a brief series of whirring sounds while it struggled back and forth out of its parking place, and then, like a thin cry, its noise evaporated into the night.

When Neddie woke her, the sky was still gray. The light in the room was gray too, gentle and chaste. The snow had stuck in the mesh of the screens still left on the windows from summer and the house seemed wrapped in gauze. It still fell outside, heavy and soft, but from somewhere on the street came the chink, chink of a lone optimist already shoveling.

"Ned. Let me sleep a minute more."

"You already slept a long time, Mumma. And I *need* you."

He was standing by the bed, his face just above her head. He wore a red baseball cap, and his brown eyes regarded her gravely.

"Why do you need me?"

"You hafta make my train go."

"What, Granpoppy's train?" He shook his head solemnly. "Oh, Christ!" she swore, and violently threw the covers back, swinging her legs out in the same motion. He looked fearful, and instantly she felt remorseful. "No, Neddie, it's all right. I'm just mad at the *train.* I'll fix it."

Her parents had given Ned the train, an expensive Swedish model of painted wood. The cars fastened together with magnets. Occasionally, by chance, Ned would line them up correctly, but most often, one or two cars would be turned backwards, north pole to north pole, or south to south, and the more he would try to push them together, the more they repelled each other. Her parents' extravagance since her divorce, their attempts to ease her way and Ned's with things she didn't want and couldn't use, annoyed her. She must have bent down to correct the magnetic attraction on this thing thirty times since they had given it to Ned.

He came and squatted by her. He had laid the track out and there were miniature pigs and sheep and ducks heaped up in the tiny open train cars. The thought of his working silently for so long, trying not to wake her, touched her. As they squatted together she began to try to explain to him the idea of polar attraction, turning the brightly painted cars first one way and then the other, so he could see the greedy pull at work.

Suddenly his head dipped slightly to look underneath her and his expression changed. She stopped. "Mumma's leaking?" he asked, pointing to the floor. She shifted her weight to one leg and looked on the floor, where she'd been squatting. Thick drops of whitish liquid, reminders of lovemaking the night before, glistened like pearls on the nicked wood. She laughed and got up to get some Kleenex.

"It's all right, Neddie. Mommy can clean it up in a second. See?" she said. "All gone."

She smiled down at him as he squatted, fuzzy and compact in his sleeper, like a baby bear. He turned away and began to pull the toy train, now perfectly attached, around the expensive track.

Shoptalk #3
On Rejection and Persistence

There was, I knew, disappointment, hurt, and pain associated with any rejection of one's work. But there were also, coincident with this, I was now reminded by letters from writers, things that—along with crushed hopes and bitterness and envy—joined us to one another: the knowledge of our common lot, of a shared struggle; the desire, most simply, to write the books and stories one yearned to be able to write; the desire to see one's work into print; the desire to be read. And there was, always, no matter the quality of the work and the energy that produced it, the common fact and possibility of not seeing one's work into print, of not being read.

(Jay Neugeboren, "Introduction," vol. 6, no. 3, 1980)

CAROLYN CHUTE

"Ollie, Oh . . ."

Carolyn Chute has written her own headnote, as follows:

"*Nineteen-eighty-something. I was sitting in on classes at the new Stonecoast Writers' Conference. I didn't have the money to be a real student but the director Ken Rosen said that wouldn't be a problem. So I used to skip around in different classes, George Garrett, Alix Kates Shulman, one doing short story, the other the novel. Shop talk. That's the thing you need badly as a writer, since you are otherwise alone with yourself and nobody in the REAL WORLD understands you.*

"*At this conference, Ellen Wilbur, the short story writer, was a guest. Ken Rosen suggested she read a story of mine. She graciously said yes.*

"*I mailed her the story, '"Ollie, oh . . ."' and she read it and suggested to Don Hall, the* Ploughshares *editor for that quarter's issue, that he look at it.*

"*He did. He took the story.*

"*After that,* Best American Short Stories *used it in their 1982 edition. Shannon Ravenal was the editor of that [John Gardner was guest editor].*

"*Meanwhile Madison Bell, a buddy of George Garrett's who had also been at Stonecoast, as an assistant to George, read some of a novel I had called* The Beans. *He suggested to his agent, Jane Gelfman, that she look at this novel. She did. And she sent it to Cork Smith, who took it as his first book on his first day at Ticknor & Fields.*

"*Getting published is kind of like sneezing on someone, and then it gets passed on to a bunch of other people who all catch your germs, but instead of germy germs, it is your words and passions, once shy, now OUT THERE."*

Carolyn Chute's books are The Beans of Egypt, Maine *(1994),* Letourneau's Used Auto Parts *(1995),* Merry Men: A Novel *(1995),* Up River: The Story of a Maine Fishing Community *(1996), and* Snow Man *(as editor, 1999).*

I

Erroll, the deputy who was known to litter, did not toss any Fresca cans or Old King Cole bags out this night. Erroll brought his Jeep to a stop in the yard right behind Lenny Cobb's brand new Dodge pickup. The brakes of Erroll, the deputy's, Jeep made a spiritless dusky squeak. Erroll was kind of humble this night. The greenish light of his police radio shone on his face and yes, the froggishly round eyes, mostly pupil because it was dark, were humble. His lips were shut down over his teeth that were usually laughing and clicking. Humbleness had gone so far as to make that mouth look almost HEALED over like the holes in women's ears when they stop putting earrings through. He took off his knit cap and laid it on the seat beside the empty Fresca can, potato chip bag, and cigar cellophanes. He put his gloved hand on the door opener to get out. But he paused. He was scared of Ollie Cobb. He wasn't sure how she would take the news. But she wasn't going to take it like other women did. Erroll tried to swallow but there was no saliva there to work around in his throat.

He looked at Lenny Cobb's brand new Dodge in the lights of his Jeep. It was so cold out there that night that the rootbeer-color paint was sealed over every inch in a delicate film like an apple still attached, still ripening, never been handled. Wasn't Lenny Cobb's truck the prince of trucks? Even the windshield and little vent windows looked heavy-duty . . . as though congealed inside their rubber strips thick and deep as the frozen Sebago. And the chrome was heavy as pots. And the plow! It was constricted into travel gear, not yet homely from running into stone walls and frost heaves. And on the cab roof an amber light, the swivel kind, big as a man's head. Of course it had four-wheel drive. It had shoulders! Thighs. Spine. It might be still growing.

The Jeep door opened. The minute he stood up out in the crunchy driveway he wished he had left his cap on. The air was like paper, could have been thirty below. His breath leaving his nose turned to paper. It was all so still and silent. With no lights on in Lenny Cobb's place, a feeling came over Erroll of being alone at the North Pole. Come to his ears a lettuce-like crispness, a keenness . . . so that to the top arch of each ear his spinal cord plugged in. A cow murred in the barn. One murr. A single note. And yet the yard was so thirsty for sound . . . all planes gave off the echo: a stake to mark a rosebush under snow . . . an apple basket full of snow on the top step. He gave the door ten or twelve thonks with his gloved knuckles. It HURT.

Ollie Cobb did not turn on a light inside or out. She just spread open the door and stood looking down at him through the small round frames of her glasses. She wore a long rust-colored robe with pockets. The doorway was outside the apron of light the Jeep headlights made. Erroll had to squint to make her out, the thin hair. It was black, parted in the middle of her scalp, yanked back with such efficiency that the small fruit-shape of her head was clear: a lemon or a lime. And just as taut and businesslike, pencil-hard, pencil-sized, a braid was drawn nearly to her heels . . . the toes, long as thumbs, clasped the sill. "Deputy Anderson," she said. She had many teeth. Like shingles. They seemed to start out of her mouth when she opened it.

He said: "Ah . . ."

Erroll couldn't know when the Cobb house had rotted past saving, yet more certain than the applewood banked in the stove, the smell of dying timbers came to him warmly . . . almost rooty, like carrots . . .

"What IS it?" she said.

He thought of the great sills of that old house being soft as carrots. "Lenny has passed away," he said.

She stepped back. He was hugged up close to the openness of the door, trying to get warm, so when the door whapped shut, his foot was in it. "ARRRRR!" So he got his foot out. She slammed the door again. When he got back in his Jeep, his coffee fell off the dash and burned his leg.

2

The kitchen light came on. All Ollie's white-haired children came into the living room when she started to growl and rub her shoulder on the refrigerator. This was how Ollie grieved. She rolled her shoulders over the refrigerator door so some of the magnetic fruits fell on the floor. A math paper with a 98 on top seesawed downward and landed on the linoleum. The kids were happy for a chance to be up. "Oh, boy!" they said. All but Aspen who was twelve and could understand. She remained at the bottom of the stairs afraid to ask Ollie what the trouble was. Aspen was in a lilac-color flannel gown and gray wool socks. She sucked the thumb of her right hand and hugged the post of the banister with her left. It was three-fifteen in the morning. Applewood coals never die. All 'round the woodstove was an aura of summer. The socks and undershirts and mittens pinned in scores to a rope across the room had a summer stillness. They heard Ollie growl and pant. They giggled. Sometimes they stopped and looked up when she got loud. They figured she was not getting her way about something. They had seen the

deputy, Erroll, leave from the upstairs windows. They associated
Erroll with crime. Crime was that vague business of speeding tickets and expired inspection stickers. This was not a new thing. Erroll had come up in his Jeep behind Ollie a time or two in the village. He said: "Red light." And she bore her teeth at him like a dog.
She was baring her teeth now.

There was an almost Christmas spirit among the children to
be wakened in the night like that. There was wrestling. There was
wriggling. Tim rode the dog: Dick Lab. He, Dick Lab, would try
to get away, but hands on his hocks would keep him back. Judy
turned on the t.v. Nothing was on the screen but bright fuzz. The
hair of them all flying through the night was the torches of after-
dark skiers: crackling white from chair to couch to chair to stair-
way, rolling Dick Lab on his side, carouseling twelve-year-old
Aspen who sucked her thumb. Eddie and Arnie, Tim and Judy.

The herdsman's name was Jarrell Bean. He was like all Beans,
silent and touchy, and had across his broad coffee-color face a look
which made you suspect he was related somehow, perhaps on his
mother's side, to some cows. The eyes were slate-color and were of
themselves lukewarm-looking, almost steamy, very huge, browless,
while like hands they reached out and patted things that interested
him. He inherited from his father, Bingo Bean, a short haircut . . .
a voluntary baldness: Father's real name was also Jarrell, killed
chickens for work and had the kind of red finely lined fingers you'd
expect from so much murder. But Bingo's eyes everybody knows
were yellow and utility. It was from Mother's side that Jarrell the
herdsman managed to know what tact was. He came to the Cobbs'
door from his apartment over the barn. He had seen the deputy
Erroll's Jeep and figured Lenny's time had come. He was wearing
a black and red checked coat and the spikes of a three-day beard,

auburn. It was the kind of beard men adrift in lifeboats have. Unkind weather had spread each of the hairs its own way.

He had traveled several yards through that frigid night with NO HAT. This was nudity for a man so bald.

In his mouth was quite a charge of gum. He didn't knock. The kitchen started to smell of spearmint as soon as he closed the door behind him. Ollie was rolled into a ball on the floor, grunting, one bare foot, bare calf and knee extended. He stepped over the leg. He made Ollie's children go up the stairs. He dragged one by the arm. It howled. Its flare of pale hair spurted here and there at the herdsman's elbow. The entire length of the child was twisting. It was Randy who was eight and strong. Dick Lab sat down on the twelve-year-old Aspen's ankles and feet, against the good wool. Jarrell came down the stairs hard. His boots made a booming through the whole big house. He took Dane and Linda and Hannah all at once. Aspen kept sucking her thumb. She looked up at him as he came down toward her, seeing him over her fingers. She was big as a woman. Her thumb in her mouth was longer and lighter than the others from twelve years of sucking. He fetched her by the blousey part of her lilac gown. She came away from the banister with a snap: like a bandaide from a hairy arm . . . "Cut it out!" she cried. His hands were used only to cattle. He thought of himself as GOOD with cattle, not at all cruel. And yet with cattle what is to be done is always the will of the herdsman.

3

When Jarrell came downstairs, Ollie was gone. She had been thinking of Lenny's face, how it had been evaporating for months into the air, how the lip had gotten short, how the cheeks fell into the bone. While Jarrell stood in the kitchen, he picked up the magnetic fruits and stuck them in a row on the top door of the refrigerator. He figured Ollie had slipped into her room to be alone.

He walked out into the yard past Lenny's new rootbeer-color truck. He remembered how it roared when Leo at the Mobil had fiddled with the accelerator and everyone: Merritt and Poochie and Poochie's brother and Kenny, even Quinlan stood around looking in at the big 440 and Lenny was resting on the running board. Lenny's neck was getting much too small for his collar even then.

Jarrell went up to his apartment over the barn, his head stinging from the deep-freeze night, then his lamp went out and the yard was noiseless.

Under the rootbeer truck Ollie was curled with her braid in the snow. She had big bare feet. Under the rust-color robe the goosebumps crowned up. Her eyes were squeezed shut like children do when they pretend to be sleeping. Her lip was drawn back from the elegantly twisted teeth, twisted like the stiff feathers of a goose are overlayed. And filling one eyeglass lens a dainty ice fern.

4

It was Ollie whose scheduled days and evenings were on a tablet taped to the bathroom door. Every day Ollie got up at 4:30 a.m. Every evening supper was at 5:45. If visitors showed up late by fifteen minutes, she would whine at them and punish them with remarks about their character. If she were on her way to the feedstore in the pickup and there was a two-car accident blocking the road up ahead, Ollie would roll down the window and yell: "MOVE!!"

Once Aspen's poor body nearly smoked, a hundred and two temperature, and blew a yellow mass from her little nose holes . . . a morning when Ollie had plans for the lake . . . Lenny was standing in the yard with his railroad cap on and his ringless hands in

the pockets of his cardigan, leaning on the new rootbeer truck . . .
Ollie came out on the porch where many wasps were circling between her face and his eyes looking up: "She's going to spoil our
time," Ollie said. "We've got to go down to the store and call for an
appointment now. She couldn't have screwed up the day any better." Then she went back inside and made her hand like a clamp on
the girl's bicep, bore down on it with the might of a punch or a kick,
only more slow, more deep. Tears came to Aspen's eyes. Outside
Lenny heard nothing. Only the sirens of wasps. And stared into the
very middle of their churning.

Oh, that Ollie. Indeed, Lenny months before must have
planned his cancer to ruin her birthday. That was the day of the
doctor's report. All the day Lenny cried. Right in the lobby of the
hospital . . . a scene . . . Lenny holding his eyes with the palms of
his hands: "Help me! Help me!" he wailed . . . she steered him to a
plastic chair. She hurried down the hall to be alone with the snack
machine . . . HEALTHY SNACKS: apples and pears, peanuts.
She despised HIM this way. THIS was her birthday.

5

In the thirty below ZERO morning jays' voices cracked from the
roof. Figures in orange nylon jackets hustled over the snow. They
covered Ollie with a white wool blanket. The children were steady
with their eyes and statuesque as they arranged themselves around
the herdsman. Aspen held the elbow of his black and red coat.
Everyone's breath flattened out like paper, like those clouds car-
toon personalities' words are printed on. It may have warmed up
some. Twenty below or fifteen below. The cattle had not been
milked, shuffling and ramming and murring, cramped near the
open door of the barn . . . in pain . . . their udders as vulgar and
hard as the herdsman's velvet head.

6

At the hospital surgeons removed the ends of Ollie's fingers, most of her toes and her ears. She drank Carnation Instant Breakfast, grew sturdy again, and learned to keep her balance. She came home with her thin hair combed to cover her ear holes. In the back her hair veiled her ruby coat.

She got up every morning at 4:30 and hurtled herself out to the barn to set up for milking. Jarrell feared every minute that her hair might fall away from her missing ears. He would squint at her. To-gether they sold some of the milk to the neighborhood, those who came in cars and pulling sleds, unloading plastic jugs and glass jars to be filled at the sink, and the children of these neighbors would stare at Ollie's short fingers, the parents would look all around everyplace BUT the short fingers. Jarrell: "Whatcha got today, only two . . . Is ya company gone?" or "How's Ralph's team doin now? . . . That's good ta hear" or "Fishin any good now? I ain't heard." He talked a lot these days. When they came around he brightened up. He opened doors for them and listened to gossip and passed it on. They teased him a lot about his lengthening beard. Sometimes Tim would stand between Jarrell and Ollie and somehow managed to have his hand on the backs of Jarrell's knees most the time. As Ollie hosed out the stainless steel sink there in the wood and glass white white room, Tim's eyes came over the sink edge and watched the water whirl.

At night Jarrell would open Mason jars and slice carrots or cut the tops off beets. Ollie would lift things slowly with her purpley stubs. She set the table. She would look at Jarrell to see if he saw how slick she did this. But he was not looking. The children, all those towheads, would be throwing things and running in the hall.

There had come puppies of Dick Lab. Tim and a buff puppy pulled on a sock. Tim dragged the puppy by the sock across the rug. Ollie would stand by the sink and look straight ahead. She had a spidery control over her short fingers. She once hooked small Marsha up by the hair and pressed her to the woodbox with her knee. But Ollie was wordless. Things would usually go well. By 5:45 forks of beets and squash were lifted to mouths and glasses of milk were draining.

After supper Jarrell would go back to his apartment and watch Real People and That's Incredible or Sixty Minutes and fall asleep with his clothes on. He had a pile of rootbeer cans by the bed. Sometimes mice would knock them over and the cans would roll out of the room, but it never woke him.

Jarrell could not go to the barn in the morning without thinking of Lenny. He would go along and pull the rows of chains to all the glaring gray lights. He and Lenny used to stand by the open door together. That black and white pokadot SEA of cows would clatter between them. And over and between the blowing mouths and oily eyes, Lenny's dollar-ninety-eight-cent gloves waved them on, and he'd say: "Oh, girl . . . oh, girl . . ." Their thundering never ever flicked Lenny's watered-down auburn hair that was thin on top. And there was the hairless temples where the chemotherapy had seared from the inside out.

Jarrell could recall Lenny's posture, a peculiar tired slouch in his p-coat. Lenny wore a watch cap in mid-winter and a railroad cap in sweaty weather and the oils of his forehead was on the brims of both.

Jarrell remembered summer when there was a big corn on the cob feast and afterward Lenny lay on the couch with just his dungarees on and his veiny bare feet kicking. His hairless chest was stamped with three black tattooes; two sailing ships and a lizard. Tim was jumping on his stomach. A naked baby lay on its back, covering the two ships. Lenny put his arm around the baby and it seemed to melt into him. Lenny's long face had that sleepy look of someone whose world is interior, immediate to the skin, never reaching outside his hundred and twenty acres. That very night that Lenny played on the couch with his children, Jarrell left early and stayed awake late in his apartment watching Tim Conway dictating in a German accent to his nitwit secretary.

Jarrel heard Ollie yelling. He leaned out his window and heard more clearly Ollie rasping out her husband's name. Once she leaped across the gold square of light of their bedroom window. Jarrell knew that Lenny was sitting on the edge of the bed, perhaps with his pipe in his mouth, untying his gray peeling workboots. Lenny would not argue, nor cry, nor turn red, but say: ". . . Oh, girl . . . oh, Ollie, oh . . ." And he would look up at her with his narrow face, his eyes turning here and there on his favorite places of her face. She would be enraged the more. She picked up the workboot he had just pulled off his foot and turned it in her hand . . . then spun it through the air . . . the lamp went out and crashed.

Lenny began to lose weight in the fall. In his veins white blood cells roared. The cancer was starting to make Lenny irritable. He stopped eating supper. Ollie called it fussy. Soon Ollie and Jarrell were doing the milking alone. Sometimes Aspen would help. Lenny lay on the couch and slept. He slept all day.

7

One yellowy morning Ollie made some marks on the list on the bathroom door and put a barrette on the end of her braid. She took the truck to Leo's and had the tank filled. She drove all day with

Lenny's face against her belly. Then with her hard spine and con-
vexed shoulders she balanced Lenny against herself and steered
him up the stairs of the Veterans' hospital. She came out alone and
her eyes were wide behind the round glasses.

8

Jarrell had driven Lenny's rootbeer Utiline Dodge for the first
time when he drove to the funeral alone. Lenny had a closed casket.
The casket was in an alcove with pink lights and stoop-shouldered
mumbley Cobbs. They all smelled like old Christmas cologne.
There must have been a hundred Cobbs. Most of the flowers
around the coffin were white. Jarrell stood. The rest were sitting.
The herdsman's head was pink in the funny light and he tilted his
head as he considered how Lenny looked inside the coffin, under
the lid. Cotton was in Lenny's eyes. He probably had skin like those
plaster of Paris ducks that hike over people's lawns single file. He
was most likely in there in some kind of suit, no p-coat, no watch
cap, no pipe, no babies, no grit of Flash in his nails. Someone had
undoubtedly scrubbed all the cow smell off him and he probably
smelled like a new doll now. Jarrell drove to the interment at about
80 to 85 miles per hour and was waiting when the headlighted cara-
van dribbled into the cemetery and the stooped Cobbs ambled out
of about fifty old cars.

9

Much later, after Lenny was dead awhile and Ollie's fingers were
healed, Ollie came into the barn about 6:10. They were running
late. The dairy truck from Portland was due to arrive in the yard.
Ollie was wearing Lenny's old p-coat and khaki shirt with her new
knit pants. Tim was with her. Tim had a brief little mouth and

freakish coarse hair, like white weeds. His coat was fastened with safety pins. Ollie started hooking up the machines with her quick half-fingers. They rolled like sausages over the stainless steel surfaces. Jarrell, hurrying to catch up, was impatient with the cows when they wanted to shift around. Ollie was soundless but Jarrell could locate her even if he didn't see her, even as she progressed down the length of the barn. He had radar in his chest (the heart, the lungs, even the bladder) for her position when things were running late. God! It was like trying to walk through a wall· of sand. Tim came over and stood behind him. Tim was digging in his nose. He was dragging out long strings of discolored matter and wiping it on his coat that was fastened with pins. One cow pulled far to the right in the stanchion, almost buckling to her knees as a hind foot slipped off the edge of the concrete platform. The milking machine thunked to the floor out of Jarrell's hands. Ollie heard. Her face came as if from out of the loft, sort of downward. HER HAIR WAS PULLED BACK caught up by her glasses when she had hurriedly shoved them on. SHE DID NOT HAVE EARS. HE SAW FOR THE FIRST TIME THEY HAD TAKEN HER EARS. His whole shape under his winter clothes went hot as though common pins were inserted over every square inch. He squinted, turned away . . . ran out of the milking room into the snow. The dairy truck from the city was purring up the hill. The fellow inside flopped his arm out for his routine wave. Jarrell didn't wave back, but used both hands to pull himself up into the rootbeer truck, slid across the cold seat, made the engine roar. He remembered Lenny saying once while they broke up bales of hay: "I just ordered a Dodge last week, me and my wife . . . be a few weeks, they said. Probly for the President they'd have it to him the next day. Don't it HURT to wait for somethin like that. Last night I dreamed I was in it, and was revvin it up out here in the yard when all of a sudden it took off . . . right up in the sky . . . and all the cows down in the yard looked like dominoes."

10

That afternoon Jarrell Bean returned. He came up the old Nathan Lord Road slow. Had his arm out the window. When he got near the Cobb place he ascended the hill in a second-gear roar. As he turned in the drive he saw Ollie in Lenny's p-coat standing by the doorless Buick sedan in which the hens slept at night. She lined the sights of Lenny's rifle with the right lens of her glasses. One of her sausage fingers was on the trigger. She put out two shots. They turned the right front tire to rags. The Dodge screamed and plowed sideways into the culvert. Jarrell felt it about to tip over. But it only listed. He lay flat on the seat for a quarter of an hour even after he was certain Ollie had gone into the house.

Aspen and Judy came out for him. He was crying, lying on his stomach. When they saw him crying, their faces went white. Aspen put her hard gray fingers on his back, between his shoulders. She turned to Judy . . . Judy, fat and clear-skinned with the whitest hair of all . . . and said: "I think he's sorry."

11

Ollie lay under the mint-green bedspread. The window was open. All the yard, the field, the irrigation ditches, the dead birds were thawing and under the window she heard a cat digging in the jonquils and dried leaves. She raised her hand of partial fingers to her mouth to wipe the corners. She had slept late again and now her blood pressure pushed at the walls of her head. She flipped out of the bed and thunked across the floor to the window. She was in a yellow print gown. The sunrise striking off the vanity mirror gave Ollie's face and arms a yellowness, too. She seized her glasses under

the lamp. She peered through them, downward . . . STARTLED.
Jarrell was a few yards from his apartment doorway, taking a pair
of dungarees from the clothesline. There were sheets hanging
there, too, so it was hard to be sure at first . . . then as he strode
back toward his doorway, she realized he had nothing on. He was
corded and pale and straight-backed and down front of his chest
dripped wet his now full auburn beard. The rounded walls of his
genitals gave little flaccid jogglings at each stride and on all of him
his flesh like unbroken yellow water paused satisfyingly and sel-
domly at a few auburn hairs. On top, the balded head, a seamless
hood, trussed up with temples all the way in that same seamless
fashion to his eyes which were merry in the most irritating way.
Ollie mashed her mouth and shingled teeth to the screen and
moaned full and cowlike. And when he stopped and looked up, she
screeched: "I HATE YOU! GET OUT OF HERE! GET OUT
OF HERE!"

  She scuttled to the bed and plunked to the edge. Underneath,
the shoes which Lenny wore to bean suppers and town council
meetings were still criss-crossed against the wall.

12

That summer Jarrell and the kids played "catch" in the middle of
the Nathan Lord Road. Jarrell waded among them at the green
bridge in knee-deep water, slapped Tim a time or two for per-
sisting near the drop-off. They laughed at the herdsman in his
second-hand tangerine trunks and rubber sandals. He took them
to the drive-in movies in that rootbeer truck. They saw Benji and
Last Tango in Paris. They got popcorn and Good n Plentys all over
the seat and floor and empty paper cups were mashed in the truck
bed, blew out one by one onto different people's lawns. He

splurged on them at Old Orchard Beach, rides and games, and co-ordinated Aspen won stuff with darts: a psychodelic poster, a stretched-out Pepsi bottle and four paper leis. Then under the pier they were running with huge ribbons of seaweed and he cut his foot on a busted Miller High Life bottle . . . slumped in the sand to fuss over himself. It didn't bleed. You could see into his arch, the meat, but no blood. Aspen's white hair waved 'round her head as she stooped in her sunsuit of cotton dots, blue like babies' clothes are blue. She cradled his poor foot in her fingers and looked him in the eye.

Ollie NEVER went with them. No one knew what she did alone at home.

One afternoon Ollie stared through the heat to find Jarrell on the front porch, there in a rocking chair with the sleeping baby's open mouth spread on his bare arm. Nearly grown puppies were at his feet. He was almost asleep himself and mosquitoes were indus-triously draining his throat and shirtless chest. On the couch after supper the little girls nestled in his auburn beard and rolled in their fingers wads of the course stuff. The coon cat with the abcesses all over his head swallowed whole the red tuna Jarrell bought for him and set out at night on an aluminum pie plate. Jarrell whenever he was close smelled like cows.

13

Ollie drove to the drugstore for pills that were for blood pressure. Aspen went along. The rootbeer truck rattled because Jarrell had left a yarding sled and chains in the back. Ollie turned her slow rust-color eyes onto Aspen's face and Aspen felt suddenly pan-icked. It seemed as though there was something changing about her mother's eyes: one studied your skin, one bored dead center in your soul. Aspen was wearing her EXTINCT IS FOREVER t-shirt. It was apricot-colored and there was a leopard's face in the middle of her chest.

"Do you want one of those?" Ollie asked Aspen who was poking at the flavored Chapsticks by the cash register.

"Could I?"

"Sure." Ollie pointed somewhere. "And I was thinking you might like some colored pencils or a . . . you know . . . movie magazine."

Aspen squinted. "I would, yes, I would."

A trio of high-school-aged Crocker boys in stretched-out t-shirts trudged through the open door in a bow-legged way that made them seem to be carrying much more weight than just their smooth long bones and little gummy muscles. One wore a baseball hat and had sweat in his hair and carried his sneakers. He turned his flawless neck, and his pink hair cropped there in a straight line was fuzzy and friendly like ruffles on a puppy's shoulders where you pat. He looked right at Aspen's leopard . . . right in the middle and read: "Extinct is forever."

His teeth lifted in a perfect cream-color line over the words and his voice was low and rolled, one octave above adulthood. Both the other boys laughed. One made noises like he was dying. Then all of them pointed their fingers at her and said: "Bang! Bang! Bang!" There are the insightful ones who realize a teenager's way of flirt-ing and then there was Aspen who could not. To see all the boys' faces from her plastic desk in school was to Aspen like having a small easily destructible boat with sharks in all directions. Sud-denly self-conscious, suddenly stoop-shouldered as it was for all Cobbs in moments of hell, Aspen stood one shoe on top of the other and stuck her thumb in her mouth. There is something about drugstore light with its smells of sample colognes passing up like moths through a brightness bigger and pinker than sun which made Aspen Cobb look large and old and the long thumb there was nasty looking. The pink-haired Crockers had never seen a big girl do this. They looked at each other gravely.

She walked over to where her mother was holding a jar of vitamin C. Her mother was arched over it, the veils of her thin black hair covering her ear holes, falling foreward, and her stance was gathering, coordinated like a spider, the bathtub spider, the horriblest kind. She lifted her eyes. Aspen pulled her thumb out of her mouth and wiped it on her shirt. Ollie put her arm around Aspen. She never did this as a rule. Aspen looked at her mother's face disbelievingly. Ollie pointed with one stub to the vitamin C bottle. It said: "200% of the adult minimum daily requirement." Aspen pulled away. The Crocker boys at the counter looked from Ollie's fingers to Aspen's thumb. But not til they were outside did they shriek and hoot.

On the way home in the truck Aspen wished her mother would hug her again now that they were alone. But Ollie's fingers were sealed to the wheel and her eyes blurred by the glasses were looking out from a place where no hugging ever happened. There was a real slow Volkswagen up ahead driven by a white-haired man. Ollie gave him the horn.

14

The list of activities on the bathroom door became more rigidly ordered . . . with even trips to the flush, snacks and rests, and conversations with the kids pre-scheduled . . . peanutbutter and Saltines: 3:15 . . . clear table: 6:30 . . . brush hair: 9:00 . . . and Ollie moved faster and faster and her cement-color hands and face were always across the yard somewhere or in the other room . . . singular of other people. And Jarrell looked in at her open bedroom door as he scooted Dane toward the bathroom for a wash . . . Ollie was CLEANING OUT THE BUREAU AGAIN, THE THIRD TIME THAT WEEK . . . and she was doing it very fast.

In September there was a purple night and the children all loaded into the back of the truck. Randy strapped the baby into her seat in the cab. The air had a dry grasshopper smell and the truck bed was still hot from the day. Jarrell turned the key to the rootbeer-color truck. "I'm getting a Needham!" he heard Timmy blat from the truck bed. He pulled on the headlights knob. He shifted into reverse. The truck creaked into motion. The rear wheel went up, then down. Then the front went up and down. Sliding into the truck lights was the yellow gown, the mashed gray arm, the black hair unbraided, the face unshowing but with a purple liquid going everywhere from out of that hair, the half-fingers wriggling just a little. She had been under the truck again.

From the deepest part of Jarrell Bean the scream would not stop even as he hobbled out of the truck. Oh, he feared to touch her, just rocked and rocked and hugged himself and howled. The children's high whines began. They covered Ollie like flies. As with blueberry jam their fingers were dipped a sticky purple. The herdsman reached for the twelve-year-old Aspen. He pulled at her. Her lids slid over icy eyes. Her breath was like carrots into his breath. He reached. And her frame folded into his hip.

Shoptalk #4

On Incantatory Style

An author's style represents not simply a technical know-how, but a way of seeing, the manner in which consciousness apprehends experience.

(Scott Turow, "Yonnondio: From the Thirties," vol. 2, no. 2, 1974)

Shoptalk #5

On Directive Ironies

One notices in most contemporary realism gaps between sentences such that . . . the reader is made to leap from one bit or fragment to the next as the writer asserts: this sensibility, my own or my narrator's, is strong enough to make leaps, to need little in the way of ground transportation. It is not a voice asserting, "Watch me," like an imperialist, and the leaps are something we do as a thing of beauty or athletic feat. To get over the gaps, to keep jumping, to keep wondering where one now is, is to be aware of a writer asserting a kind of strength that, especially in its cumulative effects, is very strong indeed.

(Roger Sale, "The Golden Age of the American Novel," vol. 4, no. 3, 1978)

EDWARD P. JONES

A Dark Night

A feature article on Edward P. Jones by Pamela Woolford, "Stories from Our Nation's Capital" (Poets & Writers Magazine, *November/December 1995), recounts how the death of Jones's mother in 1975 led him to write the story that became his first published piece of fiction, "Harvest," in* Essence. *On the basis of this story, he was admitted to a workshop at George Washington University with Susan Richards Shreves, and later he received a Henry Hoyns Fellowship to attend the University of Virginia, where he studied with James Alan McPherson. "McPherson, a contributing editor at the* Atlantic Monthly, *asked editors at* Atlantic Monthly, Ploughshares, *and* Callaloo *to read Jones's work," the article continues. "The first story Jones sent to the* Atlantic Monthly *was 'A Dark Night.' . . . It was rejected with a note saying that the magazine did not publish stories about old women. This same piece was later published by* Ploughshares. *Another editor at* Atlantic Monthly, *unaware that the story had been submitted to and rejected by* Atlantic Monthly *first, read it in* Ploughshares *and wrote to Jones asking to see his work."*

"A Dark Night" appeared in a 1981 Ploughshares *edited by James Randall, and was reprinted in* The Ploughshares Reader: New Stories for the Eighties *(ed. DeWitt Henry, 1985). A second story, "Island," appeared in a 1983 issue edited by George Garrett. Other stories appeared in* Callaloo *and the* Seattle Review *before Jones started writing most of the selections in* Lost in the City, *a volume of*

fourteen stories that seeks to convey "the multiplicity of blacks in Washington, D.C."

Lost in the City *was published by Morrow in 1992 and was winner of PEN's 1993 Hemingway Foundation Award for best first fiction. It was also a National Book Award finalist.* Newsday *commented, "The stunning success of* Lost in the City *. . . is amplified by the knowledge that the world whose news this author brings is precisely the one that many of us who live in urban America are standing in but do not see. . . . [Jones] brings a Chekovian patience, respect, and reserve to the world he describes, and it is, somehow, precisely this old-fashioned quality, brought to bear on the modern African-American community, that makes* Lost in the City *so bracingly new."*

Jones's work appears in numerous anthologies, including The Vintage Book of Contemporary Short Fiction; Brotherman: The Odyssey of Black Men in America—An Anthology; Street Lights: Illuminating Tales of the Urban Black Experience; *and* Children of the Night: The Best Short Stories by Black Writers 1967 to the Present. *Jones is also a widely published essayist and a playwright. He is currently teaching at Virginia Commonwealth University.*

About four that afternoon the thunder and lightning began again. The five women seated about Mrs. Boone's one-room apartment grew still and spoke with lowered voices and in whispers, when they spoke at all: they were no longer young, and they had all been raised to believe that such weather was the closest thing to the voice of God. And so each in her way listened.

They heard a door down the hall open and shut, and within seconds they saw Mrs. Garrett move almost soundlessly past Mrs. Boone's open door, a rubber-tipped brown cane in her hand. She went down the hall and knocked again and again at a door. The door did not open and she came back, just as soundlessly, and suddenly she was standing small and silent in the doorway. There was something forlorn about her as she stood there, about her face, the way her glasses rested near the end of her nose, beyond where they could possibly do her any good.

"I was passin'," she said to Mrs. Boone, "and I saw your door." Leaning against the doorjamb, she looked at no one else, and several times she shifted the scarred cane from one hand to the other. "I was passin' and saw your door was open, Boone, so I thought I'd stop . . . I was passin' and saw your door, Boone . . ."

She continued to repeat herself until Mrs. Boone stood and went to her, touched her hand lightly. "Come on in. You know you always welcome here, Mis Garrett." She took the woman's elbow and led her to a chair near the dining table. "I was thinkin' 'bout you, me and Mis Frazier, but somebody said you'd been under the weather, so I thought I shouldn't bother you."

It began to rain, a soft tapping at the window.

"I'm fine, by the help of the Lord," Mrs. Garrett said, sitting down. She settled herself, making sure her dress was well down over her knees, and her movements seemed affected, like those of a little girl who had recently been taught the way a woman should act. She placed her cane across her lap and leisurely began to pick pieces of lint off her dress, a silk-like polka-dotted thing that seemed alive with staring green eyes. A flash of lightning and the accompanying burst of thunder caused her to raise her head slowly and look wearily at the window. She sighed, she began to take note of the small group of women. They had been watching her intently, exchanging glances, but when she looked at them, they lowered their eyes or deftly turned their heads away. Only when they were addressed did the women look at her, smile, ask how she was, make some trivial comment. The last one—an attractive woman knitting on the couch—did not look up.

"I'm surprised to see you here, Timora," Mrs. Garrett said to her.

"I'd say the same 'bout you, Mis Garrett," the woman said, smiling, but the smile seemed more about something she had not said. "I've come for the prayer meetin'."

"So is *that* what this here crowd's all about?" Mrs. Garrett said and turned to Mrs. Boone who nodded with a smile. Suddenly, Mrs. Garrett appeared more relaxed. "Oh, but I hope y'all ain't gonna have that Reverend Sawyer again. He ain't nothin' but jack-leg, Boone. I could tell that the first time I laid eyes on him. 'Jack-leg,' I said to myself, 'as jackleg as they come.'"

Mrs. Boone glanced at the others. "It's him. But he got a church of his own, Mis Garrett. Out in Northeast, just off Bladensburg Road."

"Havin' a church, Boone, don't mount to a hill of beans," Mrs. Garrett said with a touch of exasperation, as if she had said that to the woman a thousand times. "It don't make a man a preacher, called by God. I could say I'm a man a God but that don't make it so. All havin' a church means is you got a little money and a few fools to come to it and give you that money."

"I ain't a member, don't plan to be a member. And I ain't never give him money to come here to pray with us." She spewed out the words and looked at the others, as if waiting for someone to speak in her defense. Mrs. Garrett smiled pleasantly and nodded. "I do have some food for us all when he gets here. But that's a every day normal courtesy. Some sandwiches and cake and punch . . . Just things I got 'round the corner . . . Wasn't no trouble . . ."

Mrs. Garrett looked askance at the food. "He'll fill hisself up off that." She leaned down and carefully placed her cane on the floor beside her. "And what time is this here man a God 'spected on the premises?"

"He said Three-thirty."

"Three-thirty and all the clocks say it's past four."

A woman shut the window just as the rain began to come inside. With only a small, inadequate lamp burning on the dining table, the room was dimly lit. Each flash of lightning would brighten the place and for a moment everything could be clearly seen.

"And what you doin' over in that corner, Timora, workin' away like a little tiny mouse?" Mrs. Garrett said.

"Sewin'," Mrs. Timora said. "Makin' somethin' for my new grandchild."

"Oh Lani had another? You didn't even tell me."

"A girl. A little over a month ago." Mrs. Timora sat back in a corner on the couch, out of sight of the window, and if there had been no words from her, she might well have gone unnoticed.

"And you never told me," Mrs. Garrett said, seemingly hurt. "I always thought well of Lani." She turned slowly to Mrs. Boone, and as she turned that pleasant smile gradually formed itself again. "But then Lani's husband keeps her havin' babies. Who can keep up with how many they have? She's the babiest-havin' woman I ever knowed of in my life. One after the other."

Silent and still except for the motion of the hand with the needle, Mrs. Timora never looked up.

For a year or so after Mrs. Timora moved in they had been friends, good friends, but already it was more than two years since they had not been friends. And when they had been close, people said, it was very rare to see one and not see the other: they ate and shopped together, went to each other's church, though one was a Baptist and the other a Methodist. When Mrs. Timora was invited to this or that function—as she invariably was—people thought it only natural that she should bring Mrs. Garrett along. They were like that. It got around in that apartment building for the elderly that one of the things that made for a good evening was having Mrs. Timora tell some of those funny stories about her life in Alabama. And though most everyone had heard the story of how Mrs. Garrett—who had lived in the building longer than anyone—had been saved when she was only nine, those who had invited Mrs. Timora to dinner found they could stand to hear her tell it once again.

Whatever it was that ended what the two women had, came suddenly, people said, and everyone had an opinion: Mrs. Timora wasn't quite religious enough for Mrs. Garrett, or Mrs. Garrett owed her more money that she could ever pay back, or Mrs. Timora, being much younger, had a yearning to get out and do some of the things a woman her age was still capable of doing. But no matter what had caused the break, people were certain reconciliation was impossible. They now lived their lives apart and when they happened to see each other in the halls, the recreation room, at the mailboxes, one would look through the other as though through glass. And in those rare moments when someone chanced to see Mrs. Garrett, a notorious borrower, enter or leave Mrs. Timora's apartment, he or she felt certain it was to borrow something that no one else had or wanted to lend her.

Toward five-thirty, not long after Mrs. Garrett had asked again what time the Reverend Dr. Sawyer was supposed to arrive, the telephone rang. Mrs. Boone answered and spoke but a few words before hanging up. She announced that it had been Reverend Sawyer's wife, that his car would not start and he apologized to everyone for not being able to make the meeting. Waving her hand over the table, she told her guests there was no need to waste the food, and one by one they got up and helped themselves. The storm had ceased, but there was still the rain, an insistent, almost scratching sound at the window.

Once they were seated again, the conversation took varied turns, and the evening wore away. At one point, looking out into the rain, the woman at the window commented on how particularly bad the weather had been lately. They all agreed, and Mrs. Garrett, capping her hands over her knees, said that she could not remember when her arthritis had caused her so much pain, that sometimes she felt she would never walk again. Two of the women gave sympathetic nods, mentioning their own pains, and they all began to exchange remedies. Then Mrs. Timora stuck her needle into the piece she was working on and laid it beside her. Looking up, she quietly said, "All of it reminds me of one summer back home. It was kinda like it is now." She was speaking to no one in particular, as if she was just giving voice to her thoughts.

"Oh now, Timora, we ain't gonna have one a your down home, way-back-when stories, are we?" Mrs. Garrett said. "We ain't had a evenin' of prayer, but we tryin' to keep it as close to that as we can."

"How, Evelyn?" Mrs. Boone asked, looking past Mrs. Garrett who sat between her and Mrs. Timora. "How does this 'mind you of back home." Mrs. Garrett clasped her hands and put them in the center of her lap, looking neither right nor left.

Mrs. Timora said nothing for several seconds. "It thundered and lightened a lot," she said. "I guess I was nineteen or twenty, and this fella I was keepin' company with was sittin' with me and my daddy on my daddy's porch. There was a storm goin' on while we was sittin' there. There had been a lotta rain, but not anough to do that much damage to the crops, just anough to be more than what people was used to. It was late in the evenin' and so dark I could barely make out what was three feet in front a me. It was rainin' that evenin', too, and we was just sittin' and talkin'.

"By and by I noticed this figure that kinda just stood in that corn patch in my mother's garden. It was no further than from here to that television there. I looked and looked, tryin' to see into that dark, and I told myself it was just a corn stalk leanin' out heavy with the rain. It made a move but I didn't think nothin' 'bout it. 'It's corn,' I said to myself. But when this figure moved again—moved different from all the other corn—I said this real quiet Oh. Real surprised. I touched this fella and pointed and we looked together. My father looked, too. This corn stalk, this thing, said, 'Uncle . . . Uncle . . . Evie . . .' Then it moved a few steps toward us. I saw that it was a cousin of mine, John Henry. He came a few steps more and just dropped heavy to the ground, cryin' and cryin.'

"I said, 'John, what's the matter? What is it?'

" 'It's them,' he said after a bit. He was cryin' so hard that I could barely make out what he was sayin'. 'It's them . . . It's them . . . ,' he kept sayin'. 'They just sittin' there.'

"My daddy went down the steps to him, and when he touched John, John Henry just jumped up real quick-like, like he was some doll and somethin' had pulled him up by the shoulders. He took off on down this path that led to where they lived. The three a us—my daddy, me, and this fella—took off after him. It was rainin' way harder than it is now and we was soaked through 'fore we even took a few steps.

"When we got to his house, John Henry was there lookin' in the front door. 'John,' my daddy said. 'John.' We got there and looked in. Everybody was just sittin' around like he said. My uncle Joe, his wife Ebbie, her mother, and my Uncle Ray. There was a pipe stickin' in Uncle Ray's mouth, not lit, just stickin' there like he did it sometimes. The only light was from a oil lamp on the mantlepiece and from a real small fire in the fireplace. It never crossed my mind as to why they would have a fire burnin'. But there was this one log that they had kept there all spring and all summer, and it was steady burnin' right in the center. They was all kinda gathered about the fireplace, which wasn't too strange 'cause y'all know how many folks use the fireplace for the center of the house all the year. There was a buncha smells in that room. One was the kind you get when wood gets wet, but around all of the smells was this one I hadn't smelled before and ain't smelled since. It was sour and sweet and yet it wasn't. One moment you smelled and it stunk, the next moment it wasn't that bad to the nose.

"'Joe,' my daddy said to his brother. Uncle Joe was sittin' in that chair starin' at us. No, not really *at* us, kinda through us and around us at the same time. 'Joe.' My daddy went over to him. '*Joseph.*' He touched him and my uncle fell into his arms, right over, like some dime story dummy. And somethin' told us right then that he and everybody else was gone. It told me anyway. The fella I was keepin' company with just said, 'Jesus!' I fixed my eyes on him when he said that. I was feelin' all kinds of things standin' there, and you know, one a them was this feelin' that I couldn't ever keep company with that boy again. And I didn't after that. He used to always come around and ask me why, but I could never think of an answer for him . . .

"I looked down. This long black line that had done cut a rut in the floor went from the fireplace through that little group a people right out the room to the kitchen—like somebody had took a big fireball of barbed wire and run 'cross the floor with it.

"They was just sittin' there and they was all gone. You could see where Ebbie's mother had been rockin' the crib with Ebbie's baby in it. A wind comin' through the door was still rockin' the crib, rockin' Ebbie mother's hand along with it. I thought the baby was dead, too, but it twitched and I knowed it was alive. I picked him up and put Ebbie mother's hand in her lap. I did it calm-like and I was surprised at myself, the way I was actin'. I must a been scared somewhere inside, but it was a long time 'fore I knowed it. And then it stayed and never went away.

"'Lightnin',' the fella said. 'Lightnin'.' My daddy had put his brother back in the chair and was standin' there lookin' down at him. The fella pointed at the way the line ran along the floor and out the room. 'Just came down the chimney, Mista Davenport,' he said. 'Look at it!' And we looked again when he said that, not so much 'cause a what he said, but 'cause somethin' in our own brains told us to.

"John Henry came into the house and went on out into the kitchen, his mud tracks walkin' right over that black line. I followed him and I seen where the line came to the kitchen table and hopped right up to it, then went over it and down and out the back door. Like whatever made it had a mind all its own. One a the straightest lines you'd ever wanna see. John Henry's sister was sittin' at the table. Alma was alive. She was cryin', and I don't think she'd moved since it happened. John Henry sat down and put his head in his hands. He started cryin' again. All of a sudden I got weak as that dishrag there on the table. I held the baby and watched them children. Their whole family. My family, too. People who'd never done a moment's harm to nobody. Not one moment's harm. Somethin' in me was so struck by that when I thought of Uncle Ray's pipe stickin' in his mouth and when I saw that one a Alma's plaits had come loose, like they do on little girls. I didn't know what else to do so I put Alma's head against my stomach. Then I told 'em that it would be all right, though if you'd a asked, I couldn't a said what those words meant. I kept sayin' 'em till my daddy came in and picked Alma up and told us he was takin' us home . . ."

The women were all quiet, and they were quiet for a long time.

The woman at the window asked, "Evelyn, what happened to them kids?"

Mrs. Timora did not speak for several moments, as if her mind had already gone on to something else and she had to bring it back to answer. "They still down there," she said at last. "My mama and daddy raised 'em. That baby got a house fulla kids of his own. John Henry and Alma live in a house they built years and years ago. They never married, and you never see one without seein' the other."

The rain had long since stopped.

"The Lord," Mrs. Garrett said, "works in mysterious ways." Her dentures made a soft clicking sound as she spoke. "For good or bad, the Lord seeks you out and finds you. There ain't no way around that." She looked about as if for confirmation, and when no one said anything, she seemed to fold up into silence.

They were quiet again until Mrs. Garrett began to talk about the eleventh day of August, 1900, the day she was saved. The women looked knowingly at one another. There were several ways she had of beginning the story and they knew them all. But the story itself never changed: a huge tent and a visiting preacher and a little girl who was overcome that night with something she did not quite understand; but it had comforted her, she said, and led her up the aisle to the preacher's outstretched arms. The story was like some incantation she had to utter—to herself and to others— as if to renew the importance of that night, as if time itself—like years of water falling on rocks—was wearing down the meaning and the reality of the night; and only by telling the story again and again could she keep alive that meaning. The other women listened respectfully, exchanging glances, but their minds leaped ahead of

Mrs. Garrett, so that long before she ended the story, they were waiting with the ending.

"Yes," she said. "He said I was the youngest person in eight counties to ever be saved, to ever find the Lord. Reverend Dickinson told me." Now, with the last words, she spoke more to herself than to anyone in the room. "And I've walked in the light of the Lord ever since . . ."

"Why don't y'all have some more a this cake?" Mrs. Boone said. "Or take it home with you. I'll never eat it all."

She provided aluminum foil and each woman put two slices of cake in the foil. They did not sit again; for them the hour was late, and they stood at the door, preparing to leave. Mrs. Boone asked Mrs. Timora to tell that joke she had heard her tell once, the one about the dark night. Before Mrs. Timora had said a word, Mrs. Garrett said good-night, threaded her way through the group, and went home. The women told her good-night. When Mrs. Garrett had locked her door, Mrs. Boone asked again to hear the joke.

"Well, my daddy," Mrs. Timora said, "my daddy and my Uncle Joe would fun around a lot, mostly for us kids, like two fellas on the radio show. Every now and then my daddy would say, 'Joe, what's the darkest night you ever knowed? Tell, me Joe.' My uncle would play with his chin for a bit, like he was thinkin'. 'Les see,' he'd say. 'Les see . . . Oh, yes. *Oh,* yes. I 'member this one night I was sittin' at home all by my lonesome, nobody for company but the four walls and the memory a company. It commenced to rain and rain, and I heard this tappin' at the door. So I gets up and opened it. Well, sir, who was it but these raindrops—a whole gang of 'em—lookin' down at me, lookin' scared and cold. And one of 'em—the one in the front—he says to me in this real squeaky voice, "Mista, it's so dark out here, so very dark. Would you please mind tellin' us which way it is to the ground?" . . . And that,' my uncle would say, 'is the darkest night I ever knowed.' And we'd all bust out laughin', 'specially the little kids who thought it was the funniest thing to have talkin' raindrops."

The women laughed, too, and told Mrs. Timora that she was something else with all her stories. Then they all said good-night, that they would not be long out of bed.

About four that morning the thunder and lightning began again. And at the first sound of thunder Mrs. Garrett sprang up in her bed, like some puppet suddenly jerked to life by its master, her head first this way and then that way. Her heart began to pound demandingly, as if it wished to be free of her. "Oh dear God," she said. She flung back the covers and got out of bed, and in reaching for her glasses, she tipped over the plastic cup that contained her teeth. She did not bother to retrieve them, but threw on her robe and took up her cane. The lightning lit her way to the door. Taking her key from a table, she went out the door, and the wind slammed it viciously behind her.

As she moved down the hall she could hear the sounds of thunder and of the rushing of wind coming from under the doors of the apartments. The ceiling lights—with their half-globes—provided a long line of moons all the way down the hall. She knocked lightly at the door of an apartment near the laundry room, and when she heard the sound of thunder come from under the door of a nearby apartment, she knocked just a bit louder.

"Who is it?" someone asked after a while.

"It's me."

There was a long, long pause, then the voice asked again, "Who is it?"

"It's me. *Me!*" she whispered louder.

There was a pause again, but the lock and chain came off and the door opened a bit. Mrs. Timora stared blankly at Mrs. Garrett, who lowered her head and looked at the flame of the candle Mrs. Timora was holding.

"Evelyn, it's me." The flame swayed lightly and it reminded her of a leaf.

"Come on," Mrs. Timora said coldly, and allowed Mrs. Garrett to pass through. "You lucky," and she shut the door. "I was just about ready to go in that bathroom, and you know when I go in there, I don't come out for no one." She wore a nightgown and her hair was in plaits.

"Thank you," Mrs. Garrett said hoarsely, still looking into the flame. "Thank you."

"Well, come get along."

"Yes yes. What chair, Evelyn? What chair should I get?"

"You can sit on the floor for all I care, Mis Garrett."

"I'll take this one here." There was the tearing sound of thunder as she reached for the chair and she accidentally dropped her cane, which clattered about the floor before coming to rest. It seemed to her that it had made the noise just to spite her, and she left it.

"There are people sleepin'!" Mrs. Timora said sharply.

"Oh." And the sound was of the sincerest quality, as if the old woman had really not known there were people sleeping.

They went into the bathroom and Mrs. Timora sat the candle on the sink. After Mrs. Garrett put her chair against the wall beside the hamper, she shut the door of the windowless room. Mrs. Timora spread a blanket across the threshold. With a sigh she put down the cover of the toilet and sat down.

"How long you think it might last, Evelyn?"

"Why do you always have to ask such damn stupid questions?"

Mrs. Garrett winced. She watched the flame. It reminded her of something sad, of something she could not quite put her finger on. "Evelyn, ain't you gonna blow out the candle?"

Leaning forward, Mrs. Timora blew lightly, and in the quickest of moments the room drowned in darkness. Mrs. Garrett soon began to cry, and then she prayed, a long, monotonous string of words.

The blanket did little to moderate the sound and they could still hear the thunder almost as if the blanket were not there. Once or twice they gave a small cry of surprise when they heard it. They did not comfort one another. The intensity of the sound varied: at its worst it was horrendous, a noise like a pounding. Sometimes the thunder would sound muffled, as if it were coming from far away, from beyond mountains, but then before they knew it, it would be a loud pounding at the door.

Shoptalk #6
Encounters of the Third Kind

I'm now convinced that one of the things that could save our literature, not to mention the deeper life of culture at large, would be evidence—preferably in the form of direct contact—that there is other sentient life in the universe. What else, really, could replenish the sense of mystery that has been leached out of our lives? It is that absence of *that* that has made everything our artists venture seem inconsequential, vague, and of aluminium lightness.

(Sven Birkerts, "An Open Invitation to Extra-terrestrials," vol. 11, no. 4, 1985)

JANET DESAULNIERS

After Rosa Parks

Janet Desaulniers's second appearance in print was in a 1982 Plough-shares *that I edited. I had received "Age" perhaps a year earlier and felt compelled, after a lot of thinking, to return it because it was nearly a perfect Sherwood Anderson story, complete with Anderson's tone, metaphors, style, and the theme of a "grotesque" older man being revived by his encounter with a young woman. I wrote the author that I couldn't trust it, finally, because it was overly derivative, and I did my best, sentence by sentence, to point out what I meant. That, I felt, was that—difficult, careful decision, and I would probably never hear from the author again. To my astonishment, the story came back months later in its present, rewritten form, with all the Andersonisms transformed or deleted, and, to my reading, now utterly convincing. Underneath, in some way, I felt it was a remarkable tribute to a loved and loving "virtual" father. The old man, the narrator, is invited to dance by the girl, Lily: "I raised my arm and, with it, Lily's hand, and I said to her, 'Spin.' She looked at me for a moment, and then she smiled and did it. She spun. At that moment, our lives cracked open and held out a small, very important opportunity. In the end, I did not seduce her and she did not seduce me, but something that lived in the very center of her and even of me, that breathed and moved, seduced us both." Desaulniers's contributor's note mentioned that her first publication had been in* The New Yorker.

She writes now that the earlier New Yorker *story had been only the second story she had ever written: "My career began early. . . . A for-*

mer teacher hounded me into it. . . . A lot of people wanted to give me a break. . . . Even before the story was published, I [answered] inquiries from editors and agents . . . no, I did not currently have a collection or a novel or even lucid thoughts of such things. . . . Hollywood called to say I was sitting on a female version of The Graduate. *. . . It was sweet confusion. Eventually, I wanted it to stop. Eventually, it did. . . .* Ploughshares *came later, after I'd fought my way back to a proper apprenticeship, finished at Iowa, and gone out into the world . . . And . . . I will always be grateful because that story had a long and happy life—reprinted, awarded a Pushcart Prize, anthologized here and abroad. As I recall, the volume was even reviewed, and for the first time I saw my work considered critically alongside work by the likes of Rosellen Brown and Andre Dubus. That's what I'd aspired to. Yes, I received letters from agents and editors after my* Ploughshares *publication, and a few from readers, too, but I also received letters from writers . . . and they took the time to write to an uneven apprentice. I learned things from those letters."*

Her next publications in Ploughshares, *she writes, "offered more of the same, along with kind words from guest editors Sue Miller and Tim O'Brien and the great good luck of Don Lee." She won* Ploughshares' *Cohen Award for 1996 for "After Rosa Parks," which appeared in vol. 21, no. 4, edited by Tim O'Brien and Mark Strand, and about which she writes: "One afternoon, in front of the school where I was engaged as artist-in-residence, a student who had been marked for murder by a neighborhood gang was shot. Word was he had been shot five times: once in the chest, once in each leg, and once in the behind—the last wound, according to my students, meant to embarrass him even after he was dead. But he wasn't dead. He was at Cook County Hospital, conscious and most likely surrounded by inquiring detectives, as a bullet that missed him had grazed a teacher and raised his story to lead on the local news. . . . His fellow students wanted to talk about whether he would or could or should tell the police who shot him. All agreed he knew who did it and that he'd be killed if he told. Most thought he'd be killed even if he didn't tell, as they couldn't recall anyone in the neighborhood outliving a mark. 'He's already dead,' someone said. 'He's got no choice.' That comment enraged a young woman, who claimed the wounded student did have a choice, not a choice she'd wish on anyone, but his choice, she reminded us, the one his life had brought him. She said he'd better make up his mind fast because then, at least, when they killed him, he'd die a free man. . . . That's not the story that inspired 'After Rosa Parks,' but it's a parallel story, a true one from Chicago, to stand beside it."*

To date, Desaulniers *has published stories in* The New Yorker, Ploughshares, TriQuarterly, *the* New England Review, *the* North American Review, *and* Glimmer Train, *among others. She has been anthologized in* The Pushcart Prize, The Ploughshares Reader, Love Stories for the Time Being, *and* Four-Minute Short Stories.

Janet Desaulniers has completed a collection of short fiction and is at work on a novel.

Ellie found her son in the school nurse's office, laid out on a leatherette fainting couch like some child gothic, his shoes off, his arms crossed over his chest, his face turned to the wall. "What's the deal, Kid Cody?"

When he heard her voice, he turned only his head toward her, slowly, as if he were beyond surprise. "I have a stomachache," he said.

"Yeah?" Ellie sat down beside him and stroked his bare arm. "That's the message I got."

"It's a nervous stomachache, Mom. It's right in the middle." He pointed to his belt buckle, a nicked metal casting of a race car. "It's right where Mrs. Schumacher said my nerves are."

Cody was in kindergarten, and he did not like school. He told anyone who would listen that he did not like school. Yesterday, from just inside their back door, Ellie overheard him telling their next-door neighbor Mrs. Schumacher that school gave him a bad feeling behind his stomach, "the kind of feeling," he said, "that you get before something happens." Ellie stood still in the doorway and watched as Mrs. Schumacher looked up from grooming one of her half-dozen cats. Mrs. Schumacher was a stringy, wild-haired widow—dirt poor, bone thin, and half-crazy with loneliness and neglect. Sometimes when Cody and Ellie would haul trash back to the cans in the alley, she'd wave and call out her kitchen window to Ellie, "You pull those shoulders back, girl. Divorce is no sin." Yesterday she picked cat hair out of a long metal comb and told Cody, "There are two kinds of stomachaches, you know. Now a sick one just swirls through your gut like a bad wind, but a nervous one sits real still." She pressed one gnarled hand to Cody's belly. "Almost like you've swallowed a baseball," she said. "And it glows."

"That's the one I get at school," Cody told her. "That's the one."

After he said it, Ellie pressed her head against the cool storm door and felt sorry for herself, sorry she lived in the only run-down pocket of this suburb on probably the only street for miles where a woman could put her hands on her child and tell him such things.

The school nurse, a young, red-haired woman strangely overdressed in a carnation-pink suit, came from behind her desk to the couch. Ellie leaned back as the nurse ran her hand over Cody's forehead. "He doesn't have a fever, as far as I can tell. But he won't take the thermometer in his mouth. He says he wants it under the arm."

"Axillary," Ellie said. "That's how we do it at home."

Cody lay still under the nurse's hand. "I told her that," he said.

"Well, at school we do it by mouth," the nurse said. "You need to try doing it that way at home so it won't be new at school."

Cody and Ellie both looked at the nurse, then Cody looked back at the ceiling. "It's a nervous stomachache, Mom," he said softly. "I can tell."

"Let's sit up, Cody," Ellie said. "You look sicker than you are like that, and lying down is not what you need. A break is what you need. Put your shoes on now." Ellie stood up and took the nurse's elbow, led her to a window that looked out over an empty play yard. "He gets nervous," she said quietly. "It seems to happen most often when too many people treat him like a child." The nurse looked at her. "I mean when too many people try to tell him what to do," Ellie said. "See, he's an only child, and he lives half his time with his dad in their house and half his time with me in ours. So he's accustomed to partnership, you know, to being a partner in his own management. I mean, you live alone with a child, and there's none of that usual 'us versus him' kind of thing. You live alone with a child, and he's part of the us."

"Oh," the nurse said. She took a step back. People often did that when they learned how Cody lived. A social worker, new to their city from California, had concocted the scheme during the divorce. To Ellie and her ex-husband, it had sounded humane, but Ellie and her ex-husband did not live in California. They lived in an old and mostly refined Midwestern suburb, a place where tall trees and wide driveways led back behind big houses to double and triple garages. "I'm wondering," the nurse said, "if I have the correct home phone number for you. A man took the message when I called." She looked Ellie in the eye, insinuating now. "I think I woke him up."

"That's my brother. He's been staying with us to help out." Disappointed in herself for revealing more of their life than was necessary to this woman, Ellie added, "I'm sure you did wake him up. He's ill today."

Cody looked up from struggling with his shoelaces. "Uncle Frank is a night person," he said. "When I'm asleep, he's awake. He does life the opposite."

Ellie smiled at him and looked back at the nurse. "Frank works nights, is what he means." The nurse's face said that even this fact made her suspicious. "Look, I think Cody just needs extra time is all," Ellie said. "This is his first year of school. He didn't go the play group and preschool route. His father and I kept him home so he could get wise to both of us still being there for him, even though it was in different houses. He's fine about that, but he's no wise guy when it comes to school. Are you, Cody?"

Cody stood up and smiled. "I get stomachaches," he said. Both his shoes tied, he was ready to go now. Ellie saw that he believed the hard part of this day was behind him. Next to her, the nurse narrowed her eyes at his sudden good humor, and Ellie felt her hesitate, weighing for a moment whether Cody was a liar or only a new and distinct form of damaged child. Then she looked at Ellie, and Ellie saw that what the nurse had decided was that Cody was an odd child, that he was an ill-equipped child—a child with a strange and probably damaged life—and probably, Ellie understood the nurse was thinking, probably it was Ellie's fault. They stared at each other a moment. Then Ellie went to Cody and took his hand.

"I'll just take him now. We'll just be on our way. We'll try school again tomorrow, right, Cody?"

"Okay," he said.

"You have to sign him out." The nurse pointed to a binder on her desk. "For our records."

"Right," Ellie said. "No problem."

They drove away slowly from the school. Cody rolled the window down and rested his head on the doorframe so that the wind lifted his hair off his forehead. Ellie didn't know if he was pensive or only relieved. Maybe he had sensed what the nurse thought of her. Or of him. She turned the radio on low.

"Do you want to drive by the lake?" she said. "It's warm today. We could climb down the rocks to the beach." The beach was where Cody told Ellie things, where he confided in her. The wide expanse of sand and water loosened something in him. It was there, digging a hole one day last spring with a new miniature folding spade, that he had looked up and said, "Do you want to hear something secret?"

"Sure," Ellie told him, and then he recited, nearly word for word, an ugly desperate argument she and her ex-husband had had just before they gave it all up. He recited it so precisely that the night came back to Ellie. She'd made a formal dinner in the middle of the week—cornish hens stuffed with herbs and rice. A friendly Greek man at the liquor store had helped her choose a nice wine which she served in their wedding crystal. She'd left the bottle on the table, tucked in a hammered silver ice bucket, while she and her ex-husband said horrible, hurtful things they'd never said before or since. On the beach that day, Cody recited it all. He paused in his digging and looked up at her. "I was under the table," he said. "You just didn't see me there."

For a moment, Ellie believed him. Then she remembered another moment, carrying their salad plates to the kitchen, when she'd been so ashamed she'd gone back to Cody's room to check on him. He lay sideways in his youth bed, one foot wedged between the bars. From the doorway she listened to his breathing before she went to his bed and straightened him, sliding his foot from the bars, folding his quilt up over his shoulders. On the beach, she felt the same relief she'd felt at his door. He'd been asleep. He'd slept through it. She watched him dig the hole, throwing sand over his shoulder, hunkering down to his work, and suddenly she was shaken again.

"Daddy didn't tell you those things, did he? Did Daddy tell you those things?"

"No." He looked up from his digging, a little wary of her.

"Oh."

"Daddy says I probably dreamed it."

They were both quiet then. He finished his hole and sat back on his heels to admire it. It was deep, the deepest he'd dug, and he fingered his new shovel lightly. Then he crawled into the hole, tucking his legs up to his chest and folding his arms around them. "Cover me up, Mom," he said, smiling then.

She slid the warm sand over him as he watched her. When the sand covered the tops of his knees, she smoothed it around his chest. He looked up at her. "I did see it," he said.

She took her hands away from him and sat back. "I know," she said. "I know you did."

Now, in the car, she looked at him. "How about it?" she asked.

"No thanks. I don't feel like the beach."

"We could try the library."

"No," he said. "Thanks."

"Well, I need a milkshake. I'm going to pull into that hot dog stand under the train tracks and have a chocolate shake."

He didn't answer, but Ellie pulled in anyway, and settled him outside under a striped umbrella, where she brought his milkshake out to him. He drank it quickly, tipping his head back, while Ellie looked up at the train platform, where a few late commuters stood next to their briefcases. She was glad now she and Cody were not going anywhere, glad she had taken the rest of the day off when she got the call at the office, glad they could sit here half the morning and then stop at the park if they felt like it. The gift of her child was that, in his presence, life lengthened and uncoiled. Though it was nearly eleven o'clock, this day spread out before them as sweetly as at dawn.

"I like ice cream in the morning," Cody said. "This is the first time I've had ice cream this early."

"It's a quiet pleasure," Ellie said. "That and the weather. This is the warmest January we've ever had, I think."

"I remembered this was your day," Cody said. "So I told her to call you and not Dad."

Ellie touched his wrist. "You were right. Exactly right. You're getting very good at this. You're becoming a big boy."

Cody looked out over the parking lot. The umbrellas rippled in the breeze like sails, and above them late commuters swayed lightly like distant buoys. "I would kick a bad guy in the stomach if he came near our table."

"That would do it," Ellie said.

"I'd karate-kick him in the stomach and then in the knee."

"He'd go limping off to the other side of the world," Ellie said. This was something new for them that had started with school— this imagined violence, her child's sense of himself as a warrior and her quiet affirmation. School had forced Ellie to see how divorce had changed her—that she had become a cautious person, a person who lived as if she were allowed only one mistake in life and had already made it—and school had forced her to see that she was sending her son off into the world with the rigid moral sense of a saint. He'd see a child steal another child's hat in the play yard, and he'd suffer it all day. When he came home, he'd tell her the story of the theft and then lie on the rug, exhausted, looking up at her to say, "That was a terrible thing, don't you think, Mom? Don't you think that was an awful thing to do?"—as if he'd witnessed a murder. So now she let Cody talk this way, imagining his own power, and lately she had begun to surprise him with figures from a set of fierce dinosaurs and cavemen as a way of making up for all the early years she'd encouraged a pristine sensibility.

"Cody, did anything happen today? I mean, before you went to the nurse with a stomachache?"

"No."

"Nothing?"

"Well, the playground lady made me take a time-out."

"Why was that?"

"I was swinging on my belly."

"Uh-huh."

"And that's all." He rolled the edge of his cup around one finger. "There's a rule against swinging on your belly."

"I didn't know that."

"I didn't know that, either, but the lady said that now I would know and now I would remember."

"Oh. Well, I guess she's the boss."

"She is."

Ellie ran her hand along the rough close-cropped hair at the nape of his neck. He looked away from her when she did it. "So then what happened?"

"I had to sit on the ground by her feet for a while and then I had to say I was sorry."

"Did you?"

"Yes."

"And then what?"

"Then she called me Cory and told me I could go."

"She called you by the wrong name."

"Uh-huh. Yes."

"Did you tell her?"

"No." He leaned against her then and tilted his head back to look into her face. "I didn't want her to know me by my right name, Mom."

She put one arm lightly around his shoulders and rested her chin on the top of his head. "What should we do now?" she said softly.

"Go home."

At home, Frank was on the couch, an afghan pulled over his legs, watching the noon news.

"You're awake early," Cody said.

Frank looked up. "You're home early."

Cody quieted when he said it. He dropped his knapsack under the hat rack, pulled out his box of dinosaurs and cavemen, and began to arrange them delicately, as though he were being watched. Frank raised his eyebrows at Ellie. She shook her head. "I guess I'll make soup or something," she said.

A few minutes later, Frank joined her in the kitchen. He moved stiffly to the sink, leaned there a moment, then drew a glass of water from the tap and sat down at the table.

"It's vegetable soup." Ellie turned from the pot on the stove. "Can you tolerate it?"

"Not today." He raised his glass. "Today I'm drinking water." Frank suffered from colitis—at least that's what he said it was. He'd been a medic in the Army and learned just enough about medicine to believe he could treat himself. Last week, though, he'd been so sick that Ellie had convinced him to let her drive him to the VA hospital for some tests. Nudged into a pocket of darkness between two high-rise office buildings, the hospital was a spooky place—cavernous and forbidding and full of old and middle-aged men shuffling the hallways in paper slippers. "This is awful," Ellie whispered to Frank as they stood in some line. "Why don't you get real health insurance?"

"Forget it," Frank said. "I spent three years of my life defending the Golden Gate Bridge to earn this." She noticed as he walked away from her that day, and again this morning as he came into the kitchen, that he had begun to look like those men at the VA. He'd begun to look like a damaged man. Though he was tall and thick with muscle, he carried himself lightly, his arms held away from his body, as though he were hollow. Today his rumpled hair stood up from his head. Under each eye was a white translucent spot of pain. "You look pale, Frank."

"I feel pale."

"Did you call on your test results?"

"They said they'd call me."

"You should check."

"They said they would call, Ellie."

She turned back to the stove and then shouted, "Soup in twenty minutes, Cody."

"And biscuits, please," he shouted back.

"Okay, and biscuits." She peered into the refrigerator, looking for the plastic container of dough.

"That is not a sick child," Frank said.

"He was nervous. Something happened on the playground."

Ellie went about her work quietly, spreading flour on the countertop, rolling out the dough, but she felt like Cody had looked in the other room a moment ago. She felt like she was being watched. Frank sat at the table, the glass of water between his broad hands. Her brother was an odd man. There was such power to him, in his

hands and legs and the set of his jaw, but around other people—
even Ellie and Cody—he was always quiet and watchful, slightly
ill at ease. Ellie believed that life—real life, life in society, whatever
it was she was living—was a confusion to Frank. She wasn't sure
why. Sometimes she blamed the Army. Frank had been one of the
last men drafted into Vietnam. Though the war ended not long
after he finished basic, the Army had changed him—perhaps in
ways worse than a year fighting in the jungle might have changed
him. She didn't know. She wasn't even sure exactly what he had
done during those years or what had been done to him. Occasionally, he'd written to Ellie of demotions, restrictions, extra duty, a
few short stays in the brig. She had tried to imagine what circum-
stances could have landed her brother in a military jail, in a cage.
As a boy he had been cocksure and strong-willed, and sometimes
he'd had a smart mouth, but all boys had seemed like that to Ellie
back then.

When the war ended, Frank wrote again to say that he was glad,
but for an odd reason. If he'd gone to war, he'd written, his resistance might have become inflated even in his own mind into some
kind of grand refusal. He might have gone the rest of his life thinking that what he had learned was that he could not kill anyone or
that a big country should keep its nose out of a little country's
affairs. Then he would have missed what he said was the only real
lesson of the Army, which was that people who tell you what to
do—no matter what reasons they claim—are performing an act of
aggression. You're in their way, is what Frank had written to her;
they'd just as soon you die.

When he was discharged, he roamed the world—Ellie imagined he roamed it with that credo—crewing sailboats to New
Zealand, working illegal shrimp boats out of Key West, leading
tourists across the Yucatán Peninsula. For fifteen years he lived like

that, never settling long enough for anyone or anything to impose itself upon him. That he came when she needed him had surprised her—though both their parents had died and there was no one else to help her. Frank spotted her first at the airport, and when she recognized him, it was by the easy certain smile she remembered. When she came close, though, he stepped lightly away from her. He shook her hand first and then he shook Cody's.

The nature of his support was also a surprise. He said very little, never entered into the acrimony of her divorce, never said more to her son than a benevolent stranger might say. He simply sat nearby while she found a job, a place to live, a car, while she went about the business of solving her life, and each Saturday morning, on the hall stand outside her bedroom door, he left two one-hundred-dollar bills folded under an old candy dish of their mother's.

Only once, just after he arrived, while they sat next to each other on a commuter train bringing them back from the courtroom where she had been ordered to sell her home, had he spoken up. "You're getting screwed," he told her.

"I know."

"You're just standing there letting it happen."

"It's worse if you make a fuss. I tried that once and even my own attorney yelled at me. You're just supposed to stand there and take it. It's all a glorified trip to the principal's office." She looked out the window when she said it.

"You're nuts. You're only seeing what's in front of you." When she didn't turn around, he leaned closer to her and lowered his voice. "For what you'll end up paying that lawyer, we could buy a little guest camp I once stayed at in Bali. It's real popular with the Australians, but far enough away that you'd never be found. Cody could grow up knowing how to catch his own dinner."

Still looking out the window, she considered it. She could take a few books, a bag of mementos, and her son, and disappear into a tropical life of light, loose clothing, modest shelter, balmy breezes. She turned to Frank. Perhaps this was how he had solved his life—not so much by running away from danger as by following closely the slender path of peace. "It's against the law," she said.

He shook his head. "If you're not careful, that's the law you're going to leave your kid. You have a choice, you know."

Ellie looked out the window again. Maybe she had never known she had a choice. She was a woman, a divorced mother of a young child. For a long time, her life had been one of necessity and ultimatum, not choice. But Frank was different, and she realized that his time in the Army most likely marked the beginning of a deal he'd struck with himself, because since those years ended, she could not name one thing he had done that he had not chosen to do. She turned to face him again. "I can't do it, Frank."

He looked at her then with the same expression she had seen flash over him in the courtroom earlier that day. His face became blank and quizzical as an aborigine's. As he settled back into his seat and looked past her at the city dimming into twilight, she saw something else, too. She saw his resignation. Never would they live together in a tropical guest camp. She had slipped, somehow, away from him. She felt that loss carve out a hole next to the loss of her marriage, her home, the life she had believed would be hers and her son's, and she felt the nature of Frank's love for her, and of her for him, change from hope to regret.

Moved suddenly at this memory, she sat down with him at the kitchen table. She felt tears behind her eyes and pressed the palms of her hands against them. "What?" Frank said.

"Nothing. I don't know. Maybe I should talk with his dad. We could put him in a different school, I guess."

"All schools are the same." Frank placed his thick hands flat on the table and looked at them. "They're the same man in a different hat."

"Maybe he'll get used to it. Maybe it just takes time."

Frank took a small sip of water and then looked to the pot of soup which was boiling too fast on the stove. "Look," he said. "Why don't you go back to work? I'll watch him. You can work late and make up the hours. He and I'll walk up to the chicken place for dinner and then I'll get him to bed."

She looked at him, suddenly tired, but acquiescent, too.

"Go on," he said.

She worked until past nine that night, leaving for home when lightning from a sudden thunderstorm flickered the lamp at her desk. On the drive home, the rain turned to a fraudulent snow—huge wet flakes out of a sentimental movie. She could still hear thunder out over the lake, though, rumbling distantly like doom, and she leaned over the steering wheel, anxious to be home. More and more lately, the thought came to her that in all the world, she had only two blood relatives. In the company of that fact, she felt skittish and threatened, as if two blood relatives were too slender a tie to bind her to the world.

The front of the house was dark except for the flicker of the TV in the living room. Frank was asleep on the couch, his breathing ragged and shallow. She stopped to turn off the TV and then saw the slant of light from Cody's doorway down the hall.

"Hey," she said. He was sitting up in bed with a big book open in his lap.

"Uncle Frank felt sick so I'm reading my own night story."

She came to sit beside him. "That was good of you. But it's late. Lights out."

"We went to Chicken in a Basket and I got a Coke. A large. That's why I'm so awake."

"Still." She closed his book and slid him down so that his head settled on his pillow.

"I saw the snow. Is that why you're late?"

"I worked extra so I could take you to story hour at the library tomorrow."

"Oh," he said, already drifting off. Then he opened his eyes. "After dinner, we watched the freak feature on TV. It was about giant ants that hide in the sewer. Have you seen that one?"

"I think so. It's a scary one. Don't tell about it now. You'll have bad dreams. Tell about it in the morning."

He closed his eyes again and rolled on his side to sleep. She stroked his hair off his forehead, and he took her hand and tucked it under his chin. Without opening his eyes, he said, "I'm going to tell Daddy, too, when I see him, and I'm going to find out if they have that giant ant movie at the movie store so he can watch it, too."

"You're full of plans," she said, leaning down to kiss him. Before she had sat up again, he was asleep, and he had let go of her hand.

In the kitchen she gathered their paper cups and the boxes of chicken bones. At the trash can she stopped, holding the lid open with one hand, and stared at four empty beer cans. Drinking was something Frank had chosen not to do in her home. He never used the word *alcoholism,* but he had asked her when he moved in not to keep liquor in the house. "It distracts me," he told her. For the first month or so of his time with them, he drank a lot of everything else—water, soft drinks, iced tea—and he slept a lot. Occasionally, too, he took long hushed phone calls from men Ellie believed must belong to AA or some support group—extremely polite, low-voiced men, men she thought of as veterans of another kind. She closed the lid of the trash can and moved to stand by the sink, still holding the chicken boxes and paper cups.

Frank came in then from the living room. "What's up?" he said when he saw her face. "Is Cody okay?"

She set the trash back on the kitchen table. "You drank."

"I know."

"Well, why? I mean, what am I supposed to do now, Frank? Am I supposed to kick you out?"

"You're not supposed to kick me out. Jesus, Ellie. You're supposed to drive me downtown to detox or something."

She sat down at the table, the vision of those men in paper slippers at the VA clanging around in her head. Frank filled a tall glass with water from the tap and sat down across from her. When she looked at him, he straightened his spine and set his shoulders, but his eyes drifted unsteadily. He lowered his head. "What's going on?" she asked.

"The VA called."

"What is it? Is it colitis?"

"A long time ago it was probably colitis." He looked at her. "Now it's cancer, Ellie."

She put her hand on his. He leaned back in his chair, and she felt his privacy, his strict isolation. His hand was still on the table beneath hers. It did not seem fair that he be forced to suffer more isolation. "I'm sorry," she said and took her hand away.

He shook his head. "It gets worse," he said, smiling lightly. "They went ahead and scheduled me for more tests and then this clerk called back and told me I don't qualify for treatment. 'This is not a service-related ailment,' he told me. 'The VA treats only the indigent and service-related ailments.'"

"You didn't know that?" she said softly.

He rubbed his temples with both hands and pushed his hair roughly away from his face. "No."

"So what this means . . . ," she began slowly.

"What this means is I have cancer and no health insurance."

She sat back in her chair, stunned by the precision of this cruelty. Her brother had stepped off a plane just over a year ago tanned and strong, his only weakness that he would not keep track of rules. He had balked even when she suggested he get a driver's license. She closed her eyes at the memory. She was the reason he'd come back to this place where his weakness could turn on him so cruelly. "We'll figure it out, Frank. We'll figure something out."

"No. No. I've already done that. I just hate to leave you in a bind. I've got a little money I was saving to go back to Negril this spring. I'll leave you some of it and still make out pretty well there myself."

"What are you saying?"

"I'm saying I'm going to Negril." He looked sad for her when he said it, as if he believed she were the one with the greater loss. "I'll leave in a couple days."

"Frank, my God. You have to take care of this. You can't just walk away from it."

"I'm not walking away, Ellie. There are doctors in Negril. I'm not saying I won't take care of it. I'm just saying I can't take care of it here."

He was lying, she thought. He had decided somehow that to die whole on ground he understood would be better than struggling here. She sat rigidly across from him, her mind wildly in search of hope, of a kindly Jamaican doctor down there who would take Frank in and cure him for no more reward than the satisfaction of having preserved such a man. But she had never met a doctor like that. She wasn't sure the world was a large and varied enough place to hold even one doctor like that. "How can I stop you," she said, "from doing this?"

"You can't." He pushed back his chair and stood up. "I'm tired, Ellie. I'm going to go to bed now."

He didn't go to bed. For hours she heard his silence as he moved through the house. She wondered if perhaps he was saying good-bye to the house, to its small comforts, but then she understood that he no longer saw her home as a safe place. She was frightened for herself, knowing that. He stood in the kitchen a long time, the house so quiet around him she felt she could hear his resolve building. Then he went into Cody's room. She sat up in bed and put one foot on the floor, listening until he came out again.

When she opened her eyes next, Cody stood at her bedside. "Is it morning?" he asked.

She looked to the window. Outside the snow was gone and the sun shone brightly. "Yes."

"I had a bad dream. I had a dream someone got into our house."

"Uncle Frank was up late last night. You probably heard Uncle Frank."

"I dreamed it was someone else."

"It wasn't," she said. "It was Uncle Frank."

They washed and dressed hurriedly, though it was still early. Ellie let Cody watch cartoons as he ate, grateful for the noise and distraction. As they were leaving, she lingered in the quiet front room, looking down the hallway to Frank's closed door. Cody stood in his coat and hat, watching her. "Let's go now." She took his hand. "Time to go."

They were early to Cody's school, and his teacher looked up surprised from a table in the back of the room, but she came to greet them in the hallway. "A new day and a new start," she said merrily. Cody reached up to hold on to a corner of Ellie's jacket. "Today the Green Star group is going to spend the morning at the sand table," his teacher said to him. "Why don't you hang up your coat and get started?" She looked to Ellie. "Cody is in the Green Star group."

Ellie nodded.

"I have to tell my mom something," Cody said.

"Well, hurry along. We don't want to make Mom late for work or whatever."

"Okay," Cody said, and then stood mute next to Ellie, still clutching her jacket. His teacher watched him for a moment and then went back into the classroom. "Hurry along," she called. "I'll take the top off the sand table."

Cody stiffened and began to cry as Ellie slipped his coat off his shoulders. She took his hands, warm with the moist heat of emotion and fear. "What is it you want to tell me, Cody?"

He shook his head, his eyes a little desperate and lost.

"You don't know what it is?"

He shook his head again.

She nodded and pulled him close. "I love you, child," she said into his ear. Then she drew him away from her. "I think you can do this. I think it's important that you do this." He wouldn't look at her when she said it.

Pulling up to the school that afternoon, she saw his face at the door, a bobbing pale moon in the glass that drew an ache up from her own stomach, but he ran down the slope to her car like the other children, trailing his knapsack behind him. "Did it go okay?"

"Yeah." He closed his door, locked it, and drew the seat belt around him. "At the bad parts, I just pretended I was somewhere else. I pretended it wasn't really happening."

They were early to story hour, and Cody hovered near the librarian at her desk, telling her the story of the giant ant movie he had seen. She was a kind older woman, wise in the ways of children, and she listened raptly to Cody's story, then led him off to a far corner of the children's room. Ellie sat with their coats in a small low chair and watched the other mothers and children arrive. A few minutes later, Cody came running back carrying some books the librarian had found for him. They were junior novelizations of old monster movies: *The Mummy, Frankenstein,* and *King Kong.* "Oh, these are too scary for you, Cody. These things even give me the willies."

"Mom," he said. "She gave them to me. I was going to show them to Uncle Frank."

"Oh. Well, let me see." She flipped the pages while he leaned against her shoulder. Mainly they were just a collection of black and white stills from the old movies.

"Maybe they give you the willies because the monsters are always after a lady." Cody pointed to a picture of the Mummy carrying a woman into a dark wood.

"Maybe," she said, closing the book. "I don't know."

"Could I show them to Uncle Frank? They won't scare him, I bet."

"Sure," she said. "I guess."

He crawled into her lap then, and Ellie watched the preparations for story hour while Cody paged through his books. "I read the sign," Ellie said. "Today is a special puppet show for Martin Luther King's birthday."

"Our teacher told us about him in school."

"I'm glad. He was a good brave man."

"Once nothing was fair for brown-skinned people."

"Martin Luther King changed some of that, though."

Cody turned around and looked at her. "He got killed," he said. "I know. I was a girl. It was very sad."

Cody leaned back against her then and fingered his monster books. His body grew slack against hers, and she thought he must be tired, but then she felt heat move out of him, the same heat she had felt in his hands that morning. She turned him around in her lap. "What's wrong, Cody?" He shook his head, and she remembered this morning, how he had wanted to tell her something he didn't know. "What is it?"

"Don't tell Daddy," he said.

He had never spoken those words to her before. Perhaps because of the way he lived or perhaps because of his own good nature, Cody had always been unstintingly fair in his attachments to each of his parents. "I don't know," Ellie said. "Why not Daddy?"

"It's not a man's secret."

"It's a woman's secret?"

"Uh-huh. I think so."

"What is it?"

"I'm afraid about dying. Do you just fall down one day and then it hurts forever?"

After he said it, she pulled him close. Children did this, she had read somewhere, picked up the unspoken cues and terror in their homes. "It doesn't hurt," she told him. "It stops all the hurt." She drew her hand across his forehead. "It feels like this," she said.

She knew when she said it that something was terribly wrong with her. To portray death to her own child as more dignified and easeful than life was some sort of abomination larger than she could fathom. But she did not take it back. She rocked Cody gently as the librarian rang a small bell and called for the children to gather around the puppet theater. She sat blankly, Cody curled against her, as the show began with a cardboard cutout of a strictly segregated bus—a cluster of white circles at the front, a cluster of black circles at the back. *Before Rosa Parks,* the caption under the bus read. Then the librarian explained to the children that Rosa Parks was tired and believed she had as much right to sit down and rest as anyone else.

It's a woman's secret, Ellie thought. This was what her son believed. How he must have wondered to find a woman's secret in his own mind, to understand that to the teeming power and circumstance of the world he would lose many things—one day even his life. Cody's head lolled against her shoulder. She realized he was asleep in her arms. The monster books slid out of his hands, and she held them a moment, looking into the shy, quizzical pain on King Kong's face. She shook Cody lightly. "We have to go," she said. "We have to hurry."

At home, Frank was on the couch in front of the news. He smiled briefly when they came in, then looked back at the television. Cody ran to him with the monster books. He wanted Frank to read them to him.

"In one minute," Frank said. "When the news is over, I'll read all three."

While Ellie hung up their coats, Cody eased himself onto the couch next to Frank and sat stiffly next to him, thumping his feet against the cushion. Frank lay one hand on his knee to quiet him. An old newsreel of Martin Luther King's last speech was playing on the TV. "I saw him at the library," Cody said. "A picture of him. It's his birthday."

"Monday," Frank said.

"My friend Bennie's dad is off work Monday, and Bennie doesn't have school, but I do."

"How come you have school? I thought everyone was off," Frank said. "It's a holiday."

Cody was quiet then, and Ellie saw that he was a little teary, blinking and looking away from Frank to the TV. "I don't know," he said. "I just do."

Frank shook Cody's knee gently. "Well, that stinks," he said, smiling. "That's not fair." He shook his knee more roughly until Cody began to smile, too, and then he leaned close to him. "Just don't go," Frank said. "Stay home."

Cody looked at him. Ellie could see that Cody had not considered that an option before, that he had never completely understood he had an option before, and next she knew he was going to look to her. She turned away quickly to the front window, afraid to watch the idea of freedom dawn in her son's face, but outside in the evening sky growing up at the end of her block, she saw it anyway— the sudden knowledge loose in his mind, spreading like the shadows that spilled from under stoops, crawled across lawns, and bloomed up from the dark center of even her own scraggly hedgerow. Her son was free. Behind her, music signaled the end of the news. It was late. She knew she should turn around, start on dinner, but she stood a moment longer, staring out at the dark, and felt rising in her own mind the strangest and most fearsome comfort.

Shoptalk #7
What's a Story?

The ability to tell a story, like the ability to carry a tune, is nearly universal and as mysteriously natural as language. Though I've met a few people who can't tell stories, it has always seemed to me they really can but refuse to care enough, or fear generosity, or self-revelation, or misinterpretation (an extremely serious matter these days), or intimacy. They tend to be formal, encaged by prevailing opinion, and a little deliberately dull. Personally, I can't carry a tune, which has sometimes been a reason for shame, as though it were a character flaw. Worse than tuneless or storyless people are those with a gift for storytelling who . . . go on and on in the throes of an invincible narcissism, while listeners suffer brain-death. The best storytellers hardly ever seem to know they're doing it, and they hardly ever imagine they could write a story.

(Leonard Michaels, "What's a Story?" vol. 12, nos. 1 & 2, 1986)

MONA SIMPSON

Approximations

Raymond Carver published "Approximations" in his 1983 issue of
Ploughshares *(vol. 9, no. 4), which Mona Simpson considers "my first
real publication." By then, she had already served a lengthy apprenticeship, including a B.A. in creative writing at Berkeley in 1979, writing
features for the* San Francisco Chronicle, *the* East Bay Express, *and
other area newspapers, then enrolling in the graduate writing program
at Columbia University. She tried to write poetry at Columbia, then
switched to fiction, receiving her M.F.A. in 1983. That same year, she
placed stories in the* Iowa Review, *the* North American Review, *and
the* Paris Review, *and was hired by the* Paris Review *as senior editor.*

According to Publishers Weekly *(November 4, 1996): "It was a
short story that James Atlas fished out of the slush pile at the* Atlantic
Monthly *that fortunately introduced her to an agent. He didn't publish
it, Simpson recalls, but sent it to Amanda Urban at ICA. 'She called
me out of the blue, and took me to a very fancy lunch.' . . . Four years
later . . . [Simpson] sent Urban a manuscript of* Anywhere But Here,
*which had begun to germinate at Columbia, under the guidance of Eliz-
abeth Hardwick and Richard Price. Urban sold the novel to Ann Close
at [Alfred A.] Knopf for $15,000. Shortly thereafter, subsidized by a
Guggenheim grant, [Simpson] quit her job at the* Paris Review *to take
a [Hodder] fellowship at Princeton."*

*Reviewing the 1987 novel, the critic Sven Birkerts wrote that
Simpson had "earned a place beside domestic pioneers like Anne Tyler
and Alice Munro. She has not only shaken the family tree, she has*

plucked it from its soil to expose its tangled system of roots" (Chicago Tribune, *January 11, 1987). Simpson also appeared in the 1986 anthology* 20 under 30 *(edited by Debra Spark), where she was bracketed as one of "publishing's new starlets," along with Amy Hempl, Elizabeth Tallent, Lorrie Moore, and Tama Janowitz.* Anywhere But Here *went on to sell 25,000 copies in hardcover and close to 200,000 in paper.*

In 1991, Simpson published The Lost Father, *in which the protagonist of* Anywhere But Here, *now a grown woman, enlists a detective to help her find the father she's never known. Her most recent novel,* A Regular Guy *(1996), centers on a towering, isolate, mercurial technology enterpreneur and his tentative relationship with the raggedy nine-year-old girl who appears on his estate claiming to be his daughter.*

Mona Simpson lives in Los Angeles with her husband, Richard Appel, and her son, Gabriel. She is the Sadie Samuelson Levy Scholar of Languages at Bard College, where she has taught for the past ten years.

I n my family, there were always two people. First, my mother and father. Carol and John.

They danced. Hundreds of evenings at hundreds of parties in their twenties. A thousand times between songs her eyes completely closed when she leaned against him. He looked down at the top of her head; her part gleamed white, under and between the dark hair. He rubbed her back, trying to rouse her, but she became indistinct, blurring against his jacket. He hugged her imperceptibly closer, moving his hand in slower circles on her back, but when he talked it was to someone else over her head. He closed a big hand on her ear.

How do I know this? I don't. But there was a black and white

snapshot with my father staring at someone outside the frame.
I was looking at the picture when, for some reason, I asked my
mother where he was.

I was young, only four years old, and I had no memories of my
father. I must have been repeating a question someone else had
asked me. My mother was ironing. It was 1960 and all her summer
clothes were seersucker and cotton. Her hands stalled over the iron
when I asked the question.

"He's gone," she said, not looking at me. The windows were
open. A string of hummingbirds moved on the lilac bush outside.
"But," she said, gathering her cheeks, "he'll be coming back."

"When?"

For a moment, her mouth wavered, but then her chin snapped
back into a straight line and she pushed the iron over the perforated
pink and white fabric again.

"I don't know," she said.

So we waited, without mentioning it, for my father. In the
meantime, we got used to living alone. Just the two of us.

Other people asked me questions.

"Any news from your dad?"

"I don't know."

"You must miss him." Other mothers got maternal, pulling me
close to their soft, aproned bellies.

For a moment, but only for a moment, I'd let my eyes close.
Then I jerked away. "No," I said.

Saturday nights, we went ice skating. We wore skin-colored
tights and matching short dresses made out of stretch fabric. We
skated in tight concentrated figures, our necks bent like horses',
following the lines of an 8. Then, when the PA system started up,
we broke into free skating, wild around the rink. My mother skated
up behind me and caught me at the waist.

"This is how you really lose the pounds," she called, slapping her thigh, "skating fast."

I was always behind. Jerry, the pro, did a t-stop to impress my mother, shaving a comet of ice into the air. They skated around together and I had to slow down to wipe the melting water from my face.

When the music stopped, my mother pulled me over to the barrier, where we ran our skate tips into the soft wood. She pointed up to the rows of empty seats. They were maroon, with the plush worn down in the centers.

"See, when you're older, you can bring a boy you're dating here to see you skate. He can watch and think, hey, she's not just another pretty girl, she can really do something."

She peered into my face with a slanted gaze as if, through a crack, she could see what I'd become.

Taking the skates off, on the bench, was all joy. You could walk without carrying your own weight. Your feet and ankles were pure air. The floors were carpeted with rubber mats, red and black, like a checkerboard. In regular shoes, we walked like saints on clouds. The high domed arena was always cold.

The first time we heard from my father was 1963 in the middle of winter. We got a long distance phone call from Las Vegas and it was him.

"We're going to Disneyland!" my mother said, lifting her eyebrows and covering the mouthpiece with her hand.

Into the phone, she said she'd take me out of school. We'd fly to Las Vegas and then the three of us would drive west to Disneyland. I didn't recognize his voice when my mother held out the receiver.

"Hello, Melinda. This is Daddy."

I shrugged at my mother and wouldn't take the phone. "You'll know him when you see him," she whispered.

We waited three days for our summer linen dresses to be dry-cleaned. "It's going to be *hot*," my mother warned. "Scorching," she added with a smile. It was snowing dry powder when we left Illinois. We only saw white outside the airplane window. Halfway there, we changed in the tiny bathroom, from our winter coats to sleeveless dresses and patent leather thongs. It was still cool in the plane but my mother promised it would be hot on the ground.

It was. The air was swirling with dirt. A woman walked across the airport lobby with a scarf tied around her chest, which trailed behind her, coasting on air.

My mother spotted my father in the crowd, and we all pretended I recognized him too. He looked like an ordinary man. His hair was balding in a small circle. He wore tight black slacks, a brown jacket and black leather, slip-on shoes. His chin stuck out from his face, giving him an eager look.

He had a car parked outside and my mother got into the front seat with him. We passed hotels with bright blue swimming pools and the brown tinge of the sky hung over the water, like a line of dirt on the rim of a sleeve.

My father's apartment was in a pink stucco building. When we walked up with our suitcases, his three roommates were crowded on the porch, leaning on the iron bannister. They wore white v-neck t-shirts and thick dark hair pressed out from under them. I hadn't seen men dressed like that before.

"He told us you had long blonde hair."

"You look like your dad."

"She's prettier than her dad."

When my father smiled, the gaps between his teeth made him

look unintentionally sad, like a jack-o-lantern. He looked down and
I felt he was proud of me. He touched my hair. I loved him blindly
that moment, the feeling darkening over everything. But the feeling passed.

My mother stepped up to the porch. "Don't you want to introduce me to your friends, too?"

My father introduced each man separately and each man
smiled. Then my father gave me a present: a package of six
different-colored cotton headbands. I held it and didn't tear the
cellophane open.

My father worked as a waiter in a hotel restaurant. We had dinner there, eating slowly while he worked, watching him balance
dishes on the inside of his arm. He sat down with us while my
mother was sipping her coffee. He crossed one leg over the other,
smoking luxuriously. My mother leaned closer and whispered in
my ear.

"When are we going to Disneyland?" I asked, blankly, saying
what she said to say but somehow knowing it was wrong.

My father didn't answer me. He looked at my mother and put
out his cigarette. That night in the apartment, they fought. My
father's roommates closed the doors to their rooms.

"So, when are we going?" my mother asked gamely, crossing
one leg over the other on a dinette chair.

His shoulders sloped down. "You were late," he said finally.
"You were supposed to be here Monday. When you didn't come, I
lost the money I'd saved."

"In three days, how? How could you do that?"

"On the tables."

"You, you can't do this to her," my mother said, her voice gathering like a wave.

They sent me outside to the porch. I heard everything, even their breath, through the screen door. There was a book of matches on the ground and I lit them, one by one, scratching them against the concrete and then dropping them in the dirt when the flames came too close to my fingers. Finally it was quiet. My father came out and opened the screen door and I went in.

They set up the living room couch as a bed for me. They both undressed in my father's bedroom. He pulled off his t-shirt and sat on the bed to untie his shoes. My mother looked back at me, over her shoulder, while she unzipped her dress. Finally, she closed the door.

The next morning my father and I got up before my mother. We went to the hotel coffee shop and sat on stools at the counter. I was afraid to ask for anything; I said I wasn't hungry. My father ordered a soft-boiled egg for himself. His eyes caught on the uniformed waitress, the coffee pot tilting from her hand, a purse on the other end of the counter. The egg came in a white coffee cup. He chopped it with the edge of a spoon, asking me if I'd ever tasted a four-minute egg. I ate a spoonful and I loved it. No other egg was ever so good. I told my father how good it was hoping we could share it. But he slid the whole cup down, the spoon in it, without looking at me and signalled the waitress for another egg.

Walking back to the apartment, he kicked sand into the air. There were no lawns in front of the parked trailers, but the sand was raked and bordered with rows of rocks. My father's black slip-on shoes were scuffed. He was holding my hand but not looking at me.

"So we'll go to Disneyland next trip," he said.

"When?"

Suddenly, I wanted dates and plans and the name of a month, not to see Disneyland but to see him. Taking long steps, trying to match his pace, I wanted to say that I didn't care about Disneyland. I dared myself to talk, after one more, two more, three more steps, all the way to the apartment. But I never said it. All I did was hold his hand tighter and tighter.

"I don't know," he said, letting my hand drop when we came to the steps in front of his apartment.

On the plane home, I was holding the package of headbands in my lap, tracing them through the cellophane. My mother turned away and looked out the window.

"I work," she said finally. "I pay for your school and your books and your skates and your lessons. *And,*" she said in a louder whisper, "I pay the rent."

She picked up the package of headbands and then dropped it back on my lap.

"A seventy-nine-cent package of headbands."

It wasn't fair and I knew it.

The next year my mother went back to Las Vegas without me. She and Jerry, the ice-skating pro, got married. She came back without any pictures of the wedding and Jerry moved in with us.

She said she didn't want to bother with a big wedding since it was her second marriage. She wore a dress she already had.

My mother and I spent all that summer in the arena, where Jerry ran an ice-skating school. All day long the air conditioners hummed like the inside of a refrigerator. Inside the door of my locker was a picture of Peggy Fleming. Inside my mother's was Sonja Henie. In the main office, there were framed pictures of Jerry during his days with Holiday On Ice and the Ice Capades. In them, he didn't look like himself. He had short bristly hair and a glamorous smile. His dark figure slithered backwards, his arms pointing to two corners of the photograph. The lighting was yellow and false. In one of the pictures it was snowing.

We practiced all summer for the big show in August. The theme was the calendar; the chorus changed from December angels to April bunnies and May tulips. I couldn't get the quick turns in time with the older girls, so I was taken out of the chorus and given a role of my own. After the Easter number was over and the skaters in bunny costumes crowded backstage, I skated fast around the rink, blowing kisses. A second later, the Zamboni came out to clear the ice. I stood in back before my turn, terrified to go out too early or too late, with the velvet curtain bunched in my hand.

My mother came up behind me every show and gave me a push, saying, "Now, go," at the right time. I skated completely by instinct. I couldn't see. My eyes blurred under the strong spotlight. But one night, during the Easter dance, my mother was near the stage exit, laughing with Jerry. She kept trying to bend down to tie her laces and he pulled her up, kissing her. Finally, looking over his shoulder, she saw me and quickly mouthed "Go." I went out then but it was too late. I heard the Zamboni growling behind me. I tried to run, forgetting how to skate and fell forward, flat on the ice. My hands burned when I hurried up behind the moving spotlight and I saw that I'd torn my tights. The edges of the hole on my knee were ragged with blood.

I sat down on the ice backstage while the music for my mother's number started up. I knew it by heart. Jerry led my mother in an elementary waltz. She glinted along the ice, shifting her weight from leg to bent leg. Her skates slid out from her body. She was heavier than she had once been. She swayed, moving her head to glance off the eyes of the crowd. Under the slow spotlight, she twirled inside the box of Jerry's arms.

I quit skating after that. When my mother and Jerry went to the rink I stayed home or went out to play with the other kids in the neighborhood. The next year I joined the girl scout troop.

Eventually, my mother stopped taking lessons, too. Then Jerry went to the rink himself every day, like any other man going to a job.

One Saturday, there was a father/daughter breakfast sponsored by my girl scout troop. I must have told my mother about it. But by the time the day came, I'd forgotten and I was all dressed in my play clothes to go outside. I was out the front door when my mother caught me.

"Melinda."

"What?"

"Where are you going?"

"The end of the block."

"Don't you remember your girl scout breakfast? You have to go in and change."

I didn't want to go. I was already on the driveway, straddling my bike.

"I don't feel like going to that. I'd rather play."

My mother was wearing her housecoat, but she came outside anyway, holding it closed with one hand over her chest.

"He took the day off and he's in there now getting dressed. Now, come on. Go in and put something on."

"No," I said, "I don't want to."

"Won't you do this for me?" she whispered. "He wants to *adopt* you."

We stood there a minute and then the screen door opened.

"Let her go, Carol. She doesn't have to go if she doesn't want to go. It's up to her."

Jerry was standing in the doorway, all dressed up. His hair was combed down and wet from just taking a shower. He was wearing a white turtle-neck sweater and a paisley ascot. I felt sorry for him, looking serious and dressed up like that, and I wanted to change my mind and go in but I thought it was too late and I flew off on my bike. None of the other fathers would be wearing ascots anyway, I was thinking.

My father called again when I was ten, to say he wanted to take me to Disneyland. He said he was living in Reno, Nevada, with a new wife. He and my mother bickered a long time on the phone. He wanted to send a plane ticket for me to come alone. My mother said either both of us went or neither. She said she was afraid he would kidnap me. She held out. Finally, they agreed he'd send the money for two tickets.

Around this time, my mother always told me her dreams, which were about things she wanted. A pale blue Lincoln Continental with a cream-colored interior. A swimming pool with night lights and a redwood fence around the yard. A house with a gazebo you couldn't see from the road.

She had already stopped telling Jerry the things she wanted because he tried to get them for her and he made mistakes. He approximated. He bought her the wrong kind of record player for Christmas and he got a dull gold Cadillac, a used car, for her birthday.

Before we went to California, my mother read about something she wanted. A New Sony Portable Color Television. A jewel. She wanted a white one, she was sure it came in white. In the short magazine article she'd clipped out, it said the TVs were available only in Japan until early 1967, next year, but my mother was sure that by the time we went, they would be all over California.

Jerry took us to the airport and he was quiet while we checked on our luggage. When we got onto the plane, we forgot about him. We made plans to get my father to buy us the New Sony. It was this trip's Disneyland. We'd either win it or lose it depending on how we played.

At the airport in Los Angeles we met Velma, my father's new wife. She was a good ten years older and rich; her fingers were full of jewelry and she had on a brown fur coat.

This trip there was no struggle. We went straight to Disneyland. We stayed in the Disneyland Hotel. The four of us went through Disneyland like a rake. There was nothing we didn't see. We ate at restaurants. We bought souvenirs.

But knowing the real purpose of our trip made talking to my father complicated. As I watched my mother laugh with him I was never sure if it was a real laugh, for pleasure, or if it was work, to get our TV. My father seemed sad and a little bumbling. With everyone else around, my father and I didn't talk much.

"How's school?" he asked, walking to the Matterhorn.

"Fine," I said, "I like it."

"That's good," he said.

Our conversations were always like that. It was like lighting single matches.

And I was getting nervous. We were leaving in a day and nothing was being done about the New Sony. The last night, Velma suggested that I meet my father downstairs in the lobby before dinner, so the two of us could talk alone. In our room, my mother brushed my hair out in a fan across my back.

I was nervous. I didn't know what to say to my father.

My mother knew. "See if you can get him to buy the TV," she said. "I bet they've got one for sale right nearby."

I said I hadn't seen any in the stores.

"I think I saw one," she said, winking, "a white one."

"What should I do?" I knew I had to learn everything.

"Tell him you're saving up for it. He'll probably just buy it for you." My mother wasn't nervous. "Suck in your cheeks," she said, brushing glitter on my face. She was having fun.

I didn't want to leave the room. But my mother gave me a short push and I went slowly down the stairs. I tried to remember everything she told me. *Chin up. Smile. Brush your hair back. Say you're saving for it. Suck in your cheeks.* It seemed I was on the verge of losing one of two things I badly wanted. With each step it seemed I was choosing.

I saw my father's back first. He was standing by the candy counter. Whenever I saw my father I went through a series of gradual adjustments, like when you step out of the ice rink, in summer, and feel the warm air. I had to focus my vision down from an idea as vague as a color, to him. He was almost bald. The way his chin shot out made him always look eager. He was buying a roll of Lifesavers.

"Would you like anything?" he asked, seeing me and tilting his head to indicate the rows of candy arranged on the counter.

I thought for a wild moment. I could give up the plan, smile and say yes. Yes I want a candy bar. Two candy bars. He'd buy me two of the best candy bars there. I could stand and eat them sloppily, all the while gazing up at my father. If I smiled, he would smile. He would bend down and dab the chocolate from my mouth with a handkerchief moist with his own saliva.

But I didn't say yes, because I knew it would end. I knew I'd remember my father's face, soft on mine, next year when no letters came. I would hate my best memory because it would prove that my father could fake love or that love could end or, worst of all, that love was not powerful enough to change a life, his life.

"No," I said, "I'm saving up my money."

"What?" he said, smiling down at me. He was unravelling the paper from his Lifesavers.

I gulped. "I'm saving my money for a new Sony portable color television," I said.

He scanned the drugstore for a moment. I think we both knew he was relinquishing me to my mother.

"Oh," he said finally, nodding.

We didn't get the Sony. On the way home, neither of us mentioned it. And when the plane landed, we didn't call Jerry. We took a taxi from the airport. When we got home, my mother collapsed on the blue-green couch and looked around the room disapprovingly. The suitcases were scattered on the floor.

"You didn't say one big word the whole time we were there," she said. "Here, you're clever. You should hear yourself kidding around with Jerry. You say three syllable words and . . . There, you didn't say one smart thing in front of him. Let me tell you, you sounded dumb."

She imitated a dumb person, stretching her eyes wide open and puffing air into her cheeks.

She sighed. "Go out and play," she said. "Go out and play with your friends."

But I just stood there looking at her. She got worse. She kicked off her shoes. She began throwing pillows from the couch onto the floor.

"Not one big word. The whole time we were there," she said.

"And you didn't smile. Here, you're sharp, you're animate. There you slumped. You looked down. You really just looked ordinary. Like any other kid around here. Well, it's a good thing we're back because I can see now this is just where you belong. With all the mill workers' kids. Well, here we are. Good."

She was still yelling when I walked out the door. Then I did something I'd never done before. I walked down to the end of our road and I hitchhiked. I got picked up by a lady who lived two blocks away. I told her I was going to the arena.

From the lobby I saw Jerry on the ice. I ran downstairs to my mother's locker and sat alone, lacing up skates. I ran up the hall on my skate points and I ran onto the ice fast, my arms straight out to the sides. I went flying towards Jerry.

He was bending over a woman's shoulders, steering her into a figure eight.

A second later he saw me and I was in his arms, breathing against the wool of his sweater. He put a hand over my ear and told his student something I couldn't understand.

A few seconds later, when I pulled myself away, the student was gone. I stopped crying and then there was nothing to do. We were alone on the ice.

I looked up at Jerry; it was different than with my father. I couldn't bury my face in Jerry's sweater and forget the world. I stood there nervously. Jerry was still Jerry, standing in front of me shyly, a man I didn't know. My father was gone for good and here was Jerry, just another man in the world, who had nothing to do with me.

"Would you like me to teach you to do loops?" he asked quietly.

I couldn't say no because of how he looked, standing there with his hands in his pockets.

I glanced up at the empty stands around us. I was tired. And cold. Jerry started skating in tight, precise loops. I looked down at the lines he was making on the ice.

"I'll try," I said, beginning to follow them.

Shoptalk #8
On Time and Consequence

We're made who we are over time. . . . By the things we remember, by the things we try to push aside. We live in time, with the consequences of our histories, of our behaviors and choices. Sometimes the story suggests that we need to be open to the past; sometimes it seems to be saying that we must recognize the implications of the present, that we must understand where we are going in the future. Several seem to deal with the experience of a kind of weightlessness, timelessness—but even these are stories which take note of that, rather than just reproducing it: they watch a character shift, marginally, into a life of consequence. They compare a character's insubstantiality with the imaginary substance of a screenplay, or a falsified memory. . . . [To] selectively shape a presentation of events playing out over time; to point to the connections, the results, the meaning, is to deal with consequence. And, I'd argue, to make consequential fiction.

(Sue Miller, "Introduction," vol. 19, nos. 2 & 3, 1993)

HOWARD NORMAN

Unicycle

Howard Norman's first fiction, "Unicycle," appeared in a 1983 issue of Ploughshares *edited by Gail Mazur (where it was followed by a poem by David Wojahn called "Bicycle"). Norman would expand the story later to over twice its length as the first chapter of the same title in his debut novel,* The Northern Lights *(1987), for which he received a Whiting Writers' Award, and which went on to be a finalist for the National Book Award. Before writing fiction, Norman had a reputation as a folklorist, translator, and poet.* The Wishing Bone Cycle: Narrative Poems from the Swamy Cree Indians *had been awarded the Harold Morton Landon Prize by the Academy of American Poets. He had also published* Where the Chill Came From: Windigo Tales and Journeys.*

Norman met the poet and sometime Ploughshares *editor Jane Shore in 1981—she later became his wife—and credits her for his turning to write fiction. In a recent interview with Margaritte Huppert* (The Writer's Chronicle, *vol. 31, no. 1, December 1998), he comments, "I began my first novel just after I met Jane. . . . I had written radio plays, especially in Canada, but no stories or novels as of yet. She was already dedicated to writing, to say the least. She had taught with and known great writers in Cambridge—Lowell, Bishop, Robert Fitzgerald. She was such a clear example to me. Sure, I was writing, but in an unfocused way, not disciplined at all. One day Jane and I had a conversation in which she said, 'Why would you think I'd want to be*

*with someone who says he wants to write this or that, but won't try it?'
It was more layered than that, but you get the idea."*

Norman *published a collection of stories,* Kiss in the Hotel Joseph
Conrad and Other Stories, *in 1987. His second novel,* The Bird Artist *(1994), was a finalist for the National Book Award, won the New
England Bestsellers Association Prize in Fiction, and was listed by*
Time *as one of the best five books of 1994. Thomas Mallon in* Gentle-
man's Quarterly *(August 1998) praised both of Norman's novels for
"their vividness and their ability to transport the reader to another
world." Norman's most recent novel is* The Museum Guard *(1999),
which is set in Halifax, Nova Scotia, in 1938. Norman himself comments, "In my other books, I've generally investigated how landscape
shapes character. . . . In* The Museum Guard, *I was more interested
in interior spaces. . . . The outside world is imported into Halifax—in
the form of paintings, and in the form of incipient news broadcasts from
Europe. Hitler. Foreshadowings of the Holocaust" (Huppert, ibid.).
Norman teaches one semester a year in the M. F. A. program at the
University of Maryland, and is working on a fourth novel,* The
Haunting of L.*

Howard Norman and Jane Shore coedited the winter 1997–98 issue of* Ploughshares *(vol. 23, no. 4). They divide their time between
Vermont and Washington, D.C., and are raising a daughter, Emma.*

The first time I listened to a radio my friend Pelly drowned.
My family—mother, cousin Jenny, father and I—lived, quite
isolated, near Paduola Lake in northern Manitoba. Jenny, a pretty
five years old when orphaned over to us, had hair black as birch
knotholes, and the staccato yet elegant movements of a wading
bird; an egret, or crane. One night, without her knowing, I watched
as she opened our old suitcases on the kitchen floor. Into each she
uttered an unfathomable secret, quickly snapping it closed.

My father was employed in mapping the Canadian interior. I only knew him in glimpses. On his rare occasions home, exhausted from rigorous snow travels with a merciless companion, his own fleeing health, I was always disquieted by his whittled appearance; in my worst moments I wondered from which locale on his maps he would not return. He was obsessive about one book, *Dictionary of Musical Instruments of the World,* by B. Duras, which he seemed more to occupy than own. As a young man in Toronto, where he met my mother, he played French horn in a weekend orchestra and worked in a music store to pay for night classes in geography and math; finally he took a degree from the cartography school, at that time connected with the national museum system. One night the horn was stolen from his small apartment, but the thief left the battered case. During the years he worked in the far north the case was my father's one irreplaceable valise; walking from home into the distance for months, in deep snow, he appeared to be intent on a mysterious solo with owls rather than meeting other men with tripod telescopes, quadrants, and scrolled-up topographies.

Born in Vancouver, my mother was a small, intelligent, somewhat taciturn woman, whose infrequent laughter was more an accompaniment to her silence than an actual change of heart. She and Jenny became virtually inseparable. Each winter when sparrows shuffled like abacus beads along the stiffened laundry ropes fastened between our stone-and-log house and the nearest tree, and enormous ravens appeared to buoy up from the snow, Mother and Jenny tossed them bread. Jenny's exuberant repertoire of hollow brays and hoarse cackles made the ravens, as they listened tilt-headed, seem lost mute souls and she their ventriloquist.

During those years, too, I was often ill in my lungs; my face moored in sweat, I squinted disgust at the radish-clots of blood I coughed up. There was seldom a forecast for these painful attacks;

once, however, I dreamed I could read, on cold days, my own
breath-clouds that warned me when to return home and to bed. At
some point during each convalescence my mother would fan out
her postcard illustrations of the Ark. I'd pick one at a time: first the
irreverent version in which a giraffe smoked a cigar and a spotted
cat rollerskated up the plank. Or the Asian naïve depicting an endless parade of color-sail junks, each filled to the brim with animals,
setting forth under a monsoon of orange teardrop rain toward the
bamboo Ark looming on the horizon. Or the ancient scene, where
a fabled Griffin—half eagle, half lion—stood in line with mortal
pairs of spiral-horned antelope, mottled horses, black foxes. (*Why
only one Griffin?* I asked. Because it is already two animals, was the
answer given.) The Arks cheered me. Until, with a sudden pen-
siveness, as if a certain remembered weather with specific textures
of breeze and light beckoned her face, my mother would say, "That
was a remarkable voyage. I was seasick only the first day. I felt un-
lonely; the birds, their sea echoes . . . other friendly faces in the
dark . . ." Slowly then the Arks were returned to their box.

Pelly Bay—his father's family name was Bay; he was named after
the iceberg waters due north, *Pelly Bay,* whose inlet moorage was
a respite to ships northbound from Repulse Bay—Pelly and I were
both fourteen when he drowned inside the radio. Like Jenny he had
been orphaned early. Taken in by his aunt Hettie and uncle Samuel, the three lived in Quill, the nearest village to us yet miles away
across woodland, caribou taiga, and marshes often eerie with shifting densities of mirage steam. Quill had the region's Hudson's Bay
Co. store, whose proprietor was a jittery and honest man, originally
from Halifax, named Einert Sohms. His store had Quill's only
porch. Supplies arrived in small planes using the tar landing strip
on the outskirts. Samuel Bay carved bird decoys, wood sculptures

really, and painted them expertly. In the store he displayed one Harlequin duck, one Merganser, and a loon, but sent the other ducks south; in cities they were purchased in order to be used by hunters back in the north. Such were their erratic migrations. A tall man, with wide bony shoulders, one got the impression that any shirt Samuel was wearing still was on its closet hanger. Except that Hettie hung their clothes on nails along the walls of their house. Samuel drove a collapsing pickup which, when new, he named *Speakeasy* because he badly stuttered. The unwavering control with which Samuel painted decoys was one end of a paradoxical see-saw whose counterpart was his stammer; often, much to his shy frustration, the end of a word he had begun to speak eluded him, yet cast him about, the way a subterranean well and the diviner's wishbone twig search each other through air and ground. Samuel painted ambidextrously. He could dab mallard green to a wooden feather with his left-hand brush while simultaneously applying beige mud-flecks to the tucked, webbed foot of the same duck.

Hettie was a stout, lively Cree woman, born in Quill, who married Samuel at eighteen. Quill was predominantly a Cree Indian village. Each late autumn most Indian families dispersed in all directions to winter hunting territories. They returned to Quill after the thaw, when geese arrived at the muskeg ponds, and marathon reunion conversations caught everyone up on winter news. Hettie was employed as translator at the store when furs were appraised, and when Cree occasionally bought rope, coffee, kettles. She moved deftly between Cree and English; whenever Einert Sohms attempted humor, Hettie saved him from double failure: she didn't translate, and informed him, "That's not funny in Cree." We heard this so many times it became something of a personal joke between Pelly and myself. Once, out rummaging a storm-ransacked forest for the most outrageous of the million antlers of fallen branches, we carelessly meandered into a *swallowing place;* one of the scattered, hidden suckholes formed by the berserk runnelling of the spring snowmelt. Mud-gulped to our waists, we pissed down our trousers and simply cried in fear. Then everything stopped. Astonished to discover we were caught, still breathing air, on a tangle of roots, Pelly—spitting mud—said, "This isn't funny in Cree." We clawed out and lay torn.

Summers I lived with Hettie, Samuel, and Pelly, talking through many porch dusks at the store, eating Hettie's three-course meals—all soups, each of a thicker more varied consistency than the one before—and being confined to bed by bad lungs days in a row. I imagined the loud, gray jays complained for me at my window. But I felt happy in Quill. In Samuel I saw a father. Hettie, no doubt sensing this, ingeniously addressed the situation by often remarking, in her funny English, "We love Pelly, ours . . . like a son. We love you, ours . . . like a nephew."

Although it was an excellent place to live, Quill had a wolverine grudge held against it. The Cree found laughable the boldness, wit, and inventiveness in which the otherwise reclusive wolverines carried out this grudge. In fact anything a wolverine did they found in character. No one told an exact origin of the *grudge.* Tales of it began, "A long time back, the *grudge* began . . ." (assigning it an almost separate animation), then separate episodes were delved into: a trapline ransacked, brooms chewed through, the mail plane's tires gnawed to ribbons, a man being circled with snarls and hissing followed by the wolverine simply loping away. The Indian nomenclature had wolverines as "skunk bears" because they resemble diminutive bears and have two pale brown stripes on the sides; there was also a separate word meaning "wolverine havoc." During the most trying, murderously cold months when even wolverines—penultimate survivors, next to the landscape itself—began to starve, they were believed able to snap the air and chew down the essence of winter itself.

Hettie enjoyed relating an incident from a time Einert Sohms kept his spare key around the neck of his goat tethered to the porch. One morning the absence of familiar bleating drew Sohms out the door, and he saw the goat had disappeared. Snow that morning had quilted away any hints. Five days later a nephew of Hettie's delivered the key to Einert Sohms, having discovered it, he calmly reported, glinting from a steaming twist of wolverine dung out on the middle of a frozen pond. Taking the key, Sohms joked, "At least the wolverine didn't use the key to break in and thieve the store!" This time not able to resist, Hettie translated. Her nephew—perhaps feeling the wolverine was listening; after all, it was the nephew who'd found the key and knew nothing was arbitrary within the *grudge*—said seriously, "A wolverine would not need a key to do that." Furthermore, he said, the wolverine had requested the snow to cover the tracks. Hettie translated all this. Sohms inquired, "How does he know *that?*" Again: Hettie. Her nephew replied, "I listened to what the droppings said." Hettie translated. Einert Sohms asked, "What else . . . ," interrupted by the nephew saying, "That the wolverine greatly enjoyed your goat."

Pelly, my summer companion, do you miss your rough coat? Are you cold? Are you homesick? Your aunt and uncle have a short-wave radio now; they hear orchestras. And why did you seldom sleep? Did you sense your waking life would be brief? It was known in Quill that Pelly sat through most summer nights staring from the porch; uncanny, without slapping even if the night was a suffer of blackflies. As if the distance was inside him staring out.

His hair each year darkened toward sloe-black. His long-fingered hands, always to my great delight, could detail shadow animals walking a moonlit wall. He was thin, though not gawky. He was moody; let's say he felt close to weather. And quiet; even I would ask if he wanted to talk before striking up a conversation. Winter nights, he painted—on school Manila paper, using Sam's brushes. His paintings were of familiar landscapes, though in each something aberrant occurred: a gigantic, quail-like bird, its head aloft the background forest, blinked down at the village; geese reflections crossed the moon on a lake, though no moon or geese were in the sky. . . . He walked around on snowshoes tacking his pictures up. On doors, on trees. People found them in the morning.

Before dawn on a March day, Pelly saw the mail plane working the region fall. It sputtered, spiralled from its spiralling oil smoke and careened into a stand of trees. Winds fluting the trees camouflaged the plane's dive-whistling and crash from the rest of Quill. Quickly fastening on snowshoes, Pelly set out for the accident. Above the wreckage he found more, and the dead pilot wedged up in the inverted broom of a birch. A few packages, and dozens of letters were strewn over the snow—tempered slightly by the partition of trees, surface winds swirled letters from their canvas mailbags as from cornucopias. Pelly intended to inform Hettie and Samuel of what he'd found, but felt the need to first gather the letters, to get things in order before the tragic news brought a lantern parade. For even that almost somnambulist motion in the bitter night, that ordering of fearful curiosity, would be intrusive on the odd serenity Pelly

then felt in the presence of the pilot and the imagined voices inside
their envelopes.

Among which Pelly found something he kept: a mail-order catalogue. *Full of everything,* he told me. *All kinds of radios.* Tucking
the catalogue under his coat, Pelly heard his first radio squawking
incoherently from its crow's nest, the tattered cockpit. He stared at
the pilot a long time then. And the pilot stared, as if trying to deci-
pher the radio's message, a last minute warning? Of a nimbus-
storm about to clot up the carburetor (the mechanic was hung
over). Or a hello from home, *Don't forget Sunday night, you remember, the get-together for . . .* The spectrum of possibilities was mind-
boggling; useless. Pelly finished placing the letters in individual
stacks weighted down by bits of plane, and one shoe. In Quill he
woke Hettie, who jostled Samuel awake; soon most citizens of that
northern village stood under one tree. Two Cree men climbed the
pilot down, who was half frozen. On a runner sled he was brought
to Quill. Until midday, the body was kept on the sudden mortuary
of the porch. All morning, though, the winds had calmed. Distant
sounds, drawn through the acoustics of condensed air, an echo's
paradise, came closer—so it was that Quill kept hearing, from the
trees, the radio's torn voice.

Late afternoon four men finished preparations for setting out east
to deliver the pilot to the train whose route, twice monthly, was
between Winnipeg and Churchill. Should clear weather hold, it
would be about two days' travel by dogsled. Given a track clear of
ice-buckling, or a locomotive not plagued by breakdowns, the men
still could be waiting for at least two weeks to flag the train to a halt.
Their sleds were packed with tents, a caribou shoulder, smoked
fish, pemmican, and ptarmigan steaks. Their thick Malamutes

would also be trailing a toboggan hearse. So, along with this funeral procession, under a hammock of moon already drifting through dusk, Pelly sent a letter.

While Hettie stayed in Quill with her aged parents, Samuel and Pelly spent much of that summer in Montreal visiting Sam's old friends, touring sporting-goods stores that stocked his decoys, and seeing movies. Pelly heard the radio every day there; but what he brought back to Quill was the unicycle he had ordered through the catalogue. He remembered the warehouse was in Montreal. There the unicycle was handed to him over a counter, in parts, in a box. A tire pump went with it, and a spoke tightener. And an illustrated history of unicycling, in which could be found a riding bear, the world's tallest unicycle, marathon racers, a man in a suit weaving through a London traffic jam, another man trolling a fishing line alongside the creek bridge he peddled back and forth over, a young woman herding sheep down a slope on a unicycle whose spokes were fretted with carnival ribbons . . .

In Quill, with Sam's help, Pelly assembled the unicycle and immediately began practicing on it; at first wobbling about the tar landing strip, and within weeks adept in peddling a straight line, stopping without toppling over, not leaning too heavily into turns. Yet where he truly revealed his artistry was on ice. After the freeze Pelly could be found on one pond in particular, whose borders he learned intuitively, adjusting his peripheral vision to accommodate the slight incline from his elevated seat. The wheel sprayed ice from abrupt stops. He peddled the alphabet in grainy, new-fallen snow. He sprinted the pond's circumference, arms spread wide, hands tilting like keels in the air, or with fists seeming to hold or release weight like a balance mechanism. Sometimes he made an elusive obstacle course of shadows, if he unicycled by snowlight, or moon. Quill's only circus ever.

That winter we broke tradition and I spent the coldest months in Quill. I joyfully observed as Pelly perfected a turnaround-in-the-air, and fake perils: tilting low to the ice; dramatically rolling a dizzy spell up in his eyes as the unicycle went forward, and Pelly's feet exaggerated peddling in midair; and a heart-stopper, a precise choreography—he swerved dangerously twice, then flopped over the snowbank rim, only to pop from the snow and then—like a film run backward—climbed on his unicycle again and reversed those antics until he stopped in the middle of the pond, and turned for my applause.

I left Quill with the anticipation of returning for summer in a few months. Late that morning, while the plane I'd ride home in took on supplies from the Bay Co. store, Pelly showed me where a mysteriously early thaw had serrated open part of the pond ice. We inspected this from the safety of shore, but couldn't figure it out. Hettie thought it was due to a "fish wedding," where pickerel line up under the ice like exclamation points and breathe and chip through with their knobby heads; then the fish marry air and bring it into the water. As a child she had seen this several times.

Later that morning we had watched a lynx stalk this open water. With a whole North to lick a drink from, this crouched, bearded, uninvited wedding guest wanted something more. When his wide forepaw explored near the edge, ice webbed like cracked glass. Springing backward, the lynx swung a paw and screeched at near-death, then was quick into the trees. Noting my concern about the dubious ice, Pelly said, "I'll be careful." We hugged good-bye, and I climbed into the plane among flour sacks, writing paper, candle wax, old magazines, medicines, axes, linens, a rocking chair. When the plane taxied up, arced, and leveled, I looked down to see a wolverine—no doubt weighing as much as the lynx—standing on the same thin ice, peering and scooping in the water for fish.

The pilot did not use his radio at all. We landed on ski runners on Paduola Lake. Jenny ice-skated out to meet the plane she had heard sending its engine noise ahead of it.

In early April my father, who had followed his maps home for a visit, set a two-way radio on our kitchen table. "Next winter you can talk with people other than yourselves," he said. "Sam's got a short-wave radio at his place now, too. I was just over there. We heard an orchestra. You see, what I figure can happen is, first Sam catches an orchestra from the air . . . you could say they're floating around all the time, from the great cities. He can catch one just by turning a dial . . . like casting a net . . ." With uncharacteristic enthusiasm, he explained the workings of a radio as if trying to sell the original patent. "Now, since Sam has the duplicate two-way set," he taps ours, ". . . it's like a walkie-talkie. All he has to do is put the transmitter from *his* two-way next to his short-wave's speaker . . . and presto! a philharmonic."

"One radio talking to another," my mother responded. "We just listen in on their conversation. Why not move to Quill, listen to orchestras there, with people?"

"Why not get our own short-wave?" I offered.

Baffled that my mother's spoken options so directly revealed her loneliness, her anger toward much of our life, my father said, "Never thought of those things." It was a curiously sad moment. I think he realized suddenly, unavoidably, that his circuitous radio-strategy—given the notion of it as a private box in some symphony hall—was an extension of his own long-troubling doubts about the isolation he had placed us in. We could live in Quill. It would be *easier* on us, so why not? My father stared fixedly. Then he said, "Well, no matter, because we've got this opportunity right now . . ."

Indeed no matter, because our few classical albums, Rachmaninov's *Variations on a Theme by Paganini*, Bach's *Brandenburg Concertos*, Stravinsky's *Rites of Spring*, and their cell-battery player were worn derelict and scratchy; the thought of one pure, clear bassoon note heard through the static and distance seemed revelatory.

Adjusting dials, my father fitted the earphones of the two-way over his head and spoke into the transmitter, "Sam? Sam, do you hear me? This is Paduola Lake calling. Sam, can you . . . do you have an orchestra there?" Within a few minutes Sam's voice could obviously be heard, because my father interrupted, "Sam, one second . . . just hold on . . ." and quickly slid the earphones over my own ears. But it was Hettie's voice which then crackled through. ". . . Listen, Sam is all broken. He's sat down. Listen some bad news. I can hardly tell of it, to you, the accident on the pond. Pelly is drowned gone. Fell in the ice. He gathered us for watching him do tricks, on the unicycle. Samuel and me had chairs waiting, for us special in the snow. We sat in them. We had blankets on our laps. Especially Pelly, he was waving at us. He did some tricks, many. Funny ones. Then he did a trick, wonderful, going backward. That's when it happens. Swallowed up disappeared. From laughing and clapping, to crying everyone went. A few men walk out there, ice swallowing place, but too late. Pelly is gone, already is. We stood so long there. Waiting to believe, it was part of the wonderful trick. Everyone else, huddled home. We just don't get what next now to do . . ." Earphones still on, I stopped listening; I floated my suddenly paled face up again.

Seeing I was deeply and inexplicably shaken, my father switched off the two-way, lifted the earphones from my head, and said, "Didn't think talking with Sam would upset you so much." Then, quietly, "I mean, Son, you look like you've seen a ghost."

Shoptalk #9
Classification

Good writing resists classification, breaks it down. The closer we look at any literary category—Modernism, Minimalism, Post-Modernism, Neo-Realism—the more meaningless it becomes. Are Hemingway and Faulkner and Fitzgerald really doing the same thing? John Barth and Donald Barthelme? Do they share the same aesthetic or political ideology, express the same vision of the world or our place in it? In a pig's eye. These are terms of convenience for pedants and pedants-at-large, to give them a sense of mastery over what is too varied and complex for their patience and understanding.

(Tobias Wolff, "Introduction," vol. 18, nos. 2 & 3, 1992)

MELANIE RAE THON

Little White Sister

*Melanie Rae Thon's first publication after having attended the Univer-
sity of Michigan and Boston University was in the Montana magazine*
Cutbank. *Her second acceptance, she writes, came from* Ploughshares
in 1987.

"*This one changed my life as a writer. I lived in Boston, so I knew*
Ploughshares *was one of the finest journals in the country. I'd sent
them a few stories over the years, and one finally caught the eye of De-
Witt Henry. He wrote me a note and said he couldn't publish that one,
but . . . I should send him everything I had. I gave him my five or six
strongest pieces. DeWitt chose 'Catch You Later,' my most daring story,
which had been rejected by a reader at* Ploughshares *several months
earlier. . . . 'Catch You Later' was written from the point of view of
a drug-addicted transvestite. I'd tried writing the story from a 'safer'
perspective, but the people didn't live until I ventured into more disturbing territory, until I tried to imagine every detail of my narrator's
life as if it were my own. DeWitt's appreciation of the piece gave me
faith and courage about the turn my work had taken. Soon after, he
offered me a job at Emerson, teaching literature and writing classes.
This too was a huge breakthrough. After graduate school, I worked as
a waitress for five years. . . . Teaching saved me. I discovered I loved to
be in the classroom. . . . [When] my story 'Iona Moon' appeared in the*
Hudson Review, *the agent Irene Skolnick (who is still my agent!)
came to Boston to meet me. I was working on my novel* Meteors in

August *at the time. When it was done she sold it to Random House with my first collection of stories,* Girls in the Grass. . . .

"There seems to be a trend toward 'truth' in fiction. Perhaps that's spillover from the current interest in memoir. Some editors and readers want fiction writers to be similar to their narrators. I find this strange and limiting. That's one reason I respect the editors of Ploughshares. *They've never seemed burdened by this constraint. DeWitt never asked if I was a transvestite when he agreed to publish 'Catch You Later' in 1987; Don Lee and Russell Banks knew for sure I wasn't a fifty-year-old black man when they published 'Little White Sister' in 1993.*

"I teach in the M.F.A. program at the Ohio State University, and our students are fine in every way: smart, diverse, dedicated, and remarkably generous with one another. Any one of them is gifted enough to 'succeed.' But I've learned that talent alone won't keep a person writing. Young writers must be consumed, must be willing to give themselves over to the work for many years in order to develop their skills and discover their true tales. I can't predict who will have the will and persistence to keep writing."

Melanie Rae Thon has published two novels, Meteors in August *and* Iona Moon, *and two collections,* Girls in the Grass *and* First, Body. *She has received grants from the Massachusetts Artists Foundation, the New York Foundation for the Arts, and the National Endowment for the Arts. In 1997 she received a Whiting Writers' Award.*

Mama warned me, stay away from white girls. Once I didn't. So, thirty years too late I'm minding my mama. That's how it happened.

I saw her. Flurries that night and she's running, bare-legged, wearing almost nothing at all, and the snow's rising up in funnels, like ghosts, spinning across the street till they whip themselves against the bricks, and I'm thinking, Crazy white girl don't know enough to come in from the cold.

Crackhead most likely, not feeling the wind. I'd seen the abandoned car at the end of the block, ten days now, shooting gallery on wheels, going nowhere. One of them, I told myself, pissed at her boyfriend or so high she thinks her skin is burning off her. Most times crackheads don't know where they are. Like last week. Girl comes pounding on my door. White girl. Could've been the same one. Says she's looking for Lenny. Says she was here with him last night. And I say, *Lenny ain't here;* and she says, *Let me in.* I don't like arguing with a white girl in my hallway so I let her in. I say, *Look around.* She says, *Shit—this isn't even the right place.* She says, *What're you tryin' to pull here, buddy?* And I back away, I say, *Get out of here.* I say, *I don't want no trouble;* and she says, *Damn straight you don't want no trouble.* Then she's gone but I'm thinking: You can be in it that fast and it's nothing you did it's just something that happens.

See, I've already done my time. Walpole, nine years. And I'm not saying Rita's the only reason I went down, but I'm telling you, the time wouldn't have been so hard if not for the white girl.

Cold turkey in a cage and I know Rita's in a clinic, sipping methadone and orange juice. I'm on the floor, my whole body twisted, trying to strangle itself—bowels wrung like rags, squeezed dry, ribs clamped down on lungs so I can't breathe, my heart a fist, beating itself. And I think I'm screaming; I must be screaming, and my skin's on fire, but nobody comes, and nobody brings water, and I want to be dead and out of my skin.

Then I'm cold, shaking so hard I think my bones will break, and that's when the rabbitman slips in between the bars. The rabbitman says: *Once an axe flew off its handle, split an overseer's skull, cleaved it clean, and I saw how easily the body opens, how gladly gives itself up; I saw how the coil of a man's brains spill from his head—even as his mouth opens, even as he tries to speak. Then I saw a blue shadow of a man—people say he ran so fast he ran out of his own skin and they never found him, the rabbitman, but I tell you, they took my skin and I was still alive.* Then the rabbitman whispered: *I got news for you, little brother, I been talkin' to the man and he told me, it ain't time, yet, for this nigger to die.*

So no, I don't go chasing that girl in the street. I know she'll be cold fast, but I think, Not my business—let one of her friends find her.

See, since Rita, I don't have much sympathy for white girls. And I'm remembering what my mama told me, and I'm remembering the picture of that boy they pulled out of the Tallahatchie, sweet smiling boy like I was then, fourteen years old and a white girl's picture in his wallet, so he don't think nothing of being friendly with a white woman in a store. Then the other picture—skull crushed, eye gouged out, only the ring on his finger to tell his mama who he was, everything else that was his boy's life gone: cocky grin, sleepy eyes, felt hat, his skinny-hipped way of walking, all that gone, dragged to the bottom of the river by a cotton-gin fan tied to his neck with barbed wire. Mama said she wasn't trying to turn me mean but she wanted me to see—for my own good—because she loved me, which is why she did everything—because she'd die if anything happened to me—and I thought, even then, something was bound to happen, sooner or later, the fact of living in my black skin a crime I couldn't possibly escape. I only had to look once for one second to carry him around with me the rest of my life, like a photograph in my back pocket that didn't crack or fade, that just got sharper instead, clear as glass and just as dangerous till I pulled it out one day and realized I'd been staring at myself all those years.

I thought about that boy when I met Rita. He breathed on my neck and I laughed to make him stop. I didn't go after her. It was nothing like that. It was just something that happened—like the white girl pounding at my door—I was watching it, then I was in it.

We were at Wally's, me and Leo Stokes, listening to the music, jazz—we liked the music. Mostly I'm listening to the drummer thinking he don't got it right. He thinks he's too important. He don't know the drums are supposed to be the sound underneath the sound. That's why I'm good—that's why I want to play—I got a gift. I hear a sound below horn and piano, the one they need, like I did back in Virginia living in one room—Mama and Daddy, Bernice and Leroy and me, and there were lots of sounds all the time, but I'm always listening for the one sound—like at night when Mama and Daddy are fighting and her voice keeps climbing higher and higher like it's gonna break, and his is low and hard and slow, and then they're tangled together and the words don't make sense, but I'm not scared—no matter how bad it gets—because I'm listening. I hear a whippoorwill or grasshoppers, the wings of cicadas in July, a frenzy of wings rubbing, trying to wear themselves down, and I know what they want—I know what we all want—and it's like that sound is holding everything else together, so even if Mama starts crying, and even if Daddy leaves and don't come back till afternoon the next day, and even if they stop arguing and the other sounds start, even if Daddy has to put his hand over Mama's mouth and say, *Hush now, the children,* even if they get so quiet I can't hear their breathing, I know everything's okay and I'm safe, because the cicadas are out there, and they've been there all along, even when I didn't know I was hearing them, that one sound's been steady, that one sound's been holding everything tight. So I'm listening to the music, thinking, This drummer don't know his place. He thinks he's got to get on top of things. And I hear Leo say, *Luck or trouble, little brother, heading this way,* and then she's there, standing too close, standing above me. She's saying, *Spare a cigarette?* She's whispering, *Got a light?* And then she's sitting down with us and she's got her hand on my hand while I light her cigarette and I'm thinking she's pretty—in a way, in this light—and she's older, so I think she knows things—and I ask myself what's the harm of letting her sit here, and that's when I laugh to make the boy's breath and my mama's voice go away.

Then later that night I'm looking at my own dark hand on her thin white neck and it scares me, the difference, the color of me, the size, and she says, *What color is the inside of your mouth, the inside of your chest?* She says, *Open me—do I bleed, do my bones break?* She says, *Kiss me, we're the same.* And I do. And we are. When we're alone, we are.

She came to see me once. Cried, said she was sorry, and I sat there looking like I had stones in my stomach, ashes in my chest, like I didn't want to put my hands around her neck to touch that damp place under her hair. I told myself, She's not so pretty anymore. She looked old. The way white women do. Too skinny. Cigarettes and sun making her skin crack. Purple marks dark as bruises under her green eyes, I said, *Look, baby, I'm tired, you get on home.* I'm acting like I can't wait to get back to my cell, like I'm looking forward to the next three thousand nights smelling nothing but my own rotten self, like I've got some desire to spend nine years looking at the bodies of men, like I haven't already wondered how long it's gonna be before I want them. She says she didn't know, she didn't mean to make it worse for me, and I say, *Where you been living, girl? What country?* She's not crying then, she's pissed. She says, *You know what they did to me when I came in here? You know where they touched me?* And I say, *One day. One friggin' hour of your life. I live here, baby. They touch me all the time. Whenever they want. Wherever.*

I'm not saying she stuck the needle in my arm and turned me into a thief. I'm saying I wasn't alone. Plenty of things I did I shouldn't have. I paid for those. Three burglaries, nine years, you figure. So yeah, I paid for a dozen crimes they never slapped on me, a hundred petty thefts. But the man don't mind about your grandfather's gold pocket watch; he don't worry when the ten-dollar bill flies out of your mama's purse and floats into your hand. He don't bother you much if he sees you shoving weed on your own street. But that was different. Back when I was peddling for Leo I had a purpose, doing what I had to do to get what I needed. Then things turned upside down with Rita, and I was robbing my own mama, stealing to buy the dope instead of selling it, smack instead of grass. Rita said: *Just once—you won't get hooked, and it's fine, so fine, better than the music, because it's inside.* She was right—it was better than the music, and it was inside: it made me forget the sound and the need.

Now my mama is singing me to sleep, humming near my ear, *Bless the child,* and I'm waking as a man twenty-one years old, and I'm going to Walpole till I'm thirty. Sweet-faced Rita has scrubbed herself clean for the trial. She says it was all my idea and she was afraid, who wouldn't be? Seven men see their own wives, their own daughters, and pray no man like me ever touches their pretty white things. They think they can put me away. They think locked doors and steel bars keep them safe. Five women see their own good selves and swear they'd never do what Rita did if not by force.

I want to tell them how different she can be, how she looks when she's strung out, too jittery to talk, when her jaw goes so tight the tendons pop in her neck. I want to tell them how she begged me, *Please Jimmy please,* how she said it was so easy, her old neighborhood, her own people, habits she could predict, dogs she could calm. I want to ask them, *Do black men drive your streets alone?* I want to tell them, *I was in the back, on the floor, covered by a blanket. She drove. She waited in the car, watching you, while I broke windows, emptied jewelry boxes, hunted furs.*

Next thing I know I'm in prison and she's on probation and Mama's telling me, *You got to stay alive.* Ninety-two times she says it. Once a month for eight years, then one month she doesn't show, and the next week Bernice comes, says Mama's sick and aren't I ashamed. Then Mama comes again, three more times, but she's looking yellowish, not her high yellow but some new dirty yellow that even fills her eyes. She's not losing her weight but it's slipping down around her in strange ways, hanging heavy and low, so when she walks toward me, she looks like a woman dragging her own body. *My baby.* That's all she says. But I know the rest. Then Bernice is there again, shaking her head, telling me one more time how Mama gave up her life to give us a decent chance and she's got reason to be proud—little Leroy a schoolteacher, Bernice a nurse. I mean to remind her, *You feed mashed-up peas to old ladies with no teeth. You slip bedpans under wrinkled white asses. Wearing a uniform don't make you no nurse, Bernice.* But I just say, *Lucky for Mama the two of you turned out so fine.* I grin but Bernice isn't smiling; Bernice is crossing her big arms over her big chest. I see her fall to her knees as if her body is folding under her. I see her face crumple as if she's just been struck. And I'm not in prison. I'm free, but just barely, and I see my own dark hands in too-small white gloves, five other men like me, lifting the box and Mama in it, the light through stained glass breaking above us and that terrible wailing, the women crying but not Mama, the women singing as if they still believe in their all merciful God, as if they've forgotten their sons: sacrificed, dead, in solitary, on the street, rotting in a jungle, needles in their arms, fans tied around their necks, as if they don't look up at Jesus and say, *What a waste.*

I remembered my own small hands in the other white gloves; I thought my skin would stain them. The bull was dead. I would never be washed clean. But I was, baptized and redeemed. The white robes swirled, dragged me down, blinded me, and I thought, I can't swim, I'm going to die, and this is why my father wouldn't come to church today—the preacher in black is letting me die, is holding my head under—he wants me to die, it's necessary—I remember the stories my mother and I read, forbidden stories, our secret: cities crumbling, land scorched, plagues of frogs and gnats, plagues of boils and hail, seas and rivers turned to blood, and then, suddenly, I am rising and I am alive, spared by grace. The whole church trembles around me, women singing, telling Moses to let their people go, sweet low voices urging the children to wade in the water, but I know it's too deep, too dark, and I wasn't wading, I was drowning, but the voices are triumphant, the walls are tumbling down. Easter morning light blazes through colored glass; John baptizes Jesus above the water where we are baptized. I am shivering, cold, crying. Mama is sobbing, too; I hear her voice above the others, but I know she's happy. I know that Jesus is alive again just as I am alive, and I have never been this clean, and I am going to be good forever, and I am going to love Jesus who has saved me through his suffering, and I am going to forgive my father who has forsaken me. I am high and righteous and without doubt. I am ten years old.

These same women are still singing about that same damn river, like this time they're really going to cross it, when everybody knows they're stuck here just like me and not one of us can swim; the only river we see is thick as oil and just as black, so what's the point of even trying when you'd be frozen stiff in two minutes and sinking like the bag of sticks and bones you are, and still they won't stop swaying, as if they have no bones, as if the air is water and they are under it, and they are swimming, and they cannot be drowned, as if women have a way of breathing that men don't. I'm choking. I look at Leroy to see if he's drowning, too, to see if he's gasping, remembering Mama, our love for her, our guilt, but he's not guilty, he's a good clean boy, a teacher, clever little Leroy making numbers split in pieces, making them all come together right again. *Nothing can be lost,* he says, and he believes it. I say, *Didn't you ever want anything?* And he looks at me like I'm talking shit, which I suppose I am, but I still wonder, *Why didn't you feel it, that buzz in your veins, the music playing; why didn't you ever close your eyes and forget who it was Mama told you not to touch? Didn't we have the same blind father? Didn't you ever wonder where Mama got her gold eyes? Didn't the rabbitman ever fly through your open window?*

Twenty years now and I still want to ask my brother the same questions. Twenty years and I still want to tell our mama I'm sorry—but I know there are times *sorry* don't mean a thing. I want to ask her, *Do you blame me?* And I want to ask her, *Should I go out in the snow?* I almost hear her answer, but I don't go.

Digging graves, hauling garbage, snaking sewers—I've done every filthy job, and now, two years, something halfway decent, graveyard shift but no graves. It's good work, steady, because there are always broken windows, busted doors. Fires burst glass; cars jump curbs; bullets tear through locks; police crack wood—always—so I don't have to worry, and Mama would be proud.

I'm alone with it, boards and nails, the hammer pounding. I strike straight, hold the place in my mind, like Daddy said. It's winter. My bare hands split at the knuckles, my bare hands bleed in the cold. Wind burns my ears but I don't mind. I don't want anything—not money, not music, not a woman. I know how desires come, one hooked to the other, and I'm glad my heart is a fist, shattered on a prison wall, so I don't have to think I might still play— because I can't, and it's not just the bones broken. But sometimes I hear the sound underneath the sound: it's summer, it's hot, the radios are blasting—brothers rapping, Spanish boys pleading, bad girls bitching—nobody knows a love song—then the gun goes off, far away, and I hear that, too, and later, sirens wailing. There's an argument downstairs, the Puerto Rican girl and her Anglo boyfriend, cursing in different languages. All those sounds are the song, pieces of it, but I'm listening for the one sound below it all, the one that pulls us down, the one that keeps us safe. Then I catch it: it's the rain that's stopped—it's the cars passing on the wet street—it's the soft hiss of tires through water, and it almost breaks me.

If I could find Rita now I'd tell her she was right: junk is better than jazz. It's fast and it doesn't hurt you the way the music does. It's easy. It takes you and you don't have to do anything. It holds you tighter than you've ever been held. You think it loves you. It knows where to lick and when to stop. When it hums in your veins, it says, *Don't worry, I'm with you now.*

I'd tell her, The blues scare everybody. They make you remember things that didn't happen to you, make you feel your bones aren't yours only—they've been splintered a thousand times; the blood has poured out of you your whole life; the rabbitman's skin is your skin and the body you share is on fire. Or it's simpler than

that, and you're just your own daddy, or your own mama sitting
beside him. Then you wish you didn't have to feel what they feel,
and you get your wish, and you're nobody but your own self,
watching.

Every beat I played was a step closer to my uncle's house where
I listened to my cousins breathe in the bed above me, where I slept
on the floor because Daddy was blind in our house, Daddy's legs
were swollen twice their size and stinking, Daddy was cut loose on
his own poison and Mama was there, alone, with him—giving him
whiskey, washing him, no matter what he said, no matter who he
cursed.

My cousins take me to the woods, Lucy and Louise, one older,
one younger; they say, *Touch me here, and here.* They dare me, they
giggle. They touch *me* and make me forget what's happening across
the field, in my house; then they run away and I hear the grasshoppers chirping all around me, buzzing—frantic, invisible—and
then, I remember.

But smack, it makes you forget, it makes you not care, just like
Rita said. It promises: *There's nothing more you need to know.* So I
didn't have to see my father's never-clean clothes snapping on the
line. I didn't have to remember Mama bent over the washtub in the
yard, flesh of her arm quivering like she wanted to wash out evil as
well as filth. I didn't have to go in the truck with Daddy that morning when he said it was time I saw my future. I didn't have to swing
the sledgehammer with my boy's arms or see the bull's eyes, mad
with disbelief.

But now I remember everything, how I struck the head but too
close to the nose, so there was the crack, and blood spouting from
the mouth but no crumpling, and Daddy said: *Hold the place in
your mind.* I swung a second time, grazed the face, and the bull

swelled with his own breath, filling the stall. Three strikes in all before my father grabbed the hammer: one blow, and the animal folded, knees bending, neck sagging, the whole huge beast collapsing on itself.

Then the others came, sawed off head and legs, slit skin from flesh, peeled the animal—*strange fruit*—and there was blood, a river of it, hot, and there was blood, swirling at my feet. The body opened and there was blood weeping from the walls and the rabbitman ran so fast he ran out of his own skin and the bowels spilled, an endless rope, thick and heavy, full, and the smell, but the men work in the heat of the animal: kidneys, bladder, balls—saved, and the blood spatters them: faces, hands, thighs—they are soaked with it, I am soaked; I will never be clean, and even the ceiling is dripping until at last the carcass is hung on a hook in the cold room full of bodies without legs or heads or hearts.

But I am washed clean and I do forgive my father and my father dies and my grandparents forgive my mother for her bad marriage. I am fifteen. It's November, still warm in Virginia but not in Boston, which is where we're going, on the train, with my grandfather, who is kind enough but doesn't know us, who won't come inside our house, who's brought a suitcase full of clothes we have to wear and shoes that hurt our feet. He and Granny Booker mean to save us, mean to *compensate.* They say we can be anything. But all I want to be is the music, all I want to hear is the sound. Doctor Booker means I can be like him, and I think about that, the sharp razor's edge of his scalpel, all his delicate knives. I feel his clamps. I touch speculum and forceps, imagining how precisely he opens the body, what he finds there when he does. I see the familiar brown spatters on shirt cuffs and pant legs, his never-clean clothes, and I think, For all your pride, you're no better than my father, no different, and the distance from his house to yours is only the space it takes a man to turn around.

I remember my father crying. It frightened me more than anything, more than the bull, more than the water where I thought I'd drown. And this is all it was: scarecrow on a fence. He must have been going blind even then. He thought it was another one, body tangled in barbed wire. But it was only clothes stuffed with rags, pillowcase head tied off at the neck, straw hat and empty sleeves blowing in hot wind.

In prison I learned that my body itself is the enemy, my skin so black it reflects you. You want to take it from me. I terrify. Even when I am one and you are twenty. Even when I am cuffed and you have clubs. Even when I show you my empty hands and you show me your guns. I alarm you. I do what any animal will do: no matter how many times you strike, I try to stand. I mean to stay alive.

Which is why the girl in the street scared me. I thought, Maybe she's not a crackhead. Maybe she's just a woman from the other side, lost in another country, running deeper into it because once you're here you can't see your way out. Cross a road; walk under a bridge; that's how far. No signs, no stone wall, but the line is tight as a border crossing. If you close your eyes it glitters like broken glass, pale and blue, a thousand shattered windshields. Here, every gesture is a code. Boys patrol their turf, four square blocks, pretend they own something. They travel in packs and arm themselves because they're more afraid than any of us, because every time they look up the sky is falling, so they're rapping about the cops they're gonna dust, the cities they're gonna torch. The little brothers are spinning on their heads, like this is some dance, some game—their bodies twist in ways they were never meant to bend, and then everybody in the street just falls down dead.

And the old men like me sit in the bars, drinking whiskey, going numb, talking about snatch and getting even all in the same breath, and we sound just like our own pitiful mamas, saying: *Judgment Day gonna come, righteous gonna be raised up, and the wicked gonna suffer, rich or poor, don't make no difference.* Except the men, the justice they're talking don't have nothing to do with God. They're full of the old words, saying, *We can't come in the house we're gonna knock it down;* then they sound just like the boys in the street, only tired and slurred, and the boys out there, they're quick, they got matches and gasoline, they talk fast as spit and don't ever need to sleep. But the flames burst at their backs, and they're the ones on fire.

We know the rules. Mess with white folks, you pay. Kill a white man, you hang. Kill a black man? That's just one more nigger off the street. So when I think about that girl, when I think, If she's still out there, she's in trouble, when I think even my mama would tell me I should go, I remind myself: I already done enough time for a white girl. I know how they are, how she'd be scared of me even if I said, *I just want to help you.* And I know how it would look in the alley—big black man's got his hands on a skinny white girl. Just my luck the boyfriend would come looking, shoot me dead. Nobody'd ask him why.

I think, Maybe she's already dead and I'll find her, touch her once and leave the perfect print of my hand burned on her thigh. I don't have a phone and anyway, too late to call. They'd wanna know, *Why'd you wait so long,* and I'd be gone.

Last time they found a white woman dead on this hill police turned into a lynch mob, got the whole city screaming behind them. Roadblocks and strip searches. Stopped every dark-skinned man for miles if he was tall enough and not too old. Busted down doors, emptied closets, shredded mattresses, and never did find the gun that was already in the river. But they found the man they wanted: tall, raspy voice, like me. He's got a record, long, shot a police officer once. He's perfect. He can be sacrificed. No education, string of thefts. Even his own people are glad to turn him over, like there's some evil here and all we got to do is cut it out. I'm thinking, Nobody kills the woman and leaves the man alive. Even an ignorant nigger. But the police, they don't think that way. They need somebody. Turns out the husband did it. Shot his wife. Pregnant, too. Months later, white man jumps, bridge to river, January, he's dead, then everybody knows. But that black guy, he's still in jail. Violating parole. Some shit like that. Who knows? They got him, they're gonna keep him.

I hear two voices, and they both sound like my mama. One tells me, *She's human, go.* And one whispers, *You got to keep yourself alive.* One's my real mama and one a devil with my mama's voice.

Something howled. I thought it was the wind. I wanted to lean into it, wrap my arms around it. I wanted it to have a mouth, to swallow me. Or I wanted to swallow it, to cry as it cried, loud and blameless.

It was nearly dawn and I was ashamed, knowing now which voice belonged to my mama. I held the girl in my mind. She was light as a moth, bright as a flame. I knew she was dead. It was as if she'd called my name, my real one, the one I didn't know until she spoke it. I felt her lungs filling under my hand. She said: *There's one warm place at the center of my body where I wait for you.*

Stray finds her. Mangy wolf of a dog. Smells her. Even in this cold, he knows. And it's like he loves her, the way he calls, just whining at first, these short yelps, high and sad, and when nobody comes he starts howling, loud enough to wake the dead, I think, but not her. And it's day, the first one.

We're out there in the cold, nine of us in the alley, hunched, hands in pockets, no hats, shivering, shaking our heads, and one guy is saying, Shit, *shit*, because he remembers, we all remember, the last time.

I see her, close, thirty-five at least but small, so I thought she was a girl, and I think of her that way now. I kneel beside her. Her eyes are open, irises shattered like blue glass. Wind ruffles her nightgown, exposes her. Snow blows through her hair, across bare legs, between blue lips. I see bruises on her thighs, cuts on her hands, a face misaligned, and I think, I have bones like these, broken, healed, never the same. My hand aches in the cold.

I know now what happened, why she's here. I see her keeper. She smokes his cigarettes, he whacks her. She drinks his beer, he drags her to the toilet, holds her head in the bowl. He's sorry. I've heard the stories. I've seen the women. And I've been slammed against a cement wall for looking the man in the eye. I've been kicked awake at three a.m. because some motherfucker I offended told the guards I had a knife. The keepers make the rules, but they're always shifting: we can't be good enough.

Police stay quiet. Don't want to look like fools again. And nobody's asking for this girl. Stray, like the dog. They got time.

I know now what her body tells them: stomach empty, liver enlarged, three ribs broken, lacerations on both hands—superficial wounds, old bruises blooming like yellow flowers on her back and thighs. Death by exposure. No crime committed here. And they don't care who cut her, and they don't care who broke her ribs, because all her people are dead or don't give a shit, and she was the one, after all, who ran out in the snow, so who's to say she didn't want to die.

I drink port because it's sweet, gin because it's bitter, back to back, one kills the taste of the other. I can't get drunk. Three days now since we found her and I see her whole life, like she's my sister and I grew up with her. She's a child with a stick drawing pictures in the dirt. She's drawn a face and I think it must be her own face but I say, *What are you drawing;* and she says, *Someone to love me.* I say, *What are you trying to do, break my heart?* And she says, *If you have a heart, I'll break it.* I say, *Where's your mama?* And she says, *She's that pretty lady with red lips and high heels—you've probably seen her—but sometimes her lipstick's smeared all down her chin and her stockings are ripped and she's got one shoe in her hand and the spike is flying toward me—that's my mother.* I say, *Where's your daddy?* And she says, *He's a flannel shirt torn at the shoulder hanging in the closet ever since I've been alive and my mother says, That's the reason why.*

Then I see she's not a child; she's a full-grown woman, and her hands are cut, her hands are bleeding, and I say, *Who did this to you?* She won't answer, but I know, I see him, he's her lover, he's metal flashing, he's a silver blade in the dark, and she tries to grab him but he's too sharp. Then she's running, she's crying, and I see her in the street, and I think she's just some crazy white girl too high to feel the cold, and I don't go.

Now she's talking to me always. She's the sound underneath all other sounds. She won't go away. She says, *I used to make angels in the snow, like this; I used to lie down, move my arms and legs, like this, wings and skirt, but that night I was too cold, so I just lay down, curled into myself, see, here, and I saw you at your window, and I knew you were afraid, and I wanted to tell you, I'm always afraid, but after I lay down I wasn't so cold, and I was almost happy, and I was almost asleep, but I wanted to tell you, I'm your little white sister—I know you— we're alone.*

Shoptalk #10
Borders

In search of plausibility . . . if not the simple truth, I
have been drawn more and more to fiction by writers
who see themselves as situated in a society that puts
every American man and woman on the borders of race,
culture, language, gender, and class, and who view their
world not from the privileged center of their own private Idaho, but from out there on the edges, where they
are obliged to look both ways, as if at a dangerous crossing, and say what they see coming.

(Russell Banks, "Strictly in the Interests of Plausibility," vol. 19, no. 1, 1993)

DAVID WONG LOUIE

Displacement

*David Wong Louie graduated in 1981 with an M.F.A. from the Iowa
Writers' Workshop, where he studied with Frederick Busch, Vance
Bourjaily, Hilma Wolitzer, and Janet Burroway. David Hamilton
published his first stories in* the Iowa Review; *other stories appeared
in the* Chicago Review, Kansas Quarterly, Agni Review, *the* Mid-
American Review, *and* Fiction International, *as well as in the 1988
"Fiction Discoveries" issue of* Ploughshares. *His collection* Pangs of
Love *appeared in 1991 and was featured by* Publishers Weekly *in an
article by Gayle Feldman with other new Chinese American fiction by
Gish Jen, Gus Lee, Frank Chin, and Amy Tan. Here Louie is quoted
on the difficulty of both writing and placing the collection. "I tried at
least a half-dozen agents, but with no luck. So in spring 1989 I sent it
out to a few houses myself, and that summer I got an offer from Barbara
Grossman, who was then at Crown. I told her I thought I needed an
agent and she agreed. Suddenly, agents were very happy to have me
come by. I signed with Elaine Markson. . . . Elaine tried to get Barbara
to up her offer, and she also sent the manuscript to other houses. Sonny
Mehta tendered the most money and a two-book deal, so we signed
with Knopf."*

*Elsewhere in the article, Louie recollects, "When I began writing
stories, I had a lot of difficulty figuring out the point of view. I tried
writing from a voice that didn't necessarily identify the characters as
Chinese American, because I didn't think anybody wanted to read
about such characters. I didn't see much Chinese American fiction out*

*there, and I suppose from early on I was trying to erase ethnicity. . . .
Then I began teaching and thinking more about the literature of people
of color, and I began to revise my writing to bring it in line with a new
sense of who I am." After graduating from the University of Iowa,
Louie taught at Berkeley and at Vassar College. He now teaches at
UCLA.*

In my introduction to "Displacement" for the 1988 Ploughshares,
I wrote, "[The story] developed at Ploughshares *through three submissions and two revisions. Don Lee, then associate fiction editor, orgi-
nally singled it out and passed it on to me with close commentary that
later formed the basis of my response. The problem, then, was bringing
the two main sections of the story together and clarifying the narrative
sequence. What we loved, from the outset, was the outsideness of Mrs.
Chow; and, for me, the way it was registered in physical irritation. . . .
To the extent all writers are outsiders, paranoia becomes one of the hall-
marks of a promising writer. Others here include the female point of
view; the Chagall-like surrealism in the metaphors; the central image /
vision of the roller coaster through Mrs. Chow's eyes: 'blowing away
the top layers of dailiness,' and which leads through an intuitive sequence to her 'grasp at something once there, now lost.' Dramatizing
vision also gives us the comic exaggeration of Ed the baby's tantrum, a
locus, as they say, that has become part of my thinking. . . . The complexity of the story, involving and beyond all this, is the complexity of
Mrs. Chow's character—her aristocratic origins, her oppression (and
rebellion) as an artist and as a woman, her additional displacement
by the Red Chinese, her marriage to a peasant and reluctance to have
children, and her anger at the witless arrogance of the Snopish white
Americans to whom she is subjected. The story as I read it resolves not
with assimilation, but with her resigned and forward-looking ironic accommodation."*

Subsequently, "Displacement" was chosen for Best American

166   DAVID WONG LOUIE

Short Stories, 1989. Pangs of Love *received both* Ploughshares *1991 John C. Zacharis First Book Award and the* Los Angeles Times *Art Seidenbaum Award for first fiction. Louie's first novel is due in 2000 from Holt.*

M rs. Chow heard the widow. She tried reading faster but kept stumbling over the same lines. She thought perhaps she was misreading them: "There comes, then, finally, the prospect of atomic war. If the war is ever to be carried to China, common sense tells us only atomic weapons could promise maximum loss with minimum damage."

When she heard the widow's wheelchair she tossed the copy of *Life* down on the couch, afraid she might be found out. The year was 1952.

Outside the kitchen Chow was lathering the windows. He worked a soft brush in a circular motion. Inside, the widow was accusing Mrs. Chow of stealing her cookies. The widow had a handful of them clutched to her chest and brought one down hard against the table. She was counting. Chow waved, but Mrs. Chow only shook her head. He soaped up the last pane and disappeared.

Standing accused, Mrs. Chow wondered if this was what it was like when her parents faced the liberators who had come to reclaim her family's property in the name of the People. She imagined her mother's response to them: What people? All of my servants are clothed and decently fed.

The widow swept the cookies off the table as if they were a canasta trick won. She started counting again. Mrs. Chow and the widow had played out this scene many times before. As on other occasions, she didn't give the old woman the satisfaction of a plea, guilty or otherwise.

Mrs. Chow ignored the widow's busy, blue hands. She fixed her gaze on the other woman's milky eyes instead. Sight resided at the peripheries. Mornings, before she prepared the tub, emptied the pisspot, or fried the breakfast meat, Mrs. Chow cradled the widow's oily scalp and applied the yellow drops that preserved what vision was left in the cold, heaven-directed eyes.

"Is she watching?" said the widow. She tilted her big gray head sideways; a few degrees in any direction Mrs. Chow became a blur. In happier days Mrs. Chow might have positioned herself just right or left of center, neatly within a line of sight.

Mrs. Chow was thirty-five years old. After a decade-long separation from her husband she finally had entered the United States in 1950 under the joint auspices of the War Brides and Refugee Relief Acts. She would agree she was a bride, but not a refugee, even though the Red Army had confiscated her home and turned it into a technical school. During the trouble she was away, safely studying in Hong Kong. Her parents, with all their wealth, could've easily escaped, but they were confident a few well-placed bribes among the Red hooligans would put an end to the foolishness. Mrs. Chow assumed her parents now were dead. She had seen pictures in *Life* of minor landlords tried and executed for lesser crimes against the People.

The widow's fondness for calling Mrs. Chow a thief began soon after the old woman broke her hip. At first Mrs. Chow blamed the widow's madness on pain displacement. She had read in a textbook that a malady in one part of the body could show up as a pain in another locale—sick kidneys, for instance, might surface as a mouthful of sore gums. The bad hip had weakened the widow's brain function. Mrs. Chow wanted to believe the crazy spells weren't the widow's fault, just as a baby soiling its diapers can't be blamed. But even a mother grows weary of changing them.

"I live with a thief under my roof," the widow said to the kitchen. "I could yell at her, but why waste my breath?"

When the widow was released from the hospital she returned to the house with a live-in nurse. Soon afterward her daughter paid a visit, and the widow told her she didn't want the nurse around anymore. "She can do me," the widow said, pointing in Mrs. Chow's direction. "She won't cost a cent. Besides, I don't like being touched that way by a person who knows what she's touching," she said of the nurse.

Nobody knew, but Mrs. Chow spoke a passable though highly accented English she had learned in British schools. Her teachers in Hong Kong always said that if she had the language when she came to the States she'd be treated better than other immigrants. Chow couldn't have agreed more. Once she arrived he started to teach her everything he knew in English. But that amounted to very little, considering he had been here for more than ten years. And what he had mastered came out crudely and strangely twisted. His phrases, built from a vocabulary of deference and accommodation, irritated Mrs. Chow for the way they resembled the obsequious blabber of her servants back home.

The Chows had been hired ostensibly to drive the widow to her canasta club, to clean the house, to do the shopping, and since the bad hip, to oversee her personal hygiene. In return they lived rent-free upstairs in the children's rooms, three bedrooms and a large bath. Plenty of space, it would seem, except the widow wouldn't allow them to remove any of the toys and things from her children's cluttered rooms.

On weekends and Tuesday afternoons Chow borrowed the widow's tools and gardened for spending money. Friday nights, after they dropped the widow off at the canasta club, the Chows dined at Ming's and then went to the amusement park at the beach boardwalk. First and last, they got in line to ride the Milky Way. On the day the immigration authorities finally let her go, before she even saw her new home, Chow took his bride to the boardwalk. He wanted to impress her with her new country. All that machinery, brainwork, and labor done for the sake of fun. He never tried the roller-coaster before she arrived; he saved it for her. After that very first time he realized he was much happier with his feet set on the ground. But not Mrs. Chow: Oh, this speed, this thrust at the sky, this UP! Oh, this raging, clattering, pushy country! So big! And since that first ride she looked forward to Friday nights and the wind whipping through her hair, stinging her eyes, blowing away the top layers of dailiness. On the longest, most dangerous descent her dry mouth would open to a silent O and she would thrust up her arms, as if she could fly away.

Some nights as they waited in line a gang of toughs out on a strut, trussed in denim and combs, would stop and visit: MacArthur, they said, will drain the Pacific; the H-bomb will wipe Korea clean of Commies; the Chows were to blame for Pearl Harbor; the Chows, they claimed, were Red Chinese spies. On occasion, over-extending his skimpy English, Chow mounted a defense: he had served in the U.S. Army, his citizenship was blessed by the Department of War, he was a member of the American Legion. The toughs would laugh at the way he talked. Mrs. Chow cringed at his habit of addressing them as "sirs."

"Get out, get out," the widow hissed. She brought her fist down on the table. Cookies broke, fell to the floor.

"Yes, Missus," said Mrs. Chow, thinking how she'd have to clean up the mess.

The widow, whose great-great-great-grandfather had been a central figure within the faction advocating Washington's coronation, was eighty-six years old. Each day Mrs. Chow dispensed

medications that kept her alive. At times, though, Mrs. Chow wondered if the widow would notice if she were handed an extra blue
pill or one less red.

Mrs. Chow filled an enamel-coated washbasin with warm water
from the tap. "What's she doing?" said the widow. "Stealing my
water now, is she?" Since Mrs. Chow first came into her service,
the widow, with the exception of her hip, had avoided serious ill-
ness. But how she had aged: her ears were enlarged; the opales-
cence in her eyes had spread; her hands worked as if they were
chipped from glass. Some nights, awake in their twin-size bed,
Mrs. Chow would imagine old age as green liquid that seeped into
a person's cells, where it coagulated and, with time, crumbled, caving in the cheeks and the breasts it had once supported. In the dark
she fretted that fluids from the widow's old body had taken refuge
in her youthful cells. On such nights she reached for Chow,
touched him through the cool topsheet, and was comforted by the
fit of her fingers in the shallows between his ribs.

Mrs. Chow knelt at the foot of the wheelchair and set the washbasin on the floor. The widow laughed. "Where did my little thief
go?" She laughed again, her eyes closing, her head dropping to her
shoulder. "Now she's after my water. Better see if the tap's still
there." Mrs. Chow abruptly swung aside the wheelchair's footrests
and slipped off the widow's matted cloth slippers and dunked her
puffy blue feet into the water. It was the widow's naptime, and before she could be put to bed, her physician prescribed a warm foot-
bath to stimulate circulation; otherwise, in her sleep, her blood
might settle comfortably in her toes.

Chow was talking long distance to the widow's daughter in Texas.
Earlier the widow had told the daughter that the Chows were
threatening again to leave. She apologized for her mother's latest

spell of wildness. "Humor her," the daughter said. "She must've had another one of her little strokes."

Later Mrs. Chow told her husband she wanted to leave the widow. "My fingers," she said, snapping off the rubber gloves the magazine ads claimed would guarantee her beautiful hands into the next century. "I wasn't made for such work."

As a girl her parents had sent her to a Christian school for training in Western-style art. The authorities agreed she was talented. As expected, she excelled there. Her portrait of the King was chosen to hang in the school cafeteria. When the Colonial Minister of Education on a tour of the school saw her painting he requested a sitting with the gifted young artist.

A date was set. The rumors said a successful sitting would bring her the ultimate fame: a trip to London to paint the royal family. But a month before the great day she refused to do the Minister's portrait. She gave no reason why; in fact, she stopped talking. The school administration was embarrassed, and her parents were furious. It was a great scandal; a mere child from a country at the edge of revolution but medieval in its affection for authority had snubbed the mighty British colonizers. She was sent home. Her parents first appealed to family pride, then they scolded and threatened her. She hid from them in a wardrobe, where her mother found her holding her fingers over lighted matches.

The great day came and went, no more momentous than the hundreds that had preceded it. That night her father apologized to the world for raising such a child. With a bamboo cane he struck her outstretched hand—heaven help her if she let it fall one inch—and as her bones were young and still pliant, they didn't fracture or break, thus multiplying the blows she had to endure.

"Who'd want you now?" her mother said. Her parents sent her to live with a servant family. She could return home when she was invited. On those rare occasions she refused to go. Many years passed before she met Chow, who had come to the estate seeking work. They were married on the condition he take her far away. He left for America, promising to send for her when he had saved enough money for her passage. She returned to Hong Kong and worked as a secretary. Later she studied at the university.

Now as she talked about leaving the widow, it wasn't the chores or the old woman that she gave as the reason, though in the past she had complained the widow was a nuisance, an infantile brat born of an unwelcomed union. This time she said she had a project in mind, a great canvas of a yet undetermined subject. But that would come. Her imagination would return, she said, once she was away from that house.

It was the morning of a late spring day. A silvery light filtered through the wall of eucalyptus and warmed the dew on the widow's roof, striking the plums and acacia, irises and lilies in such a way that, blended with the heavy air and the noise of a thousand birds, one sensed the universe wasn't so vast, so cold, or so angry, and even Mrs. Chow suspected that it was a loving thing.

Mrs. Chow had finished her morning chores. She was in the bathroom rinsing the smell of bacon from her hands. She couldn't wash deep enough, however, to rid her fingertips of perfumes from the widow's lotions and creams, which, over the course of months, had seeped indelibly into the whorls. But today her failure was less maddening. Today she was confident the odors would eventually fade. She could afford to be patient. They were going to interview for an apartment of their very own.

"Is that new?" Chow asked, pointing to the blouse his wife had on. He adjusted his necktie against the starched collar of a white

short-sleeved shirt, which billowed out from baggy, pinstriped slacks. His hair was slicked back with fragrant pomade.

"I think it's the daughter's," said Mrs. Chow. "She won't miss it." Mrs. Chow smoothed the silk undershirt against her stomach. She guessed the shirt was as old as she was; the daughter probably had worn it in her teens. Narrow at the hips and the bust, it fit Mrs. Chow nicely. Such a slight figure, she believed, wasn't fit for labor.

Chow saw no reason to leave the estate. He had found his wife what he thought was the ideal home, certainly not as grand as her parents' place, but one she'd feel comfortable in. Why move, he argued, when there were no approaching armies, no floods, no one telling them to go? Mrs. Chow understood. It was just that he was very Chinese, and very peasant. Sometimes she would tease him. If the early Chinese sojourners who came to America were all Chows, she would say, the railroad wouldn't have been constructed, and Ohio would be all we know of California.

The Chows were riding in the widow's green Buick. As they approached the apartment building Mrs. Chow reapplied lipstick to her mouth.

It was a modern two-story stucco building, painted pink, surrounded by asphalt, with aluminum windows and a flat roof that met the sky like an engineer's level. Because their friends lived in the apartment in question, the Chows were already familiar with its layout. They went to the manager's house at the rear of the property. Here the grounds were also asphalt. Very contemporary, no greenery anywhere. The closest things to trees were the clothesline's posts and crossbars.

The manager's house was a tiny replica of the main building. Chow knocked on the screen door. A radio was on and the smell of baking rushed past the wire mesh. A cat came to the door, followed

by a girl. "I'm Velvet," she said. "This is High Noon." She gave
the cat's orange tail a tug. "She did this to me," said Velvet, throwing a wicked look at the room behind her. She picked at her hair,
ragged as tossed salad; someone apparently had cut it while the girl
was in motion. She had gray, almost colorless eyes, which, taken
with her hair, gave her the appearance of agitated smoke.

A large woman emerged from the back room, carrying a basket
of laundry. She wasn't fat, but large in the way horses are large. Her
face was round and pink, with fierce little eyes, and hair the color
of olive oil and dripping wet. Her arms were thick and white, like
soft tusks of ivory.

"It's the people from China," Velvet said.

The big woman nodded. "Open her up," she told the girl. "It's
okay."

The front room was a mess, cluttered with evidence of frantic
living. This was, perhaps, entropy in its final stages. The Chows sat
on the couch. From all around her Mrs. Chow sensed a slow creep:
the low ceiling seemed to be sinking, cat hairs clung to clothing, a
fine spray from the fish tank moistened her bare arm.

No one said anything. It was as if they were sitting in a hospital
waiting room. The girl watched the Chows. The large woman
stared at a green radio at her elbow broadcasting news about the
war. Every so often she looked suspiciously up at the Chows. "You
know me," she said abruptly, "I'm Remora Cass."

On her left, suspended in a swing, was the biggest, ugliest baby
Mrs. Chow had ever seen. It was dozing, arms dangling, great
melon head flung so far back that it appeared to be all nostrils and
chins. "A pig-boy," Mrs. Chow said in Chinese. Velvet jabbed two
fingers into the baby's rubbery cheeks. Then she sprang back from
the swing and executed a feral dance, all elbows and knees. She
seemed incapable of holding her body still.

She caught Mrs. Chow's eye. "This is Ed," she said. "He has no hair."

Mrs. Chow nodded.

"Quit," said Remora Cass, swatting at the girl as if she were a fly. Then the big woman looked Mrs. Chow in the eyes and said: "I know what you're thinking, and you're right. There's not a baby in the state bigger than Ed; eight pounds, twelve ounces at birth and he doubled that inside a month." She stopped, bringing her palms heavily down on her knees, and shook her wet head. "You don't understand me, do you?"

Mrs. Chow was watching Velvet.

"Quit that!" Remora Cass slapped the girl's hand away from the baby's face.

"Times like this I'd say it's a blessing my Aunt Eleanor's deaf," said Remora Cass. "I've gotten pretty good with sign language." From her overstuffed chair she repeated in pantomime what she had said about the baby.

Velvet mimicked her mother's generous, sweeping movements. When Remora Cass caught sight of her she added a left jab to the girl's head to her repertoire of gestures. Velvet slipped the punch with practiced ease. But the blow struck the swingset. Everyone tensed. Ed flapped his arms and went on sleeping. "Leave us alone," said Remora Cass, "before I really get mad."

The girl chased down the cat and skipped toward the door. "I'm bored anyway," she said.

Remora Cass asked the Chows questions, first about jobs and pets. Then she moved on to matters of politics and patriotism. "What's your feeling about the Red Chinese in Korea?"

A standard question. "Terrible," said Chow, giving his standard answer. "I'm sorry. Too much trouble."

Mrs. Chow sat by quietly. She admired Chow's effort. She had studied the language, but he did the talking; she wanted to move, but he had to plead their case; it was his kin back home who bene-fited from the new regime, but he had to bad-mouth it.

Remora Cass asked about children.

"No, no, no," Chow said, answering as his friend Bok had coached him. His face was slightly flushed from the question. Chow wanted children, many children. But whenever he discussed the matter with his wife, she answered that she already had one, meaning the old woman, of course, and that she was enough.

"Tell your wife later," the manager said, "what I'm about to tell you now. I don't care what jobs you do, just so long as you have them. What I say goes for the landlady. I'm willing to take a risk on you. Be nice to have nice quiet folks up there like Rikki and Bok. Rent paid up, I can live with anyone. Besides, I'm real partial to Chinese take-out. I know we'll do just right."

The baby moaned, rolling its head from side to side. His mother stared at him as if in all the world there were just the two of them.

Velvet came in holding a beachball. She returned to her place beside the swing and started to hop, alternating legs, with the beachball held to her head. "She must be in some kind of pain," Mrs. Chow said to her husband.

The girl mimicked the Chinese she heard. Mrs. Chow glared at Velvet, as if she were the widow during one of her spells. The look froze the girl, standing on one leg. Then she said, "Can Ed come out to play?"

Chow took hold of his wife's hand and squeezed it, as he did to brace himself before the roller-coaster's forward plunge. Then in a single well-rehearsed motion Remora Cass swept off her slipper and punched at the girl. Velvet masterfully sidestepped the slipper and let the beachball fly. The slipper caught the swingset, the beachball bounced off Ed's lap.

The collisions released charged particles into the air that seemed to hold everyone in a momentary state of paralysis. The baby's eyes peeled open, and he blinked at the ceiling. Soon his distended belly started rippling. He cried until he turned purple, then devoted his energy to maintaining that hue. Mrs. Chow had never heard anything as harrowing. She visualized his cry as large cubes forcing their way into her ears.

Remora Cass picked Ed up and bounced on the balls of her feet. "You better start running," she said to Velvet, who was already on her way out the door.

Remora Cass half-smiled at the Chows over the baby's shoulder. "He'll quiet down sooner or later," she said.

Growing up, Mrs. Chow was the youngest of five girls. She had to endure the mothering of her sisters who, at an early age, were already in training for their future roles. Each married in her teens, plucked in turn by a Portugese, German, Brit, and New Yorker. They had many babies. But Mrs. Chow thought little of her sisters' example. Even when her parents made life unbearable she never indulged in the hope that a man—foreign or domestic—or a child could save her from her unhappiness.

From the kitchen Remora Cass called Mrs. Chow. The big woman was busy with her baking. The baby was slung over her shoulder. "Let's try something," she said as she transferred the screaming Ed into Mrs. Chow's arms.

Ed was a difficult package. Not only was he heavy and hot and sweaty but he spat and squirmed like a sack of kittens. She tried to think of how it was done. She tried to think of how a baby was held. She remembered Romanesque Madonnas cradling their gentle-manly babies in art history textbooks. If she could get his head up by hers, that would be a start.

Remora Cass told Mrs. Chow to try bouncing and showed her

what she meant. "Makes him think he's still inside," she said. Ed emitted a long, sustained wail, then settled into a bout of hiccups. "You have a nice touch with him. He won't do that for just anyone."

As the baby quieted, a pain rolled from the heel of Mrs. Chow's brain, down through her pelvis, to a southern terminus at the backs of her knees. She couldn't blame the baby entirely for her discomfort. He wanted only to escape; animal instinct told him to leap from danger.

She was the one better equipped to escape. She imagined invading soldiers murdering livestock and planting flags in the soil of her ancestral estate, as if it were itself a little nation; they make history by the slaughter of generations of her family; they discover her in the wardrobe, striking matches; they ask where she has hidden her children, and she tells them there are none; they say, good, they'll save ammunition, but also too bad, so young and never to know the pleasure of children (even if they'd have to murder them). Perhaps this would be the subject of her painting, a non-representational canvas that hinted at a world without light. Perhaps—

Ed interrupted her thought. He had developed a new trick. "Woop, woop, woop," he went, thrusting his pelvis against her sternum in the manner of an adult male in the act of mating. She called for Chow.

Remora Cass slid a cookie sheet into the oven and then stuck a bottle of baby formula into Ed's mouth. He drained it instantly. "You do have a way with him," said Remora Cass.

They walked into the front room. The baby was sleepy and dripping curds on his mother's shoulder. Under the swing High Noon, the cat, was licking the nipple of an abandoned bottle. "Scat!" she said. "Now where's my wash gone to?" she asked the room. "What's she up to now?" She scanned the little room, big feet planted in the deep, brown shag carpet, hands on her beefy hips, baby slung over her shoulder like a pelt. "Velvet—" she started. That was all. Her jaw locked, her gums gleamed, her eyes rolled into her skull. Her head flopped backwards, as if at the back of her neck there was a great hinge. Then she yawned, and the walls seemed to shake.

Remora Cass rubbed her eyes. "I'm bushed," she said.

Mrs. Chow went over to the screen door. Chow and the girl were at the clothesline. Except for their hands and legs, they were hidden behind a bedsheet. The girl's feet were in constant motion. From the basket her hands picked up pieces of laundry which Chow's hands then clipped to the line.

"Her daddy's hardly ever here," Remora Cass said. "Works all hours, he does. Has to." She patted Ed on the back, then rubbed her eyes again. "Looks like Velvet's found a friend. She won't do that with anyone. You two are naturals with my two. You should get you some of your own." She looked over at Mrs. Chow and laughed. "Maybe it's best you didn't get that. Here." She set the baby on Mrs. Chow's shoulder. "This is what it's like when they're sleeping."

Before leaving, the Chows went to look at Rikki and Bok's apartment. They climbed up the stairs. No one was home. Rikki and Bok had barely started to pack. Bok's naked man, surrounded by an assortment of spears and arrows, was still hanging on the living room wall. Bok had paid good money for the photograph: an aboriginal gent stares into the camera, he's smiling, his teeth are good and large, and in his palms he's holding his sex out like a prize eel.

Mrs. Chow looked at the photograph for as long as it was discreetly possible before she averted her eyes and made her usual remark about Bok's tastes. Beyond the building's edge she saw the

manager's cottage, bleached white in the sun. Outside the front
door Remora Cass sat in a folding chair, her eyes shut, her pie-tin
face turned up to catch the rays, while Velvet, her feet anchored to
the asphalt, rolled her mother's hair in pink curlers. Between the
big woman's legs the baby lay in a wicker basket. He was quietly
rocking from side to side. Remora Cass's chest rose and fell in the
rhythm of sleep.

Driving home, they passed the boardwalk, and Mrs. Chow
asked if they might stop.

Chow refused to ride the roller-coaster in the daytime, no matter how much Mrs. Chow teased. It was hard enough at night,
when the heights from which the cars fell were lit by a few rows of
bulbs. As he handed her an orange ticket, Chow said, "A drunk
doesn't look in mirrors."

The Milky Way clattered into the terminus. After she boarded
the ride, she watched Chow, who had wandered from the loading
platform and was standing beside a popcorn wagon, looking up at
a billboard. His hands were deep in the pockets of his trousers, his
legs crossed at the shins. That had been his pose, the brim of his
hat low on his brow, as he waited for her to finally pass through the
gates of Immigration.

"Go on," an old woman said. "You'll be glad you did." The old
woman nudged her young charge toward the empty seat in Mrs.
Chow's car. "Go on, she won't bite." The girl looked back at the
old woman. "Grand-muth-ther!" she said, and then reluctantly
climbed in beside Mrs. Chow.

Once the attendant strapped the girl in she turned from her
grandmother and stared at her new companion. The machine
jerked away from the platform. They were climbing the first ascent
when Mrs. Chow snuck a look at the girl. She was met by the clear-
est eyes she had ever known, eyes that didn't shy from the encoun-

ter. The girl's pupils, despite the bright sun, were fully dilated, stretched with fear. Now that she had Mrs. Chow's attention she turned her gaze slowly toward the vertical track ahead. Mrs. Chow looked beyond the summit to the empty blue sky.

Within seconds they tumbled through that plane and plunged downward, the cars flung suddenly left and right, centrifugal force throwing Mrs. Chow against the girl's rigid body. She was surprised by Chow's absence.

It's gravity that makes the stomach fly, that causes the liver to flutter; it's the body catching up with the speed of falling. Until today, she had never known such sensations. Today there was a weightiness at her core, like a hard, concentrated pull inward, as if an incision had been made and a fist-sized magnet imbedded.

Her arms flew up, two weak wings cutting the rush of wind. But it wasn't the old sensation this time, not the familiar embrace of the whole fleeting continent, but a grasp at something once there, now lost.

Chow had moved into position to see the riders' faces as they careened down the steepest stretch of track. Whenever he was up there with her, his eyes were clenched and his scream so wild and his grip on his life so tenuous that he never noticed her expression. At the top of the rise the cars seemed to stop momentarily, but then up and over, tumbling down, at what appeared, from his safe vantage point, a surprisingly slow speed. Arms shot up, the machine whooshed past him, preceded a split second earlier by the riders' collective scream. And for the first time Chow thought he heard her, she who loved this torture so, scream too.

As she was whipped skyward once more her arms were wrapped around the little girl. Not in flight, not soaring, but anchored by another's being, as her parents stood against the liberators to protect their land.

Some curves, a gentle dip, one last sharp bend, and the ride rumbled to rest. The girl's breath was warm against Mrs. Chow's neck. For a moment longer she held onto the girl, whose small ribs were as thin as paintbrushes.

The Chows walked to the edge of the platform. He looked up at the billboard he had noticed earlier. It was a picture of an American woman with bright red hair, large red lips, and a slightly upturned nose; a fur was draped around her neck, pearls cut across her throat.

"What do you suppose they're selling?" he asked.

His wife pointed at the billboard. She read aloud what was printed there: "No other home permanent wave looks, feels, behaves so much like naturally curly hair."

She then gave a quick translation and asked what he thought of her curling her hair.

He made no reply. For some time now he couldn't lift his eyes from her.

"I won't do it," she said, "but what do you say?"

She turned away from him and stared a long time at the face on the billboard and then at the beach on the other side of the board-walk and at the ocean, the Pacific Ocean, and at the horizon where all lines of sight converge, before she realized the land on the other side wouldn't come into view.

Shoptalk #11

Success

The lesson was clear, and came across in all of [Mark] Van Doren's teaching, whether in his lectures or his life and work: be true to your own deepest instincts, your own vision, the "noble voice" within you; never try to pander to the marketplace, not only because you will violate some precious part of your own being but because you won't fool anyone anyway. Another way of stating the lesson was that the self-conscious strategy for what was known in the Fifties as "selling out" was not only dishonorable, but most ironic of all, it didn't work! . . . What "worked" in the world according to Mark Van Doren was honest integrity, the courage to go to the depths of yourself to tell your story.

(Dan Wakefield, "Lion: A Memoir of Mark Van Doren,"

vol. 17, nos. 2 & 3, 1991)

SUSAN STRAIGHT

Back

When Jay Neugeboren introduced "Back" for the 1988 "Fiction Discoveries" issue of Ploughshares, *he wrote of his then graduate student, "Susan Straight's prose is as innocent and hard as the lives of the people she loves. It is this love for her characters—unidealized, tangible, as deep as time—that makes her story so extraordinary. . . . [At twenty-seven, she writes with] the wisdom of one who has seen as much of life's harshness as has her aging narrator."*

As Michael Coffey noted in a Publishers Weekly *profile (July 4, 1994), "Straight is white; she is petite, blonde, and blue-eyed. . . . And though it jars some that this fair woman has written three books about black life—and very much in the voice of black Americans—it is something she hardly thinks about. She is writing about what she knews, in a voice she knows."*

Straight grew up in Riverside, California. "The neighborhood I came from, everyone was Air Force. There were people that were half-German and half-black, half Filipino and half-white. So we had friends who were half-half-half-half." She now lives there with her husband of sixteen years, Dwayne Sims, and two daughters. She was educated at UCLA and the University of Massachusetts at Amherst, where her teachers included Jay Neugeboren, James Baldwin, and Julius Lester. She says that on arriving at U. Mass., "I went to check out Jay Neugeboren, one of the teachers, because he's written a novel about a black guy, called Big Man. *I looked at his picture in the library: he was a white guy, and the novel is about a black basketball player and I*

*thought, so maybe this guy won't laugh at me, right? So I wrote my
first Darnell story [stories written from the point of view of a black
man]. . . . And he wrote on the bottom, 'This is wonderful, stop by and
see me.' And it was like, if he'd laughed at me right then I'd've gone
home."*

In addition to Ploughshares, *Straight's early stories appeared in*
Triquarterly, *edited by Reginald Gibbons. She and Dwayne had
moved back from Massachusetts to Riverside to live and work. "We
didn't have any money. I was pretty intimidated, I didn't try to sell
anything or make any connections, and Jay again was on my case."
Gibbons bought two stories. "Once I got that little bit of encouragement,
it was like everything changed for me. My family used to say, Well what
are you staying up all night typing for, I mean c'mon. Now I had a
reason to do it, I'd say, Look, I sold this story, I made some money. I
could show that check" (Coffey, op. cit.).*

A grant from Poets & Writers Magazine *led to a reading in Min-
neapolis, where Straight met Emilie Buchwald of Milkweed Editions.
At Neugeboren's suggestion, she was taken on by agent Richard Parks
in New York, and Parks "helped her shape the collection that became*
Aquaboogie: A Novel in Stories." *The collection was published by
Milkweed as winner of the Milkweed National Fiction Prize in 1990,
and was named one of the best books of 1990 by* Publishers Weekly.
Hyperion's Pat Mulcahy bought Straight's second novel, I Been in
Sorrow's Kitchen and Licked All the Pots *(1992), which was fol-
lowed by* Blacker Than a Thousand Midnights *(1994) and* The
Gettin Place *(1996), also from Hyperion.*

Every night I use to think, I have to get up, because it always like
this. Wait, listen, hold my own breathing till I hear him. I
would breathe in his rhythm, try and take in the air he done let out
his mouth, back then when it was still sweet and warm, like years

ago. Most of the time now it smell sick, and there not enough of it for him, so how can it be any left for me to pull in? Now it stink like sores cover up too long, like the mess inside his lungs, but then when I turn away, the wind blow through the cracks in the window, pushing past my shoulders so cold, and at least L. C. air warm on my face.

His breathing use to be strong and deep, so loud I wonder how big them ribs must be. They curve up like a huge turtle shell, then his belly cave in below. I would have my face hard by his chest when we first marry, and the fold in his shirt rub my cheekbone real soft, fall and rub again, put me to sleep even if I were worried about something. I would start to sleep on his bones, be so tired after washing for all them people, and later in the night I always wake up to find my head done slid down to his stomach, resting there. Now his coughing shake the whole bed, shake loose dreams I don't want in my head. Everything just tremble for a minute when he stop, and I wait. I don't sleep at all, the whole night. Sometimes I be tired, sometimes no. But I lay here all night with my head up in L. C. back, be afraid to dream, afraid to let him breathe without me. I know each breath count.

It was a time when I would just get up with the shaking, stay out in the kitchen till the sun come up. When I first know he was sick. I would wait every minute out there at the table, wait for him to leave this world, his breath sound so bad. The air catch in his chest like a fingernail drag down a screen. I hear him cough and wonder did he still see them tiny sparkles behind his eyes like I do when I cough real deep? Them little showers of light I used to watch when I were a baby girl, red and falling I use to see, and then I would cough even more. L. C. must don't see them after all these months of coughing. They must be use up.

Back then, when I realize he were coughing all through the night, into each morning and don't stop, not worse and not better, I couldn't stay in the bed and listen. When the sky start to get purple then, I would put on the grits, the only thing he eat, and everything was quiet but for L. C. The cars ain't started yet for the morning, the people still asleep, and the pot clink just a second, like money, on the stove. The grits falling out the bag, marking the minutes like sand in a egg timer I seen at a white lady's house. One morning the light in the kitchen seem to turn pale so slow, and I couldn't hold nothing inside. I let the tears sink into the grits and disappear, not like when you catch them on your cheek or in a tissue and they stays wet and clear. Salt sinking into the grits, salt I pour on top, through my fingers. I never cry so he can see me. I heard him pushing hisself up on his elbow, heard the bed cracking exactly that, and he call, "Pashion?" the way he do. I stood there next to him holding the water glass, but he just looked at me. That weren't what he need. He lay back down, had his eyes open, shake two or three times like a cold bird. I know he trying to push that cough down in his chest so I won't get out the bed every night. I seen the windowshade moving in the draft, seen his eyes look away from me. Soon enough I be cold and trying to keep warm. I won't be making no trail, whispering my feet across the floor like the widow upstairs, rubbing over my head back and forth trying to pass the night.

I stay in the bed now, keep my head in the hollow down his back. When we first marry, forty-nine years ago, I were sixteen. That winter, I use to watch L. C. put oil on his arms, his chest, reach up and try to get it on his back. He were always in a hurry to get to work, cause we been in the bed playing, and he couldn't reach nothing but the sides of his back, under the shoulders. Gray skin got left all ashy in the valley between the muscles. I use to pull the oil in from the sides and rub it down the center, where his backbone like a river. Now when I lay here, I keep a ear to that valley and wait, listen to the bubble in his chest like water running.

The walls get settle long after midnight, cracking and popping, and I can hear the rats running through they trails. I know I'm fixing to think the same things all night, every night, like there only a few certain sounds and seeings left in me. I wait for those few. I can look at the wall and see wood, not cinderblock. When we first move to Baltimore, after the mine closed, I spent all my time looking in the street, seeing the light shine off the cars and puddles. All I want to look at then was West Virginia and my porch shadow, when the moon full and the birches outside my door look silver thin like needles in with the black trunks of the other trees. I use to watch the sun going down behind the buildings here, put my face up to the screen while I was cooking, and sometimes when it was a breeze, I could smell the night coming like we were at home, clean like water and trees was close by. The wind stop, and then I smell the air coming back out the room behind me, warm from the greens on the stove, but like somebody else's air. L. C. knew. He came up behind me and said, "It get dark too fast here. It be light and then gone. No shadows."

I look at the walls and see wood floors, the wood I split for the stove, the sides of the wooden washtub I had my face in trying to get the black out of L. C. clothes. I smell the boards and trunks of trees when they get wet, smell the smoke.

Sometimes I think I can't lay here no more, I can't wait for them seeings and listen to these walls with they little feet scrabbling and hear the sound L. C. make in his chest all night. I want to get up and be far away from him, take down them shirts I hang to dry in the kitchen, put one round my back and sit up in the front window. I see the shadows of them shirts from where I lay, I see the way they hanging over the stove. They L. C. old flannel ones, the only thing he wear now. This morning I caught myself fixing to pull out a sleeve turn the wrong way; it was light-color in the sun, all the checks and stripes pale as nothing, so I reach in to get the cuff and then I realize that is the right side. The shirt too soft and thin, like the back of L. C. arms when I pull him over on his side so he can breathe.

But if I get up, if I leave, he can feel the bed shake, and he call out for me. This bed tell you anything. Long time ago, he were trying to get in this bed real quiet, been out late and knew I was fixing to get mad. He was easing into the sheets and a spring busted and shot up through the mattress. Scratched him on the behind like a cat, long and deep, and I laughed so hard. He still got that scar. I use to run my finger down the scab when it were healing, wait for that right minute to catch him there, just to hear him cuss and fuss.

I seen how he got most all his scars, because we was together so young. When I marry him, Mama say, "Pashion, he a baby, only twenty. He got nothing." She want me to wait for someone with more, a older man from town want a young wife. But I don't want no old man like she had. I never remember my father, only my mother walking all them years, fourteen years, like the widow upstairs. A house empty from deep voices and nobody to hear her feet on the floor, only the dogs sleeping under the house.

It start to rain. I can hear the cars on the streets blocks and blocks away, moving like a fast touch of wind. And a train, so tiny calling that it could be a dog howling in somebody trees. It be so cold now, in winter, and my fingers curl up like I'm fixing to push the scrub pad round the sink or the floor with my knuckles, getting a stain off. My hands don't come straight. When I yawn, seem like my back relax and a big chill of air go in my mouth. Then I start shivering and can't stop till I stiff up my back again. It like the air inside me now, and it determine to stay cold. Mama use to say," That why you cover the mouth when you yawn, so nothin bad fly inside." But my fingers too bent up, and if I put my hand close to my mouth, the nails touch my cheek hard like a rake.

I can see by the shadows in the kitchen it about five in the morning. It get darker for a while, the darkest cause the moon gone. I push my face closer to L. C. back, and I can feel the rib bone under my cheek, feel that rasp inside him come right out the skin. What kind of black they say in his lung? What color? Black like his eyebrows use to be? Like when his fingernail use to fall off, a purple black? He use to bang one up every week at work. Black inside the nail, inside the finger. His skin still smooth like a flower petal beside his eyes, I look every day, and the sleep stay dry as dust in his lashes sometimes in the mornings. In a while cars start passing on the street, sending noise up to the window to mix with his breath, with all the feet that start to walking in the building, on the sidewalk, all shaking and humming like waiting in a church.

I think of when I were sixteen and my neck soft as powder. It still soft now, when I touch it, but the wrinkles so many L. C. finger couldn't run down the front like it use to, draw from my chin to my chestbone, not pulling hard. My neck darker now, muddy color. I hear the way he breathe wrong, it that time in the dawn when he do that, and I stop. It worse again, like rain hitting the tin roof on the shed back in the woods, coming in waves and spattering. Fortynine years and I lay in the bed thinking, long as I touch him, he still mine, and it keep me awake, listening. I keep a hand on his back and reach around with my other hand to feel the bottle. It stay under the mattress, tuck into a hole. They gave him pills at the clinic, to make him sleep. I take two out each time, and now I got eighteen, twenty, but I don't know if that enough to let me go when I want, when I choose. His breath stop raining in his chest, soon, dry and finish, but not yet, not while I touching him and listen. Next week, when I get more pills, when I know, then it *my* choosing, when it stop for good. I remember his arm cross my chest long time ago, his lips round my ear and then he fall asleep in the middle of a kiss, he so tired. How many years I listen, he always sleep before me, and wake up to call my name.

Shoptalk #*12*
Confronting Racial Difference

Most American writers and readers seem to avoid or ignore racial issues. Again, writers of color have always had to pay attention to the power culture; in their daily lives they must confront its members and its institutions, and they have had to imagine daily the inner lives of white and mostly Christian Americans, read, hear, and see their self-advertisements, their fictions, their films and TV shows. When a "minority" writer writes, there is also the problem of a double audience: he or she writes to voice and dignify the experience of a separate culture, and hence writes to members of that culture, but her or his address is mostly to the white majority— the market necessary for profitable publishing. White writers who address race are rare, because, again, they have not felt the necessity—material or moral—to pay attention. . . . But the news is that younger writers are now paying attention.

(DeWitt Henry, "On My Racism: Notes by a WASP," vol. 16, nos. 2 & 3, 1990)

CHRISTOPHER TILGHMAN

Mary in the Mountains

Christopher Tilghman's first significant publication was in the Virginia
Quarterly Review *in 1984 ("Norfolk 1969"), while he was a student
at the Bennington Writers' Conference, the only writing program he
ever attended. "Almost everything that has happened to me since then,"
he writes for this headnote, "can be traced, quite directly, to the encouragement I got at Bennington and the people I met there. Until that time,
I had written in extreme isolation, and I didn't have a clue what kept
me going.*

*"I was a big reader of quarterlies during those years. . . . Before
'Mary in the Mountains' I had sent one previous story to* Ploughshares *and got back a rejection from the managing editor that I still
remember as the most infuriating rejection I ever got. It was so bad that
I wrote her a nasty note and, needless to say, abandoned the hope of
publishing in* Ploughshares *on the spot. So then, a few years later,
comes a note from George Garrett (whom I met at Bennington) saying
he was doing a discovery issue, and he knew I was hooked into [Andre
Dubus's writing group, begun in the fall of 1987] and suggested I send
along 'Mary in the Mountains' with Andre's imprimatur."*

*Introducing Tilghman for the 1988 "Fiction Discoveries" issue,
Andre Dubus commented that Tilghman "writes from an enduring
heart about love and faith and hope and loyalty. His characters refuse
to accept the world as it appears to be. They struggle to keep their families together; to probe more deeply than their clergy into the mysteries
of spiritual life in a culture which condones more than encourages that*

life; and they summon volition and strength and love to give to their moments and seemingly mundane actions with the people in their lives. . . . It is Mary, with her ancient truths, and her great love, who blessed me when I first read this story, in manuscript, lying on my bed. That was in the winter of 1988. She is with me still, from time to time, in the way great characters in stories become parts of our memory, and of us."

"The publication of 'Mary in the Mountains' in Ploughshares," *Tilghman himself writes, "was the moment I had been waiting for and working towards for fifteen years. Based on what happened because of it, it truly was a breakthrough; it was—and probably still is—the single most powerful affirmation of my worth as a writer that I have ever received. It lifted me out of the swamp of despair." He was soon contacted by the agent Maxine Groffsky (who had previously rejected him as a client), who promptly sold the collection to Farrar, Straus, and Giroux. Tilghman was forty-three when* In a Father's Place: Stories *came out and he found himself featured on the front page of the* New York Times Book Review *as one of four "New Guys on the Block." Since then he has published a first novel,* Mason's Retreat *(Random House, 1996), and a second collection,* The Way People Run: Stories *(Random House, 1999).*

Tilghman's story "In a Father's Place" appeared in Ploughshares *15, nos. 2 & 3 (1989), edited by James Carroll, and won the Denise and Mel Cohen Award for the best story in* Ploughshares *that year. He has also received a Whiting Writers' Award (1990), a Guggenheim Fellowship (1992), and an Ingram Merrill Foundation Award in fiction (1993). He first taught at Emerson in 1990 and is presently writer in residence there. He has also taught at the University of Houston, the University of Virginia, St. Mary's College, and Yale Summer School.*

In 1993, he coedited (with poet Marie Howe) an issue of Ploughshares *featuring emerging writers. "I am still waiting for the writers I*

*included in my issue to flower," he writes. "They're taking their god-
damn time about it. . . . The truth is that apprenticeships are simply
longer than they used to be; some people lose heart and others are just
plugging away, amassing enough good work to push them over the top.
You can't get a first book published unless it is perfect and professional.
I am continuously struck by the fact that . . . big debuts seem more and
more to be coming from people in or near their forties, people like Elizabeth Strout, or George Saunders. People like me."*

S*he wrote to say this: Send me a picture of the boy we never had, the
one with blue eyes, big ears, and a smile that says, Nothing, so far,
has hurt too bad.*

   *She wrote: Yesterday, when I got your letter, I carried it with me
like a dark bloom. I took it with me when I went swimming at the dam,
and I lay down in the sun, gray-haired and white. A few feet away from
me two high school girls with long thin bodies dove into the water without a ripple or splash. They wore black bathing suits stretched from hipbone to hipbone across their flat stomachs, and I touched your letter to
make sure it was addressed to me.*

   *She wrote: I think of you now when I look at the oak tree standing
apart in the lower corner of my field. Last winter, against the snow, I
saw your profile—it was your nose—in the branches. This summer
there will be growth and the deadwood that forms your eyebrows will
not make it through the winter, but that is right: you were always leaving anyway. When I look at that tree, I think of you with your deep
tangled roots and your fresh buds, but mostly I think of you alone.*

Mary rarely laughed; she was silent in groups and was content to
pass unnoticed by anyone but Will through his boisterous college
days; she stuttered, often, on *t*'s and *w*'s. She and Will were mar-

ried in June, 1958, in a white New Hampshire church with high wooden tresses, under a cross made of spruce that had twisted and checked. She wore her grandmother's dress, petticoats and lace, but as she came down the aisle it was her black hair and white skin and green eyes that people noticed. Will mumbled, but she repeated her vows so clearly and slowly, with such conviction and determination, that husbands and wives all through the congregation squirmed and avoided each other's eyes.

Will's friends, a week out of college, were disappointed by the food, the lodging, Mary's bridesmaids, the lack of liquor and late-night bars. Will had warned them to expect little, just as he had tried to explain Mary to them for the past two years. The ushers left the quiet reception as soon as Mary and Will did, and reconvened that night in Boston for a party they all would remember for the rest of their lives. Years later Will heard about it and it hurt his feelings.

Will's mother never warmed to Mary—she had recognized, as few others ever had, that Mary was a mouse that wasn't afraid to show its teeth—but Will loved her so much he stayed awake at night counting the times she breathed.

They went to Europe for the Grand Tour. Will's mother told everyone at the reception that at least the honeymoon would be festive and gay, but they spent most of the first month in cathedrals. Will listened in the gloomy shadows as she explained the tympanum at Vezelay, the chancel at Chartres, the altar and relics of Rouen. He wore Bermuda shorts and black shoes and socks, a handsome face made featureless by his sandy crew cut and heavy black glasses. Even so, he worried what the Europeans would make of Mary in her plain cotton shifts and wide-brimmed straw hat, with her earnest look and stuttering French.

In their travels, they met, as planned, with three of his ushers making a tour of nightclubs, cafes and whorehouses. As they drove off the following morning, Will watched them go with the first stirring of regret. He said to Mary, "Sweetheart, I'm getting a little tired of cathedrals."

"But I thought you liked them. I thought you said so."

"Of course, but aren't we here to see more? I really need to understand the French for my job." He added, "It's not as if you were a Catholic or anything."

So the itinerary changed, and they completed the circuit in the sweaty thunder of Tivoli Gardens and Place Pigalle. She loved the look of excitement on his face as they descended into the loud smoky music and steamy air; even as he shouted encouragement to her across a round table, she knew he longed for something unexpected, something that might save a little piece of himself for later.

On the night before their boat left, in a hotel in Le Havre, she surprised him with a leather box. Inside were tens of objects, pieces of ephemera from every region, every country, tourist bits like miniature landmarks and local crafts like clay figurines and fishing boats made of grass. All summer she had been collecting for this box.

She said, "It's so you remember. For your job."

She wrote: I am trying to bring back all the bedrooms I have ever lived in. Now that I have returned to my father's house for good, it seems time to see where I went. I bought a pad of graph paper, and a plastic square, and a box of hard pencils, and I am making a plan of each, a quarter inch to the foot. This is not as hard as it sounds because, of course, I have always had that same bed, a yardstick, but now it has your scratch across the headboard, a straight fissure through the curly maple like a road cut. Some of my bedrooms are very painful to remember, like the house in Wellesley. Other than that, I don't know what I expect to learn from charting my rooms, unless it is that wide windows have always been good to me.

They lived in Cambridge in the bottom floor of a brown-shingled two-family, not far from the consulting firm where Will analyzed international business trends. She researched butterflies and insects for *Horticulture Magazine,* and on Friday afternoons, a few minutes before two, she would run across Massachusetts Avenue to stand in line for rush tickets at Symphony. Often she saw her mother-in-law arriving in her mink coat and yellow rubber boots, and occasionally curly-headed conservatory boys would ask her out for coffee.

Will looked forward to the day they would move out of their modest apartment with its too friendly Italian landlord, but Mary loved that collection of small rooms, each one with a purpose like jewelry boxes. There was a built-in hutch in the dining room, a small bookcase in the parlor, a window seat and mirror in the entrance hall, a linen closet outside the bedroom and a line of brass clothes hooks in the bedroom. She covered the pantry shelves with paper and made orderly rows of bright cans and colored boxes, and each time she went in she would think of her father's garden.

On Sundays, they liked to walk to the river, cross one bridge, then work down to the next, for a full circle that brought them home to hot tea. One Sunday, when spring had driven the last of the frost from the banks, Will said, "I just hope you're not getting bored. Don't you want to find something more to do? I don't know, ballet lessons?"

"But I'm never going to get bored. W-w-why do you ask that?"

"I just think someone as smart as you would want something more than that silly job."

The next Sunday, Mary went to church, alone. Inside the gray clapboard building there was order, and light, and flowers, and mystery, but still, she knew there would always be something missing from Will's life.

Mary kept going to church, but Will moved them to Wellesley anyway. They drove into town one night to have dinner with two other couples. He thought it would cheer her after the latest miscarriage. Waiting for them, in a French spot decorated with Paris scenes made out of soldered tin, were the Billings, who lived on Beacon Hill, and the Blooms, who were leaving, the very next day, for Selma.

"Tell the truth, Mort," said Will. "Aren't you scared?"

"They can't wipe out a whole bus. I don't think Sylvia should go but . . ."

Sylvia interrupted, "Kennedy *died* for this. No one has any *choice*."

"But," said Will, "playing the Devil's advocate here, isn't this a problem for the South itself to . . ."

Sylvia interrupted again. "The Jews that said that are all in *ovens*."

Mary heard this with a start. Sylvia was right, she thought, but she hadn't realized the Blooms were Jewish. It was as if that gave them something to be, something to grow into. She looked at the Billings, silent and distracted during the discussion, and wondered why they had been invited to this gathering. Then, as she had often done around Will's hearty friends, she wondered why she had been invited. Then, as he continued to debate, preparing his voice and hesitating every time he said the word "Jew" or "Negro," she wondered why Will had been invited.

On the way home, driving out Route Nine, she could see Will chewing the inside of his cheek. Halfway, they came upon a car wreck, and there were police blinkers, and the harsh light of ambulances with their doors open, and a man screaming for his wife. Mary felt empty and dark, a body that would bear no children, like their big stucco house in Wellesley, with hemlock hedges strangling every window and ivy covering the walls. As they drove up the gravel driveway, Will announced, "I'm going to go. Mort and Syl are right. I'm going to Alabama."

After a few days, there was no more mention of Freedom Riding. Instead, he kept talking about that accident, the terrible arbitrariness of it, the momentary, mad collision of circumstance. For Will, the matter ended in a great black hole, but Mary, feeling the last hormones of her pregnancy forsaking her body, was not sure, not sure at all.

It probably shouldn't surprise you to hear that however much I continue to grieve for you, which is illusory, I become more whole, which is fact. My life is a crab's life, a scavenger content to back at the pieces left behind. You're looking for the meaning of breath; I'm looking for a lost mitten. I have learned to envy your restless treasure hunt. I came to this conclusion the other day when I was working in my garden. I turned over a spade of sod that was dense with root, with seed and wildflower bulbs and tubers, and I saw a whole season of life laid out side to side, clumped and spaced, patient and forgiving. It was then I realized also how much I pitied you.

Will, at last, had been transferred to the Paris office. The assassinations and the riots at Columbia had terrified him, but the barricades of that summer in Paris gave him the quickening heady sense of being there for history. He let his hair grow well over his collar, and took to wearing tight shirts with epaulets and salmon-colored trousers. Still, when he found them an apartment, it was on the Right Bank, a peaceful untouched neighborhood just off the Etoile, a place with wrought iron gates and cast balconies, and high narrow doors and marble stairs.

Mary stayed behind for two months to wrap up her church committee work and to sell the Wellesley house to a family of seven.

When she joined Will in their new home in Paris, she found a pair of women's underpants hanging on a brass hook behind the bathroom door. They were beige, and American made. She pressed them into her palm, where they burned like a hot coin, and she went dizzy staring at the black and white tiles on the walls and floor. She had no place of her own to hide them, so she put them in her pocketbook and carried them for weeks. She spent many days at the Louvre and kept wondering if she had made fun of the silly face he made when he kissed. When the underpants became gray in the pencils, ticket stubs and loose change of her bag, she washed them and put them in her bureau. Every time she wore them she tried to picture her.

Will bought Mary a bright mini-skirt and a see-through blouse at a boutique on the Rue de Rivoli. She modeled them for him once, but never wore them outside. One day she went to lunch with a curator of Dutch paintings. He wore a cashmere suit and onyx cufflinks; he seated her with a smooth assurance, ordered an aperitif with two ice cubes on the side and snapped his long fingers at the waiter who forgot the condiments for his steak tartare. By dessert, all these stylish continental ways had reduced her to a laughing fit, which she stifled into her napkin.

She took long train rides, slow locals to Avignon, Munich, and

Amsterdam. She sat in compartments on worn seats of red velvet
that smelled of babies and tarragon, and wrote thoughts in a journal. The words came out in unfamiliar voices, loaded with paradox
and sudden turns she barely understood. Sometimes, when the
door banged opened and a businessman or a nun or a schoolgirl
would slip in, she would look up in fright.

For their vacation, in the fall, they lived for a week on a canal
boat, gliding on the silent ice through vineyards and wheatfields.
The captain's heavy wife served them fresh bread and chicken, and
picked on Will. It was on the boat, while they were sitting in aluminum lawn chairs on the foredeck, heading into a red sun, that Will
told her about trying LSD.

"In Cambridge. With Harvey and Monica. We knew you
wouldn't be interested."

"W-w-when?"

"I told you. Last winter in Cambridge."

"No. When? Where was I? W-w-where was I? Was I sitting out
in that prison in W-w-w . . . oh shit . . . in W-w-wellesley when you
and Harvey and Monica all took LSD?"

"We did it a couple of times. Three times really. Harvey and I
called in sick and it was just stupid and infantile that we had to
sneak around like that."

"Oh."

He waited for her to say more. When she didn't, he said, "You
really can't believe what it's like."

Mary's eyes widened.

He persisted. "The thing is, what I remember most vividly,
what I understood, for the first time really, truly, was you, and how
much I . . ."

She stood up and slapped him across the face, so hard he began to whimper, and whimper, and he took off his glasses and wiped his eyes, and the color drained from his face except for the outline of her hand, which was blue.

Would it please you to know I'm seeing someone? I'm not in love with him, just seeing him, and how I love that way of saying it. Because as much as I loved you I'm not sure I ever saw you. My dog Arnold is seeing him too, with his nose; when he comes over Arnold samples his shoes, his crotch, his trousers, and then curls up in the center of the floor. My friend does not talk very much, although I suspect he goes home worrying that he talked my ear off. So there the three of us sit, in that fussy parlor my mother thought so elegant, in the dark of late dusk, just seeing each other.

The Billings came to dinner to look over the new Cambridge house, but they were so busy bickering at each other they had little appetite for veal. Harvey took a place sprawled in a loveseat with his hands tucked deep into his waistband and his feet stacked heel-to-toe as if everyone was supposed to admire his shoes, and from time to time he would loll his head sideways to spew insults all over his wife.

Mary kept leaving the room, but each time she did the conversation died, as if the three of them had so exhausted each other that the only fun left was to display it to the world.

"Oh yeh, Will. Did I tell you where Monica was that other night? I can't remember if I told you this one. Hey Mary, hey wait, let me . . ."

After an hour of this Mary turned off the stove and went to her bedroom. She put on a nightgown, brushed out her hair graying quickly now, and felt the promise of an early fall as it parted the curtains and passed over her bed.

The morning of her forty-second birthday Will got up for work early and was gone by the time she came down. On the breakfast table he had set her place with a yellow placemat, and a folded yellow napkin, and a small blue box centered between the silver. She pushed the box aside and ate her breakfast, and all day long avoided the kitchen.

She opened it, finally, in the late afternoon. It was a string of pearls spaced with tiny gold balls, all strung on a fine golden chain. She stared at the pearls, cradled in satin, ran her fingertip down the line and then burst into tears. Who could he have been thinking about when he bought those pearls for her? Around what young neck had he pictured them hanging?

You have asked me if I forgive you, after all these years. You should know better than to ask a Christian that question. It's like asking a poet, Is the rain a symbol for death? If the truth were that simple, the answer would have been that simple. Forgiveness has nothing to do with time and nothing to do with me. Forgiveness is a high meadow, yellow grasses surrounded by the dense, sharp tangle of spruce trees. It exists, I promise you, but it's not a place for me to go as much as I would like to. It's a place for you to find, alone.

"Wouldn't you like to go away for a while? Maybe find a place you can think without me moping around?"

Mary jerked her head up, startled. She was reading in her study, and from the corner of her eye the plumber's helper Will was carrying looked like a club.

He repeated. "I've just been running it over and over. And I suddenly realized how selfish I've been."

"Are you asking me to leave? Is that what you want me to do?"

"No. Not at all. It's just that lately you've seemed so worn out and it's me, I know it's me doing this to you. So I thought you'd have fun planning some kind of trip. To Europe maybe."

"I don't think I'd have much fun in Paris, even you can see that."

"I did not mean France," he said curtly. She reached her hand over to his hairy thigh. He was wearing only his undershorts and watch. "Will. Sit down." She gave him a slight push toward a chair. "Sit down and talk to me."

"I really don't have time for this. I didn't want a big thing."

"Is there anything wrong?"

"Wrong? I clogged the toilet." He held up the plumber's helper for her to see.

"Is everything at work okay? Everything's all straightened out?"

"What in God's name are you after? Everything's fine at work. You know that."

"Do you want me to be your friend? Is someone treating you badly? You can talk to me about it."

He blushed.

"Do you feel okay? You're not worried about any health things, are you?"

"No."

"Then there's nothing wrong," she said, and glanced back at her book.

"Well Christ, Mary. Doesn't the world strike you as a bit peculiar? Just look out the window. Read the paper someday. You get killed these days for having a fashionable pair of sunglasses. Reagan's going to win and then you can kiss it all goodbye. The Russians are moving missiles into East Germany, the Arabs have us by the balls and the Spics, from Mexico to Tierra del Fuego are going to self-destruct, except they'll take us and our economy with them.

I've never understood why all your church stuff makes you miss these little details. Next time you're on your knees I really wish you'd think about this."

"I have noticed that the world is not a kind or generous place. That's what I think about when, as you say, I'm on my knees."

"But you don't think about me, do you?"

"I thought you said nothing is wrong with you."

"Jesus, Mary. How can you be so cruel? You're just so goddamn *cruel*." His mouth quivered and tears flooded his eyes.

She reached out again for his knee, but he bolted up and ran out into the hall where he let out a yelp, like a dog. He was still carrying the plumber's helper, and a few minutes later Mary heard a great rush of water as the toilet ran free again.

On Wednesday, or Thursday if Wednesday is rainy or bitter cold, I take my neighbor Violet for a walk. She is not much past seventy, but she says living in the same house all her life has given her arthritis and she leans very heavily on me. She would like to go out more often, but I have to take a rest between outings. Violet has never been outside the State of New Hampshire, which is fine with her really, but she loves to hear about other places and wonders if she would have the courage to climb what she calls the Iffel Tour. As we walk, picking our way around tricky stones and across frozen ruts, so entwined it's hard to know which of the four legs are the bad ones, I tell her my stories. I'm sure by now most of what I say is plain fiction, but she doesn't care. When I repeat myself, she starts jabbing a deformed knuckle into my side to urge me to get on to the parts she loves, about trains, and about people who fear for their souls. She sighs happily when I close out a chapter, as if there is now music, and sometimes, on the sad but replete close, Violet says, That was lovely. Along the way she has formed a very firm picture of you and even though I have never told her anything severe, she tenses when

*you come on stage and gives you a villain's hiss. She is Catholic, though,
and says rosaries for you. She wants me to convert so I can drive her to
Mass. I tell her to go to hell and we both laugh, two ladies with the
vague fear we're going there anyway.*

Mary's father died a few months after his eightieth birthday, and
left the house to Mary. A few months later, she and Will packed
most of her portable things into their cars, and they drove up from
Boston into the mountains in a convoy. Will insisted they stop in
Concord for a "nice lunch," and Mary sat in a renovated mill building and pictured them eating ice cream together, thirty years earlier. She could not understand why, with everything that had happened since, she didn't want this breakup.

After they had unloaded the cars she began to ache, a hollow
tightness she hadn't felt in years. Will waited in the mudroom
while she cried softly and briefly, then they kissed and he was gone.

On the pegs of the mudroom still hung the old forester's woolen
pants and mackintosh, with a sprig of fir stuck in one pocket. Six
pairs of boots, one for each working day, stood in a line and the last
pair was still caked in mud, which Mary scraped off and tasted.

The house smelled faintly of lavender and cedar, her mother's
presence decades after her death, and of woodsmoke and dogs, her
father's. In the dark parlor, upholstered in English linen with cam-
elbacks and ball and claw feet, she found the row of Staffordshire
her mother had collected: the chimney sweep, the happy milkmaid,
the sea captain home for good.

She walked into her father's study, with its rows of Kipling,
Gibbon and Tennyson, its Loeb classics, its Zane Grey and Bret
Harte. In the corner was a pile of Christmas novels, most from her
and all, how it pleased her, unread. On the desk was the last manuscript of a forestry handbook that would never be published. She

rubbed the desk surface and smelled her father's chalky forearms on her hands, and knelt down to kiss the permanent shape in the leather of his chair.

She wrote: It is a paradox I cannot escape that you, who believes the world has been so uniquely damaged by the modern age, are still capable of the deepest faith, while I, who finds the Holy Ghost in even the most hideous and ardent acts, will always be among the children at the gates. Faith is the assurance of things hoped for, the conviction of things not seen. You, on your treasure hunt that has caused me such pain, have held hopes beyond madness and you have stared at the unseen so long that your eyes are hollow. Your thirst, that sandy being I used to feel in bed with me, turning your blood to powder and your flesh to bone, will save you.

She wrote: If you send me a picture of your son I will put it on my bureau. It was kind of you to write and not just send an announcement, although an announcement is more than I would have expected. The joy, at your age, to have a child at last. But please don't think his picture would be alone on my bureau. Please don't think yours is the only face I see in the branches of oak trees. I've never lost anyone. That is what will save me. The memories are my grace and all of you, as you can hear me say, are w-w-welcome in my heart.

Shoptalk #*13*
Gender, the Writer, and Imagination

The unquestioned faith that he can, if he wants to, make a story of any character that interests him. That the sex of his character is only one of a number of significant facts to be approached and accounted for. This is a freedom, few would disagree, that has only recently begun to be available to women. . . . It is . . . a fiction writer's First Amendment. . . . Everyone has a list of successful transformations of male to female / female to male perspective. . . . At the same time that women are feeling free to explore whatever they choose to, many are single-mindedly concerned with getting their own sex's stories told, not with telling anyone else's. Every time a man writes—sensitively, accurately—from a woman's point of view, or the reverse, might we not say that we are seeing a triumph of the possibilities for understanding between the sexes? Wanting the empathy of the opposite sex, ought we not to welcome the writer's single form of it: identification? . . . When we don't like the results, we call it colonialism. . . . No story with resonance is a 'young man's' or a 'young woman's' story. Achieving resonance, a human sympathy, is the only hard part.

(Rosellen Brown, "Notes on This Issue's Issue," vol. 2, no. 2, 1978)

DAVID GATES

A Wronged Husband

David Gates has been a staff writer for Newsweek *for two decades. He finished his A. B. at the University of Connecticut, but dropped out of the Ph.D. program when his thesis on Samuel Beckett ran into trouble. "A marriage to the writer Ann Beattie brought them both to jobs at the University of Virginia and Harvard. And when Beattie's career took off, they moved to Connecticut, where she wrote and Gates 'sort of fell apart,' as he puts it" (Michael Coffey, "David Gates: Voices for Vices,"* Publishers Weekly, *May 10, 1999).*

" 'A Wronged Husband' in Ploughshares *(1991) and 'The Bad Thing' in* Esquire *were neck and neck my first published stories," Gates writes for this headnote. "But* Ploughshares *had the edge. I'd actually sold a story called 'The Crazy Thought' in 1983—I'd been writing seriously for about three years then—but . . . it never ran. So it took me another eight years to get any fiction into print. I'd been sending stories out the whole time, getting encouraging notes. . . . In those days I used to send everything first to the magazines that paid big money: first* The New Yorker, *then—in whatever order—the* Atlantic, Esquire, Harper's, *and I guess that was all. So I assume 'A Wronged Husband' was rejected by all those places and probably by some quarterlies as well. . . . I never attended a writing program or went to a writers' conference. . . . I worked on my first novel,* Jernigan *(a 1991 Pulitzer finalist), for four or five years, then made a list of agents to approach. The first to get back to me was Amanda Urban; I sent her the manuscript, she liked it, and had it sold to Knopf within a week."*

Gates's second novel, Preston Falls, *appeared in 1998, and was short-listed for the National Book Critics Circle Award. A revised version of "A Wronged Husband" appears in Gates's story collection* The Wonders of the Visible World *(1999). Asked what he sought to improve in his earlier work, Gates replies, "What embarrasses me the most is a few infelicitous or imprecise words, maybe a superfluous phrase or sentence here and there. Failures of clarity and condensation, a tendency here and there to the orotund, the sentimental, the faux-poetic. But it wasn't terrible, and these are easy fixes to make."*

I

Half awake, pawing at the night table for *The Book of Great Conversations,* I knock the bottle onto the floor. The sound hangs there: there's a ringing part of it and a shattering part of it and a splashing part of it. I smell the gin. Well, it can stay there until I feel like getting up. Nobody here to be scandalized, nobody to be protected. A mouse, I suppose, might scamper across and cut its dainty foot, but that's the mouse's lookout, no? I remember we felt sorry at first for the bright-eyed mice who started appearing a month after we'd moved in. So tiny, so *dear:* couldn't we all just *live?* It took another month for you to agree that "something"— your word—had to be done. Like what, I said, a resettlement program? Well, couldn't we? you said. Couldn't we try? And finally I went out and bought the Hav-a-Heart trap. That was only last fall. Less than a year ago. As I remember it, we were all right then.

Kid noise through the open window. Sunday morning, quarter to eleven, already hot. I lift the sheet and shake it out to make it feel cool as it floats back down to rest on my legs. The feeling doesn't last. I prop both pillows (yours and mine) together against the headboard, sit up, put on my prescription sunglasses and turn to the Great Conversation in which Shaw loses his temper when Chesterton calls him a Puritan. Shaw says Chesterton has no real self, no firm place to stand, and Chesterton calls Shaw a Puritan for thinking that was necessary. Trying to understand these ideas is waking me up. I put the book back on the night table—carefully, now that there's no reason to be careful—get out of bed and, trying not to step on glass, go to the window and tug the shade down to make it go up. Down in the street they've put a sprinkler cap on the hydrant. Otherwise the Dominicans just open it up and let it gush. So these pencil-thick streams of water come arching out and a little boy stands at the edge of the widening puddle, undecided.

But hang on: hadn't I left the car in that first space to the right of the hydrant? What's there now is a rusted-out station wagon, cloudy plastic duct-taped to where the passenger window used to be. So I've found out one more thing: they tow you after a week of tickets. Well, fine, more power *to* 'em. Unless of course somebody stole the thing to part it out. In which case fine, too. But isn't it weird. You were always the one who said it was crazy to keep a car in New York. I was always the one who said I wanted the feeling I could get out.

2

And your going off to Minneapolis (supposedly to Minneapolis) seemed a good opportunity. Drive up and get out of the heat and the noise, spend some time with my brother. We sat around his house mostly—Joey was still depressed about throwing away his marriage—though one day we did get over into Vermont, to a used bookstore run by a lady with cats. Joey beat her down on the price of some old mythology book he wanted for the illustrations; to atone, I picked *The Book of Great Conversations* off the twenty-five-

cent table and told her it was off the dollar table. The odd pair-
ings—Goethe and Napoleon, Stalin and H. G. Wells—made it
seem better than it turned out to be.

He called yesterday, speaking of Joey, to say he was doing a lot
better. I said I was doing a lot worse: that you had gone to live in
Boston, that I hadn't been out of the apartment for a week, hadn't
called work, didn't know if I had a job anymore and even if I did,
didn't know how I could face going back there and seeing Kate
every day. I said the goddamn sirens keep you awake all night long.
Car alarms and shit. Kate, he said: refresh me. I refreshed him.
Hm, he said. Listen, I said, the Kate thing had all been discussed.
Worked through. Resolved. Hm, he said. Well, he said, as far as
the job, they were probably just assuming I was taking two weeks
instead of the one and if they were seriously upset they would have
called, no? He said he was sorry about your leaving, but guessed
he'd seen it coming when we'd been up there at Christmas. What
do you mean, I said, why was that? He said, For one thing, you
never touched each other. He said speaking as somebody who'd
been through the same thing he knew I was going to come out of
this stronger. Said at least in my case there were no children. Said
maybe I could start seeing this Kate again. Joey. He runs off to the
Outer Banks for two weeks for a mad interlude with his old used-
to-be, she ends up going back to her husband (many tears), he
comes home and Meg and the children are gone. And now he dis-
covers there are no great new women in Peterborough, New
Hampshire. The night I got up there he tried to talk me into getting back in the car and driving down to Boston. Some idea of picking up college girls: just as big as real women, he said, but stupider.

"Joey," I said. "I just drove five *hours*."

"So I'll drive and you can sleep on the way down. Listen," he said, "I got a teensy thing of coke left. And we can absolutely get more once we get there. Fuck, let's do some coke, you want to?"

But as of yesterday he'd gotten the north side of the house painted, which really needed it, he'd started cutting wood for the winter, he'd got the roof all patched in the woodshed. Said he'd probably just needed some physical exercise: said it makes a tremendous difference. Said he'd started a new series of silk screens which were absolutely going to be the best things since those ducks he was doing a couple of years ago. They're going to be—whatever the plural is of phoenix. But getting back to my thing: said he'd always said that Gordon Conway was scum and he was glad at least that now everybody would see it. Said as it turned out he guessed it had been a good thing I'd talked him out of going into Boston that night. He'd been going to hit Gordon up since Gordon generally kept enough coke around to sell, and it would've been incredibly disastrous if we'd knocked on the door and so on. Said he thought you might come back once the dust had a chance to settle. If that was what we both wanted. Said it seemed to him that despite everything there'd been a lot of love there.

3

Or something. I remember speaking the vows and thinking, Maybe.

The day before, we'd had that huge thing about whether Meg's sister should be at the ceremony. "What am I supposed to do," I said, "turn around at this point and disinvite her? You know, she drives *down* with them, thinking everything is cool, and—I mean, Janey, this was, literally, *years* ago. She is now a *friend*. I mean, what should I have done, *not* told you?"

"Yes," you said. Then you said, "No." Then you began to cry.

But then there were the times when, deferring to my choice of a film or a restaurant, you used to take my hand and kiss it like a courtier. What were the proportions of sweetness and irony? Not that I ever wanted to pick it apart. At first. This gesture was still in your repertoire as late as a few weeks ago: that Saturday when you wanted to go down and hit one of the Indian joints on Sixth Street and I wanted to go someplace where we could count on its being air-conditioned. In retrospect, this last handkiss makes me wonder when exactly you and Gordon Conway had made your arrangements. Though that's not all it makes me wonder.

As far as I know, you hadn't met him before this spring, when you went up to Boston for Lynnette's show. The three of you at lunch. At some health-food place. Which all seemed fine. A friend of your friend Lynnette's. (This was the weekend Kate and I broke our rule about each other's apartments. We rented Syberberg's *Parsifal*, though we only got through the overture and the first act, and we ordered in from the good Chinese place.) I remembered him, of course, from when he'd gone to Pratt with Joey, and I decided not to be gratuitously unpleasant by saying he'd always struck me as a poseur, and therefore just the kind of person who'd fasten onto Lynnette or vice versa. This must have been in April. Now at that point I assume you were telling me everything, or why would you have told me even *that* much? Well, maybe to preclude my hearing it from somebody else. Or maybe just to get some relief. I can sympathize. I made a point of telling you what sounded like everything: how Kate and I on hands and knees had extracted misfed paper from the innards of that chronically misbehaving Xerox machine, how "I" had rented *Parsifal*, how Armin Jordan had lip-synched so undetectably as Amfortas. Such truths, told forthrightly, kept the rest of the truth away: while telling them, I could almost believe that Kate was just the funny woman who worked two offices down. With the husband who sounded so interesting.

Now the next thing I heard about your new friend Gordon was the following week: he and Lynnette were going to be in New York and could we all have dinner. This was the point, I thought, at which to get myself on record. "As you know," I said, "Lynnette is not one of my favorite people. And I truly dislike Gordon Conway."

"He speaks well of *you*," you said.

"He's a ferret," I said. "Are he and Lynnette an item?"

You said nothing.

"So where's dinner?" I said. "Elaine's?"

You put down your glass. "What's *this* about?"

"Or hey," I said, "there's always the East Village. You know, down there where the *real* artists hang out. Now me, there's nothing I like better than *real* artists, you know? Being *real*. Should I buy a beret for the occasion?"

"I thought you weren't going."

"Are *you*?" I said.

"Yes."

"Well," I said, "have a *marvelous* time."

"*Grazie,*" you said, and picked up your glass. "I intend to."

4

And then nothing (meaning nothing I was told about) until two weeks ago. A Sunday morning. Me at the kitchen table, drinking coffee.

"I've got it," you called when the phone rang. Then you came out of the bedroom. I asked if you'd turned off the fan in there. You said you had to go to Minneapolis.

"Why?" I said. "What's up?"

"Marie," you said. "She was in a car wreck. She died this morning."

"*What?*" I said.

"Look, I have to pack. Will you please call a cab? La Guardia, tell him."

"Jesus," I said. "Oh my God. Listen, I think we better take the car instead. Stick it in the long-term parking. We can't leave it on the street, you know? Without moving it."

You shook your head. "You're not coming," you said.

"Janey. Come on."

"Will you just please call the cab?"

"Janey."

"Okay, fine," you said. "Then I will call the cab." You hauled down the Yellow Pages and made a show of leafing through.

"The hell is going *on?*" I said. "I'm coming *with* you."

"You see my family once a year," you said. "At Thanksgiving. That's a grand total of five times. And once at the wedding."

"This is completely batshit," I said. "I'm your *husband.*" You rolled your eyes. "Listen," I said. "If absolutely *nothing* else, there's the proprieties. It would be incredibly disrespectful to your mother for me not to show up."

"Helen knows everything is fucked," you said. "She's not expecting you. You're so concerned with the proprieties, sit down and write her a note. Truly. I'll hand-deliver it." You went back into the bedroom and shut the door. I followed you, wondering if at a time like this I should be asking what this everything-is-fucked business was about. Or were you entitled to slip stuff in and not be called on it because your sister was dead?

I ended up agreeing to everything: not to come, not to call, to let you breathe. Not to upset your mother by sending flowers. If I'd given you more of an argument, would you have broken down and confessed? Such a bizarre lie argues that you wanted me to see through it. So: one more time I failed you. But you made it convincing. So: one more time you arranged for me to fail you. While you packed, I wrote a draft of the thing for your mother on an old manila envelope. Like the Gettysburg Address. Then I copied it over cleanly, keeping my head to the side so drops of sweat wouldn't fall on the good notepaper. I wonder what you ended up doing with it.

After helping you down with your stuff, I came back upstairs, made more coffee, and decided to call in the next morning and take the week off. I'd like to think I'd planned to spend some of the time thinking about Us instead of just hanging out up at Joey's drinking wine at his kitchen table. But I must have known it was really just a holiday. Your sister had laid down her life (as I thought) so I could have a week off from you.

5

I got back from Joey's on Thursday night. You called on Friday, around noon: you were coming in on American, seven o'clock. "I'll be glad to see you," I said. "How's your mother making it? How are *you?*"

"Look, I'll see you at seven," you said.

At seven o'clock I watched stranger after stranger after stranger come down the carpeted passageway. You came up behind me and said, "Hi."

"Hi," I said. "I don't get this. How could I have missed you?"

"Been here since five," you said.

"You're kidding," I said. "Why didn't you *call* me?" Then I smelled your breath. "Well," I said, "I can see you've used the time to advantage."

"The American Advantage," you said. "Now *I* have the advantage."

"Shall we?" I said, and took your suitcase. You followed like a little girl who had been bad. I turned around and said, "Have you eaten anything? Do you want to stop someplace?"

"Want to go home," you said, your head down.

"Fine," I said. "I don't know what there *is* there, but there's probably something."

"You don't *want* to talk with me," you said.

It was the second-to-last of our silent car rides: me sitting thinking of ways to open a conversation and imagining how you'd parry each one, you sitting thinking God knows what. I thought, I am so tired of all this. And then I thought how unfair it was of me to think that after you'd just lost your sister. As I thought. You were looking good, despite the shape you were in. Your cheeks pale, your lips fat. It was the first thing I had felt for you sexually since our confrontation over Kate. I decided to be angry instead. You showed better sense: when we got upstairs and I put down your suitcase to unlock the door, you reached for my belt. To my credit, I was gracious.

6

On Saturday afternoon, you were out grocery shopping when the phone rang. "Hi, Rick," said the voice, "it's Marie. Is Jane around? Listen, when are you guys ever going to come *see* me?"

"Who is this?" I said. "Goddamn it, who the fuck is this?"

7

When you came in, I said: "Marie called."

"Oh," you said. "Well." You shook your head. "Actually I'm

surprised it took *this* long. But—" You shrugged. "It must have been pretty awkward for you. What did you end up saying?"

"*Why?*" I said. "Why would you be so stupid? I mean, *beyond* stupid."

"Sometimes you feel like being stupid, what can I say?" You said. "Didn't you ever want to just be stupid?" You went into the kitchen.

I followed. "So where were you?" I said. "Obviously you were *with* somebody. *And* obviously you wanted me to find out. Who was the lucky man?"

"Why do you assume it was just *one* lucky man?" you said. You set the bag down on the counter and turned to face me. "Oh Rick, I can't go on living a lie," you said, clamping the edge of the countertop behind you and hopping up to sit. "The truth is, it was all of your dear friends. It was Stefan and Andy and Alex—oh, and Gregory. *Dear* Gregory. Oh, but see, now there I go *lying* again."

"Okay, forget it," I said. "I mean, I'm through anyway. I truly am."

You hopped down and gripped both my arms. "Rick," you said. "I need your compassion at this terrible moment. The truth is, it wasn't a man—it was a woman. In fact, you won't believe this, but it was your dear friend and platonic co-worker *Kate* and we just found we had *so* much in common that we decided to have gay women's sex." You started giggling. "Rick, Rick, you must believe me."

"You're stoned," I said.

"Oh yes, Rick, I *am* stoned. You're so perspicacious, always. The truth is, I'm hooked on cocaine."

"Fine," I said. "You don't want to talk, fine."

"Oh Rick, you do understand." Your fingernails dug into my

arms and you lifted your head and kissed my cheek so hard I felt teeth. Then you let go and slapped and my glasses went flying. We looked at each other. You were red-faced and breathing hard. I was thinking:

- I am sick to death of every aspect of this.
- I can't walk out with her in this kind of shape.
- This will never end.
- I will take her throat and rip it open.
- I am observing all this from a great distance.

Then you began to sob and I took you in my arms and patted your back again and again, and smoothed and smoothed your hair, thinking:

- Every minute of this is a minute out of my life.

When you finally went into the bathroom to wash your face I went and picked up my glasses. A Y-shaped crack in the left lens. I tried to think how to hide from you the evidence of what you yourself had done: all I could do was not put them back on. Then it seemed to me you were taking too long in there. The water had stopped running long ago. Cutting your wrists? Not easy with a Good News razor. Swallowing the whole thing of Sudafed? I could save your life by breaking down the door. But I would have to ask first if you were all right, and that might enrage you—might in fact be the thing that would *make* you suicidal. The thing to do was to ask something else. I rehearsed, in my head, to get the right tone: "Hey, Janey? I'm going to need to use the john pretty soon." If you answered I'd know you were all right; if you didn't I'd know that you were either not all right or sulking. But of course you'd see through it. So I waited and worried. As you either did or didn't know.

Finally you came out and sat on the sofa hugging yourself, your feet tucked under you. "I'm sorry," you said. "I am completely humiliated. And I need very much not to talk right now. I'm very confused at this point."

"*You're* confused?"

"Please," you said. "Would you do something? Would you please pretend with me, just for a while? Like until tomorrow? Can we just pretend we're all right? One more day?"

8

The way we managed it was we drank lots of wine. Or I did: I lost track of you. We called the good Chinese place for cold hacked chicken and cold sesame noodles and I found my old prescription sunglasses in the drawer and we sat on the bed in our underwear and watched an old Jackie Gleason variety show on cable. It seemed to me the show was about a fat unhappy man who dressed himself up on Saturday night to watch things happen around him. The orchestra leader was named Sammy Spear, and I pounded the mattress and said, "God, it's too *perfect*. That one's the spear and that one's the open wound. Look at him—he's the open wound. He's the walking wounded."

"You're the walking *drunk*," you said, in the old way.

"*I'm* not walking," I said. "Lying right here. Too goddamn, too goddamn *smart*, to *think* about trying to walk."

9

Sunday morning, catnapping. I opened my eyes, looked at the clock, closed them, felt your thigh against mine, opened my eyes again, saw it was ten minutes later, closed them again. Wanted to keep on and on. Then I woke up and you weren't beside me. I looked around the room: there you were, at the dresser, bareback, in underpants. I imagined a steely look on your face and closed my eyes again. But my head hurt and I couldn't get back down into sleep. When I opened my eyes you turned around. Your large, flat nipples. You came and took your watch off the night table and strapped it on. It was the look I'd imagined, more or less.

You said, "I'm going to pack some things, you know? And then I'm going to go. Okay?"

"Go where?" I said. "Would you please tell me what the fuck is going on?"

"*Please* don't be stupid," you said.

I watched you take a T-shirt out of the drawer, then closed my eyes before you pulled it over your head. "I don't want to go through this day," I said.

"Ees not my puddoblem," you said. "Listen, I think you're going to do *just fine* out of this. If your platonic friend and co-worker Kate won't take you back, you can always find another platonic friend and co-worker. And another one and another one. You know, until you find the *right* one. Now you just lie there, go back to sleep, and when you wake up—presto. Wifey just an unpleasant memory."

"Where are you *going?*" I said. I opened my eyes. You were pulling on a pair of jeans.

"To Unpleasant Memoryland. Poof." You raised your palm to your lips and blew.

"Where are you going?"

You zipped the zipper and gave me the look again. "Boston," you said. "I'll write the address for you."

I took a deep breath and let it out. "Oh," I said.

You shrugged.

"He's a lowlife," I said.

"He's not that bad," you said. "Fact, he's a little like you in some ways. At any rate, he's probably not forever."

"So then what?"

"Ees not your puddoblem," you said, sitting on the bed to put on your running shoes. "Look, I promise you, this will be very easy. I don't want money, I don't want any of the stuff except for my grandfather's chair which I'll come get at some point. I guess I want the little rug that's in the other room. My books. You can keep the VCR. I'll let you know when I'm coming. *And* I will call Marie tonight, to spare you any further embarrassment. Okay?" You picked up your pocketbook and slung it over your shoulder and said in your Robert DeNiro voice, "Don' worr'. I take care ev'ryt'ing."

"I can't believe this," I said.

"Look," you said, "I have to crank it, you know? If I'm going to make this plane."

"Could I at least drive you to the airport?" I said. "And we could talk on the way? I really need to understand what's going on."

You sighed. "Sure. Fine, what the hell. But I don't know what you think you have to understand. Your bad wife is leaving you. For another man. You're a wronged husband. Now you can be happy."

10

I pull the shade back down and go into the kitchen to find the phone book. The number for Towaways is busy. Eight million stories in the Naked City. I pull off some paper towels to mop up the gin and take care of the broken glass. I pick up the pieces gingerly, remembering I'm in a stressful period. They go into a paper bag which goes into an empty Tropicana carton which goes into the trash so no one gets hurt.

Since Kate wasn't about to leave her husband and I wasn't about to leave you, she and I had agreed to be careful. Out of consideration. No hang-up calls, no leaving the office together, no be-

ing at each other's places even if it seemed perfectly safe, no over-
nighters anywhere. But you and I had rules, too, though never
codified: the gist was that we weren't to go looking for what we
didn't want to see. You were the one who violated that rule, by following me into the subway at lunch hour, riding in the next car to
West Fourth Street, walking a block behind me to Kate's sister's
building and watching from a phone booth as I was buzzed in. I
was the one who was trying to protect you.

As I had with the Hav-a-Heart trap. We both thought it was
ingenious, the way the trapdoor would fall away from under the
mouse when he went for the bait and tumble him into the metal
box. "We could take and release them in Central Park," you said.
"By the zoo. Plenty of warm places for a mousie to hang out."

The next day, I got home before you did. I went into the kitchen
and opened the thing to check, and there was a mouse: twitching,
squealing, hopelessly wedged into a corner between sharp edges of
galvanized metal. He had tried to worm himself out through a
place where the box hadn't been put together quite right. I watched
for a second, then went looking for something. Best thing I could
find was a screwdriver: I pressed the tip of it into his neck until I
felt a snap. Then I hid him at the bottom of the trash, wrapped in
the paper towel I'd used to wipe the inside of the box. When you
came in I told you that the thing was useless.

"It's only been a *day*," you said.

"Right," I said. "But. One of them already managed to take the
bait and get away. We're either going to have to get D-Con or put
up with the mice. Or get a cat."

You shook your head. "Rick, you *know* I'm allergic to cats." You
sighed. "I don't know," you said. "I guess we can't put up with
mice, can we? I mean they do carry disease, right?" As in *The Book
of Great Conversations*, the things we said to each other would have

sounded ordinary, most of them, to anyone who didn't know the story.

A week ago, at just this time of day, we were on our way to La Guardia. I asked you what last weekend had been about: why had it been necessary for you to come back and put us both through it? You wouldn't talk. I pressed you—it seemed wrong not to press you—but I was thinking, Why not just admit you're relieved? All that traffic must have been people heading for the beaches. Sun glinting off windshields and bumpers. We weren't moving fast enough to get a breeze going and my shirt was soaked through. Shifting from low to second and back to low. Good I had the sunglasses. I remember passing a black van with an orange volcano painted on its side panel, then the van passing us. Its windows were up and the driver, a blond thug, was singing away unheard, beating time on the steering wheel, as his girlfriend painted her nails. When we finally got there you let me park and carry your suitcase as far as security. I put it on the moving belt, you put your pocketbook next to it and turned to me before stepping into the frame.

"Bye," you said.

"This is really it?" I said.

You smiled, beckoned with your forefinger and raised your chin. I cupped my hands like parentheses around your shoulders and bent to kiss at least your forehead. You laid a hand on my cheek, pushed my head to the side, and whispered in my ear, "This is what you *wanted*."

Shoptalk #14
On Responsibility

How can the contemporary disavowal movement not
affect those of us who tell stories? We begin to move
away from fiction of protagonists and antagonists into
another mode, another model. It is hard to describe this
model but I think it might be called the fiction of finger-
pointing, the fiction of the quest for blame. . . . In such
fiction, people and events are often accused of turning
the protagonist into the kind of person the protagonist
is, usually an unhappy person. That's the whole story.
When blame has been assigned, the story is over.

(Charles Baxter, "Dysfunctional Narratives," vol. 20, nos. 2 & 3, 1994)

CAROLYN FERRELL

Proper Library

Carolyn Ferrell graduated with a degree in creative writing from Sarah Lawrence College in 1984, where she studied with Allan Gurganus and Grace Paley. After living in Germany for four years, where she studied German literature and worked as a high school teaching assistant, she returned to the United States and began teaching adult literacy in Manhattan and the South Bronx. She also entered the master's program in creative writing at CCNY, and published her first stories in Callaloo, The Literary Review, *and* Fiction.

In screening unsolicited fiction at Ploughshares, *Don Lee singled out "Proper Library" in 1992 and forwarded it to guest editor Al Young, who selected it for the spring 1993 issue. When Houghton Mifflin's Janet Silver, a senior editor and in-house editor for the annual* Best American Short Stories, *read the story (which Tobias Wolff then selected for* Best American Short Stories, 1994*) in* Ploughshares, *she promptly signed Ferrell to a contract for a collection.* Don't Erase Me *was published in 1997, and subsequently won both* Ploughshares' *seventh annual John C. Zacharis First Book Award and the* Los Angeles Times *Award for First Fiction.*

*"The finished collection . . . features eight first-person stories, eight singular voices that incandescently mix lyricism and street patois to portray the lives of mostly poor black girls," Don Lee writes in announcing the Zacharis Award (*Ploughshares *23, no. 4). "The subjects are sometimes grave—sexuality, domestic violence, AIDS, incest—but somehow her characters carry with them an unfailing passion and hope.*

Ferrell says, 'Originally, I'd planned for the collection to center around the story "Wonderful Teen" and focus on the coming-of-age theme set in California, dealing with family drama, parental strife, race issues, among other things. But once I wrote "Proper Library," I decided to bring in other dimensions. I liked reading the black/interracial/over-weight girl everywhere: in California, in New York, in the South Bronx, in Germany.' "

"Ferrell gives much credit for her work to the writer Doris Jean Austin. 'Before she died in 1994, she taught me a great deal about the art of writing, through conversastions and in workshops of the New Renaissance Writers, a black writers' group that she led. Her perception of good writing and the questions writers must ask themselves as they perfect their craft influenced me profoundly.' "

Carolyn Ferrell presently teaches at Sarah Lawrence College, and is working on a novel.

B oys, men, girls, children, mothers, babies. You got to feed them. You always got to keep them fed. Winter summer. They always have to feel satisfied. Winter summer. But then you stop and ask: Where is the food going to come from? Because it's never-ending, never-stopping. Where? Because your life is spent on feeding them and you never stop thinking about where the food is going to come from.

Formula, pancakes, syrup, milk, roast turkey with cornbread stuffing, Popsicles, love, candy, tongue kisses, hugs, kisses behind backs, hands on faces, warmth, tenderness, Boston cream pie, fucking in the butt. You got to feed them, and it's always going to be you. Winter summer.

My ma says to me, Let's practice the words this afternoon when you get home, baby. I nod to her. I don't have to use any words with her to let her know I will do what she wants. When family people come over and they see me and Ma in the kitchen like that with the words, they say she has the same face as the maid in the movies. She does have big brown hands like careful shovels, and she loves to touch and pat and warm you up with them. And when she walks, she shuffles. But if anyone is like the maid in the movies, it is Aunt Estine. She likes to give mouth, 'specially when I got the kids on my hands. She's sassy. She's got what people call a bad attitude. She makes sure you hear her heels clicking all the time, 'specially when you are lying in bed before dawn and thinking things in order, how you got to keep moving, all day long. Click, click. Ain't nobody up yet? Click. Lazy-ass Negroes, you better not be 'specting me to cook y'all breakfast when you do get up! Click, click. I'm hungry. Click. I don't care what time it is, I'm hungry y'all and I'm tired and depressed and I need someone to talk to. Well, the hell with all y'all. That's my last word. Click, click, click.

My ma pats her hands on my schoolbag, which is red like a girl's, but that's all right. She pats it like it was my head. The books I have in it are: Biology, Woodworking for You, Math I, The History of Civilization.

I'm supposed to be in Math 4, but the people keep holding me back. I know it's no real fault of mine. I been teaching the kids Math 4 from a book I took out the Lending Mobile in the schoolyard. The kids can do most of Math 4. They like the way I teach it to them, with real live explanations, not the kind where you are supposed to have everything already in your head and it's just waiting to come out. And the kids don't ask to see if I get every one right. They trust me. They trust my smart. They just like the feel of the numbers and seeing them on a piece of paper: division of decimals, division of fractions. It's these numbers that keep them moving and that will keep them moving when I am gone. At school

I just keep failing the City Wide Tests every May and the people don't ask any questions: they just hold me back. Cousin Cee Cee said, If you wasn't so stupid you would realize the fact of them holding you back till you is normal.

The kids are almost as sad as Ma when I get ready to go to school in the morning. They cry and whine and carry on and ask me if they can sit on my lap just one more time before I go, but Ma is determined. She checks the outside of my books to make sure nothing is spilled over them or that none of the kids have torn out any pages. Things got to be in place. There got to be order if you gonna keep on moving, and Ma knows that deep down. This morning I promise to braid Lasheema's hair right quick before I go, and as I'm braiding, she's steady smiling her four-year-old grin at Shawn, who is a boy and therefore has short hair, almost a clean shave, and who can't be braided and who weeps with every strand I grease, spread, and plait.

Ma warns me, Don't let them boys bother you now, Lorrie. Don't let 'em.

I tell her, Ma, I have not let you down in a long time. I know what I got to do for you.

She smiles but I know it is a fake smile, and she says, Lorrie, you are my only son, the only real man I got. I don't want them boys to get you from me.

I tell her because it's the only thing I can tell her, You cooking up something special tonight?

Ma smiles and goes back to fixing pancake mix from her chair in the kitchen. The kids are on their way to forgetting about me 'cause they love pancakes more than anything and that is the only way I'll get out of here today. Sheniqua already has the bottle of Sugar Shack Syrup and Tonya is holding her plate above her nappy lint head.

Tommy, Lula Jean's Navy husband, meets me at the front door as I open it. Normally he cheers me up by testing me on Math 4 and telling me what a hidden genius I am, a still river running deep, he called it one time. He likes to tell me jokes and read stories from the Bible out loud. And he normally kisses my sister Lula Jean right where I and everybody else can see them, like in the kitchen or in the bedroom on the bed, surrounded by at least nine kids and me, all flaming brown heads and eyes. He always says: This is what love should be. And he searches into Lula Jean's face for whole minutes.

I'm leaving for Jane Addams High School and I meet Tommy and he has a lady tucked under his arm and it ain't Lula Jean. Her hair is wet and smells like mouthwash and I hate him in a flash. I never hate anybody, but now I hate him. I know that when I close the door behind me a wave of mouths will knock Tommy and this new lady down but it won't drown them. My sister Anita walks into the room and notices and carries them off into the bathroom, quick and silent. But before that she kisses me on my cheek and pats her hand, a small one of Ma's, on my chest. She whispers, You are my best man, remember that. She slips a letter knife in my jacket pocket. She says, If that boy puts his thing on you, cut it off. I love you, baby. She pushes me out the door.

Layla Jackson who lives in the downtown Projects and who might have AIDS comes running up to me as I walk out our building's door to the bus stop. She is out of breath. I look at her and could imagine a boy watching her chest heave up and down like that and suddenly get romantic feelings, it being so big and all, split like two kickballs bouncing. I turn my eyes to hers, which are crying. Layla Jackson's eyes are red. She has her baby Tee Tee in her arms but it's cold out here and she doesn't have a blanket on him or nothing. I say to her, Layla, honey, you gonna freeze that baby to death.

And I take my jacket off and put it over him, the tiny bundle.

Layla Jackson says, Thanks Lorrie man I got a favor to ask you please don't tell me no please man.

Layla always makes her words into a worry sandwich.

She says, Man, I need me a new baby-sitter 'cause I been took Tee Tee over to my mother's but now she don't want him with the others and now I can't do nothing till I get me a sitter.

I tell her, Layla, I'm going back to school now. I can't watch Tee Tee in the morning but if you leave him with me in the cafeteria after fifth period I'll take him on home with me.

She says, That means I got to take this brat to Introduction to Humanities with me. Shit, man. He's gonna cry and I won't pass the test on Spanish Discoverers. Shit, man.

Then Layla Jackson thinks a minute and says, Okay, Lorrie, I'll give Tee to you at lunch in the cafeteria, bet. And I'll be 'round your place 'round six for him or maybe seven, thanks, man.

Then she bends down and kisses Tee Tee on his forehead and he glows with what I know is drinking up an oasis when you are in the desert for so long. And she turns and walks to the downtown subway, waving at me. At the corner she comes running back because she still has my jacket and Tee Tee is waving the letter knife around like a flag. She says that her cousin Rakeem was looking for me and to let me know he would waiting for me 'round his way. *Yes.* I say to her, See you, Layla, honey.

Before I used to not go to Jane Addams when I was supposed to. I got in the habit of looking for Rakeem, Layla's cousin, underneath the Bruckner Expressway, where the Spanish women sometimes go to buy oranges and watermelons and apples cheap. He was what you would call a magnet, only I didn't know that then. I didn't understand the different flavors of the pie. I saw him one day and I had a feeling like I wanted him to sit on my lap and cradle me. That's when I had to leave school. Rakeem, he didn't stop me. His voice was just as loud as the trucks heading towards Manhattan on the Bruckner above us: This is where your real world begins, man. The women didn't watch us. We stared each other in the eyes. Rakeem taught me how to be afraid of school and of people watching us. He said, Don't go back, and I didn't. A part of me was saying that his ear was more delicious than Math 4. I didn't go to Jane Addams for six months.

On the BX 17 bus I see Tammy Ferguson and her twins and Joe Smalls and that white girl Laura. She is the only white girl in these Bronx projects that I know of. I feel sorry for her. She has blue eyes and red hair and one time when the B-Crew-Girls were going to beat her butt in front of the building, she broke down crying and told them that her real parents were black from the South. She told them she was really a Negro and they all laughed and that story worked the opposite than we all thought. Laura became their friend, like the B-Crew-Girls' mascot. And now she's still their friend. People may laugh when she ain't around but she's got her back covered. She's loyal and is trying to wear her thin flippy hair in cornrows, which in the old days woulda made the B-Crew, both boys and girls, simply fall out. When Laura's around, the B-Crew-Girls love to laugh. She looks in my direction when I get on the bus and says, Faggot.

She says it loud enough for all the grown-up passengers to hear. They don't look at me, they keep their eyes on whatever their eyes are on, but I know their ears are on me. Tammy Ferguson always swears she would never help a white girl, but now she can't pass up this opportunity, so she says, You tight-ass homo, go suck some faggot dick. Tammy's kids are taking turns making handprints on the bus window.

I keep moving. It's the way I learned: keep moving. I go and sit next to Joe Smalls in the back of the bus and he shows me the Math 3 homework he got his baby's mother Tareen to do for him. He claims she is smarter now than when she was in school at Jane Addams in the spring. He laughs.

The bus keeps moving. I keep moving even though I am sitting still. I feel all of the ears on us, on me and Joe and the story of Tareen staying up till 4 a.m. on the multiplication of fractions and then remembering that she had promised Joe some ass earlier but seeing that he was sound asleep snoring anyway, she worked on ahead and got to the percent problems by the time the alarm went off. Ha ha. Joe laughs, I got my girl in deep check. Ha ha.

All ears are on us, but mainly on me. Tammy Ferguson is busy slapping the twins to keep quiet and sit still, but I can feel Laura's eyes like they are a silent machine gun. Faggot faggot suck dick faggot. Now repeat that one hundred times in one minute and that's how I am feeling.

Keep moving. The bus keeps rolling and you also have to keep moving. Like water like air like outer space. I always pick something for my mind. Like today I am remembering the kids and how they will be waiting for me after fifth period and I remember the feel of Lasheema's soft dark hair.

Soft like the dark hair that covers me, not an afro, but silky hair, covering me all over. Because I am so cold. Because I am so alone. A mat of thick delicious hair that blankets me in warmth. And therefore safety. And peace. And solitude. And ecstasy. Lasheema and me are ecstatic when we look at ourselves in the mirror. She's only four and I am fourteen. We hold each other smiling.

Keep moving. Then I am already around the corner from school while the bus pulls away with Laura still on it because she has fallen asleep in her seat and nobody has bothered to touch her.

On the corner of Prospect Avenue and East 167th Street where the bus lets me out, I see Rakeem waiting for me. I am not supposed to really know he's there for me and he is not supposed to show it. He is opening a Pixie Stick candy and then he fixes his droopy pants so that they are hanging off the edge of his butt. I can see Christian Dior undies. When I come nearer he throws the Pixie Stick on the ground next to the other garbage and gives me his hand just like any B-Crew-Boy would do when he saw his other crew member. Only we are not B-Crew members, we get run over by the B-Crew.

He says, Yo, man, did you find Layla?

I nod and listen to what he is really saying.

Rakeem says, Do you know that I got into Math 3? Did you hear that shit? Ain't that some good shit?

He smiles and hits me on the back and he lets his hand stay there.

I say, See what I told you before, Rakeem? You really got it in you to move on. You doing all right, man.

He grunts and looks at his sneakers. Last year the B-Crew boys tried to steal them from him but Rakeem screamed at them that he had AIDS from his cousin and they ran away rubbing their hands on the sides of the buildings on the Grand Concourse.

Rakeem says, Man, I don't have nothing in me except my brain that tells me: Nigger, first thing get your ass up in school. Make them know you can do it.

I say, Rakeem, you are smart, man! I wish I had your smart. I would be going places if I did.

He says, And then, Lorrie, I got to get people to like me and to stop seeing me. I just want them to think they like me. So I got to hide *me* for a while. Then you watch, Lorrie, man: *much* people will be on my side!

I say to him, Rakeem, you got Layla and baby Tee Tee and all the teachers on your side. And you got smart. You have it made.

He answers me after he fixes his droopy pants again so that they are hanging off exactly the middle of his ass: Man, they are whack! You know what I would like to do right now, Lorrie? You know what I would like? Shit, I ain't seen you since you went back to school and since I went back. Hell, you know what I would like? But it ain't happening 'cause you think Ima look at my cousin Layla and her bastard and love them and that will be enough. But it will never be enough.

I think about sitting on his lap. I did it before but then I let months go by because it was under the Bruckner Expressway and I believed it could only last a few minutes. It was not like the kind of love when I had the kids because I believed they would last forever.

He walks backwards away and when he gets to the corner, he starts running. No one else is on the street. He shouts, Rocky's Pizza! Ima be behind there, man. We got school fooled. This is the master plan. Ima be there, Lorrie! *Be there.*

I want to tell Rakeem that I have missed him and that I will not be there but he is gone. The kids are enough. The words are important. They are all enough.

The front of Jane Addams is gray-green with windows with gates over all of them. I am on the outside.

The bell rings first period and I am smiling at Mr. D'Angelo and feeling like this won't be a complete waste of a day. The sun has hit the windows of Jane Addams and there is even heat around our books. Mr. D'Angelo notices me but looks away. Brandy Bailey, who doesn't miss a thing, announces so that only us three will hear: Sometimes when a man's been married long he needs to experience a new kind of loving, ain't that what you think, Lorrie?

For that she gets thrown out of the classroom and an extra day of in-school suspension. All ears are now on me and Mr. D'Angelo. I am beyond feeling but I know he isn't. And that makes me happy in a way, like today ain't going to be a complete waste of a day.

He wipes his forehead with an imported handkerchief. He starts out saying, Class, what do we remember about the piston, the stem, and the insects? He gets into his question and his perspiration stops and in two minutes he is free of me.

And I'm thinking: Why couldn't anything ever happen, why does every day start out one way hopeful but then point to the fact that ain't nothing ever going to happen? The people here at school call me ugly, for one. I know I got bug eyes and I know I am not someone who lovely things ever happen to, but I ask you: Doesn't the heart count? Love is a pie and I am lucky enough to have almost every flavor in mine. Mr. D'Angelo turns away from my desk and announces a surprise quiz and everybody groans and it is a sea of general unhappiness but no one is more than me, knowing that nothing will ever happen the way I'd like it to, not this flavor of the pie. And I am thinking: Mr. D'Angelo, do you know that I would give anything to be like you, what with all your smarts and words and you know how to make the people here laugh and they love you. And I would give anything if you would ask me to sit on your lap and ask me to bite into your ear so that it tingles like the bell that rips me in and out of your class. I would give anything. Love is a pie. Didn't you know that? Mr. D'Angelo, I am in silent love in a loud body.

So don't turn away. *Sweat.*

Mrs. Cabrini pulls me aside and whispers, My dear Lorrie, when are you ever going to pass this City Wide? You certainly have the brains. And I know that your intelligence will take you far, will open new worlds for you. Put your mind to your dreams, my dear boy, and you will achieve them. You are your own universe, you are your own shooting star.

People 'round my way know me as Lorrie and the name stays. Cousin Cee Cee says the name fits and she smacks her gum in my face whenever she mentions that. She also adds that if anyone ever wants to kick my ass, she'll just stand around and watch because a male with my name and who likes it just deserves to be watched when whipped.

Ma named me for someone else. My real name is Lawrence Lincoln Jefferson Adams. It's the name on my school records. It's the name Ma says I got to put on my application to college when the time comes. She knows I been failing these City Wide Tests and that's why she wants to practice words with me every day. She laughs when I get them wrong but she's afraid I won't learn them on my own, so she asks me to practice them with her and I do. Not every day, but a whole lot: look them up and pronounce them. Last Tuesday: Independence Chagrin. Symbolism. Nomenclature. Filament. On Wednesday, only: Apocrypha. Ma says they have to be proper words with proper meanings from a dictionary. You got to say them right. This is important if you want to reach your destiny, Ma says.

Like for instance the word *Library.* All my life I been saying that "Liberry." And even though I knew it was a place to read and do your studying, I still couldn't call it right. Do you see what I mean? I'm about doing things, you see, *finally* doing things right.

Cousin Cee Cee always says, What you learning all that shit for?

Don't you know it takes more than looking up words to get into a college, even a damn community college? Practicing words like that! Is you a complete asshole?

And her two kids, Byron and Elizabeth, come into the kitchen and ask me to teach them the words too, but Cee Cee says it will hurt their eyes to be doing all that reading and besides they are only eight and nine. When she is not around I give them words with up to ten letters, then they go back to TV with the other kids.

When we have a good word sitting, me and Ma, she smooths my face with her hands and calls me Lawrence, My Fine Boy. She says, You are on your way to good things. You just got to do things the proper way.

We kiss each other. Her hands are like the maid in the movies. I know I am taken care of.

Zenzile Jones passes me a note in History of Civilization. It's the part where Ptolemy lets everyone know the world is round. Before I open it, I look at her four desks away and I remember the night when I went out for baby diapers and cereal and found her crying in front of a fire hydrant. I let her cry on my shoulder. I told her that her father was a sick man for sucking on her like that.

The note says, Please give me a chance.

Estine Smith, my mother's sister who wants me and the kids to call her by both names, can't get out of her past. Sometimes I try on her clothes when I'm with the kids and we're playing dress-up. My favorite dress is her blue organza without the back. I seen Estine Smith wear this during the daytime and I fell in love with it. I also admired her for wearing a dress with the back out in the day, but it was only a ten-second admiration. Because then she opens her mouth and she is forever in her past. Her favorite time to make us

all go back to is when they lynched her husband, David Saul
Smith, from a tree in 1986 and called the TV station to come and
get a look. She can't let us go one day without reminding us in
words. I never want to be like her, ever. Everybody cries when they
are in her words because they feel sorry for her, and Estine Smith
is not someone but a walking hainted house.

Third period. I start dreaming about the kids while the others are
standing in line to use the power saw. I love to dream about the kids.
They are the only others who think I am beautiful besides Ma and
Anita. They are my favorite flavor of the pie, even if I got others in
my mind.

Most of the time there are eight but when my other aunt,
Samantha, comes over I got three more. Samantha cries in the
kitchen and shows Ma her blue marks and it seems like her crying
will go on forever. Me, I want to take the kids' minds away. We go
into Ma's room where there is the TV and we sing songs like "Old
Gray Mare" and "Bingo Was His Name O" or new ones like "Why
You Treat Me So Bad?" and "I Try to Let Go." Or else I teach
them Math 4. Or else I turn on the TV so they can watch Bugs or
He-Man and so I can get their ironing done.

Me, I love me some kids. I need me some kids.

Joe Smalls talks to me in what I know is a friendly way. The
others in Woodworking for You don't know that. They are like the
rest of the people who see me and hear the action and latch on.

Joe Smalls says, Lorrie, man, that bitch Tareen got half the per-
centage problems wrong. Shit. Be glad you don't have to deal with
no dumb-ass Tareen bitch. She nearly got my ass a F in Math 3.

I get a sad look on my face, understanding, but it's a fake look
because I'm feeling the rest of the ears on us, latching, readying. I

pause to Heaven. I am thinking I wish Ma had taught me how to pray. But she doesn't believe in God.

Junior Sims says, Why you talking that shit, Joe, man? Lorrie don't ever worry about bitches!

Perry Samson says, No, Lorrie never ever thinks about pussy as a matter of fact. Never ever.

Franklin says, Hey, Lorrie, man, tell me what you think about, then? What can be better than figuring out how you going to get that hole, man? Tell me what?

Mr. Samuels, the teacher, turns off the power saw just when it gets to Barney Moore's turn. He has heard the laughter from underneath the saw's screeching. Everybody gets quiet. His face is like a piece of lumber. Mr. Samuels is never soft. He doesn't fail me even though I don't do any cutting or measuring or shellacking. He wants me the hell out of there.

And after the saw is turned off, Mr. Samuels, for the first time in the world, starts laughing. The absolute first time. And everybody joins in because they are afraid of this and I laugh too because I'm hoping all the ears will go off me.

Mr. Samuels is laughing Haw Haw like he's from the country. Haw Haw. Haw Haw. His face is red. Everyone cools down and is just smiling now.

Then he says, Class, don't mess with the only *girl* we got in here!

Now it's laughter again.

Daniel Fibbs says, Yeah, Mr. Samuels is *on!*

Franklin laughs, No fags allowed, you better take your sissy ass out of here less you want me to cut it into four pieces.

Joe Smalls is quiet and looking out the window.

Junior Sims laughs, Come back when you start fucking bitches!

Keep moving, keep moving.

I pick up my red bag and wade towards the door. My instinct is the only thing that's working, and it is leading me back to Biology. But first out the room. Inside me there is really nothing except for Ma's voice: *Don't let them boys.* But inside there is nothing else. My bones and my brain and my heart would just crumble if it wasn't for that swirling wind of nothing in me that keeps me moving and moving.

Perry laughs, I didn't know Mr. Samuels was from the South.

With his eyelashes, Rakeem swept the edges of my face. He let me know they were beautiful to him. His face went in a circle around mine and dipped in my eyes and dipped in my mouth. He traveled me to a quiet place where his hands were the oars and I drifted off to sleep. The thin bars of the shopping cart where I was sitting in made grooves in my back, but it was like they were rows of tender fingers inviting me to stay. The roar of the trucks was a lullaby.

Layla Jackson comes running up to me but it's only fourth period because she wants to try and talk some sense into Tyrone. She hands me little Tee Tee. Tyrone makes like he wants to come over and touch the baby but instead he flattens his back against the wall to listen to Layla. I watch as she oozes him. In a minute they are tongue-kissing. Because they are the only two people who will kiss each other. Everyone says that they gave themselves AIDS and now have to kiss each other because there ain't no one else. People walk past them and don't even notice that he has his hand up her skirt, squeezing the kickball.

Tee Tee likes to be in my arms. I like for him to be there.

The ladies were always buying all kinds of fruits and vegetables for their families underneath the Bruckner Expressway. They all talked Spanish and made the sign of the cross and asked God for forgiveness and gossiped.

Rakeem hickeyed my neck. We were underneath the concrete bridge supports and I had my hands on the handle of a broken shopping cart, where I was sitting. Don't go back, Rakeem was telling me, don't go back. And he whispered in my ear. And I thought of all the words I had been practicing, and how I was planning to pass that City Wide. Don't go back, he sang, and he sat me on his lap and he moved me around there. They don't need *you*, he said, and *you* don't need *them*.

But I do, I told him.

This feeling can last forever, he said.

No, it can't, I said, but I wound up leaving school for six months anyway. That shopping cart was my school.

I am thinking: It will never be more. I hold Tee Tee carefully because he is asleep on my shoulder and I go to catch the BX 17 back to my building.

Estine Smith stays in her past and that is where things are like nails. I want to tell her to always wear her blue organza without the back. If you can escape, why don't you all the time? You could dance and fling your arms and maybe even feel love from some direction. You would not perish. *You* could be free.

When I am around and she puts us in her past in her words, she tells me that if I hada twitched my ass down there like I do here, they woulda hung me up just by my black balls.

The last day Rakeem and I were together, I told him I wanted to go back, to school, to everyone. The words, I tried to explain about the words to Rakeem. I could welcome him into my world if he wanted me to. Hey, wasn't there enough room for him and me and the words?

Hell no, he shouted, and all the Spanish women turned around and stared at us. He shouted, You are an ugly-ass bastard who will always be hated big time and I don't care what you do; this is where your world begins and this is where your world will end. Fuck you. You are a pussy, man. Get the hell out my face.

Ma is waiting for me at the front door, wringing her hands. She says it's good that I am home because there is trouble with Tommy again and I need to watch him and the kids while she goes out to bring Lula Jean home from the movies, which is where she goes when she plans on leaving Tommy. They got four kids here and if Lula Jean leaves, I might have to drop out of school again because she doesn't want to be tied to anything that has Tommy's stamp on it.

I set Tee Tee down next to Tommy on the sofa bed where I usually sleep. Tommy wakes me up and says, Hey, man, who you bringing to visit me?

I go into the kitchen to fix him some tea and get the kids' lunch ready. Sheniqua is playing the doctor and trying to fix up Shawn, who always has to have an operation when she is the doctor. They come into the kitchen to hug my legs and then they go back in the living room.

Tommy sips his tea and says, Who was that chick this morning, Lorrie, man?

I say I don't know. I begin to fold his clothes.

Tommy says, Man, you don't know these bitches out here nowadays. You want to show them love, a good time, and a real deep part of yourself and all they do is not appreciate it and try to make your life miserable.

He says, Well, at least I got Lula. Now that's some woman.

And he is asleep. Sheniqua and her brother Willis come in and ask me if I will teach them Math 4 tonight. Aunt Estine rolls into the bedroom and asks me why do I feel the need to take care of this bum, and then she hits her head on the doorframe. She is clicking her heels. She asks, Why do we women feel we always need to teach them? They ain't going to learn the right way. They ain't going to learn shit. That's why we always so alone. Click, click.

The words I will learn before Ma comes home are: Soliloquy, Disenfranchise, Catechism. I know she will be proud. This morning before I left she told me she would make me a turkey dinner with all the trimmings if I learned four new words tonight. I take out my dictionary but then the kids come in and want me to give them a bath and baby Tee Tee has a fever and is throwing up all over the place. I look at the words and suddenly I know I will know them without studying.

And I realize this in the bathroom and then again a few minutes later when Layla Jackson comes in cursing because she got a 60 on the Humanities quiz. She holds Tee but she doesn't touch him. She thinks Tyrone may be going to some group where he is meeting other sick girls and she doesn't want to be alone. She curses and cries, curses and cries. She asks me why things have to be so fucked. Her braids are coming undone and I tell her that I will tighten them up for her. That makes Layla Jackson stop crying. She says, And to top it off, Rakeem is a shit. He promised me he wouldn't say nothing but now that he's back in school he is broadcasting my shit all over the place. And that makes nobody like me. And that makes nobody want to touch me.

I put my arm around Layla. Soon her crying stops and she is thinking about something else.

But me, I know these new words and the old words without looking at them, without the dictionary, without Ma's hands on my head. Lasheema and Tata come in and want their hair to be like Layla's and they bring in the Vaseline and sit around my feet like shoes. Tommy wakes up still in sleep and shouts, Lula, get your ass on in here. Then he falls back to sleep.

Because I know I will always be able to say the words on my own. I can do the words on my own and that is what matters. I have this flavor of the pie and I will always have it. Here in this kitchen I was always safe, learning the words till my eyes hurt. The words are in my heart.

Ma comes in and shoves Lula Jean into a kitchen chair. She says, Kids, make room for your cousin, go in the other room and tell Tommy to get his lame ass out here. Layla, you can get your ass out of here and don't bring it back no more with this child sick out his mind, do your 'ho'ing somewhere out on the street where you belong. Tommy, since when I need to tell you how to treat your wife? You are a stupid heel. Learn how to be a man.

Everybody leaves and Ma changes.

She says, I ain't forgot that special dinner for you, baby. I'm glad you're safe and sound here with me. Let's practice later.

I tell her, Okay, Ma, but I got to go meet Rakeem first.

She looks at me in shock and then out the corner of my eye I can tell she wants me to say no, I'll stay, I won't go to him. Because she knows.

But I'm getting my coat on and Ma has got what will be tears on her face because she can't say no and she can't ask any questions. Keep moving.

And I am thinking of Rocky's Pizza and how I will be when I get there and how I will be when I get home. Because I am coming back home. And I am going to school tomorrow. I know the words, and

I can tell them to Rakeem and I can share what I know. Now he may be ready. I want him to say to me in his mind: Please give me a chance. And I know that behind Rocky's Pizza is the only place where I don't have to keep moving. Where there is not just air in me that keeps me from crumbling, but blood and meat and strong bones and feelings. I will be me for a few minutes behind Rocky's Pizza and I don't care if it's just a few minutes. I pat my hair down in the mirror next to the kitchen door. I take Anita's letter knife out my jacket pocket and leave it on the table next to where Tommy is standing telling his wife that she never knew what love was till she met him and why does she have to be like that, talking about leaving him and shit? You keep going that way and you won't ever know how to keep a man, bitch.

Shoptalk #15
Tribalism

It is sad to think that one day there will be no more tribes as we know them. . . . But what is our notion of tribe and tribalism as we approach the twenty-first century? . . . Some of the work directly portrays ethnic tribes . . . these writers describe their own cultures, with an underlying realization and sadness that they are being swallowed up by the dominant culture, rather than being accepted by it. . . . Other variations . . . include homosexuality, love, religion. What nearly all these works share is the desire to acknowledge the tribes of people outside the cozy confines of larger society and their inalienable right to bang at the gates.

(James Welch, "Introduction," vol. 20, no. 1, 1994)

GINA BERRIAULT

The Infinite Passion of Expectation

"The Infinite Passion of Expectation" appeared in 1979, with a redis-
covery appreciation by Richard Yates, in Ploughshares *5, no. 3, edited*
by James Randall, and was reprinted in Pushcart Prize V; *in 1980*
Gina Berriault published "Works of the Imagination" in Ploughshares *6, no. 3, edited by Jay Neugeboren (a story about the recovery*
from writer's block, where a grieving writer feels "indifference, like a
drugged sleep, to everyone else on earth"); and in 1985 "The Island of
Ven" (which went on to win an O'Henry Award and be reprinted in
Pushcart Prize XI) *in* Ploughshares *11, nos. 2 & 3, coedited by*
James Alan McPherson and myself. I recall sending her comments from
McPherson about the disturbing vaccuum of commitment reflected by
the minimalist fiction of the time. She wrote back, characteristically,
"This is the Time of No Thought and so of no thoughtful words. . . .
What I mean is that the human face in minimalist stories is not truly
there but is made to seem there by tricks of the trade. . . . [And yet, the
best minimalist stories, a rare few] make sparks fly, even one spark, or
are like poetry, or like a sotto voce or staccato voice saying in a few
words about the value of life in a time of accelerating violence against
all life, something that had to be said fast. Cocteau's 'Literature is a
written cry' may be more true now than ever." She appeared again in
1995 in Ploughshares *with "Who Is It Can Tell Me Who I Am?"*
(vol. 21, no. 4, edited by Tim O'Brien and Mark Strand), a story
about a public librarian haunted by his social conscience.

Reviewing Gina Berriault's most recent collection, Women in Their Beds: New and Selected Stories (America, *Nov 15, 1997*), *Katrin R. Burlin summarizes: "For more than forty years, Gina Berriault, a Californian, has been writing short stories, screenplays, articles, interviews and novels (four), publishing the short fiction for which she had been particularly noted, both in a variety of magazines and literary journals . . . as well as in short story collections. She has been honored with a grant from the National Endowment for the Arts and a Guggenheim Fellowship, with an Ingram–Merrill Fellowship, a Commonwealth Gold Medal for Literature. . . .* Women in Their Beds *has brought her the PEN / Faulkner Award, the Bay Area Book Reviewers Award and the National Book Critics Circle Award [and the Rea Award for lifetime achievement in the short story]. Having taught writing at the university level, she is now a full-time writer, dedicating all her publications to her daughter, Julie Elena."*

Berriault herself singles out editor Jack Shoemaker, first of North Point Press, now of Counterpoint, for particular support and encouragement in the past twenty-some years, when after an eighteen-year silence, she again began to publish new work, to have her earlier work reissued, and to be recognized by a new generation of readers. North Point Press published Lights of Earth: A Novel *(1984) and* The Infinite Passion of Expectation: Twenty-five Stories *(1989), and then brought back to print her earlier books,* The Descent: A Novel *(1960),* The Mistress and Other Stories *(1965),* The Son: A Novel *(1966), and* Conference of Victims: A Novel *(1962). Moving on to Counterpoint, Shoemaker published* Women in Their Beds: New and Selected Stories *(1996).*

Gina Berriault passed away on July 22, 1999, as I was compiling this note. In answer to my questions, Jack Shoemaker told me that her first publication was in Contact *magazine, in the late 1950s, edited by*

Evan S. Connell (followed by her later appearance in Richard Yates's
Stories for the Sixties); *that in fact Connell had been the writer to*
introduce Gina Berriault to Shoemaker in 1979 as a prospective author
for North Point Press; and that through the years of her supposed si-
lence in the 1970s, she had in fact been writing screenplays, most nota-
bly a screenplay for Kate Chopin's The Awakening, *the production of*
which later fell apart over copyright negotiations, and one for her own
widely anthologized story "The Stone Boy," *which was produced and*
released in 1984, starring Robert Duvall and Glenn Close.

The girl and the elderly man descended the steep stairs to the
channel's narrow beach and walked along by the water's edge.
Several small fishing boats were moving out to sea, passing a
freighter entering the bay, booms raised, a foreign name at her bow.
His sturdy hiking boots came down flatly on the firm sand, the
same way they came down on the trails of the mountain that he
climbed, staff in hand, every Sunday. Up in his elegant neighborhood, on the cliff above the channel, he stamped along the side-
walks in the same way, his long, stiff legs attempting ease and flair.
He appeared to feel no differences in terrain. The day was cold,
and every time the little transparent fans of water swept in and
drew back, the wet sand mirrored a clear sky and the sun on its way
down. He wore an overcoat, a cap, and a thick muffler, and, with his
head high, his large, arched nose set into the currents of air from
off the ocean, he described for her his fantasy of their honeymoon
in Mexico.

He was jovial, he laughed his English laugh that was like a bird's
hooting, like a very sincere imitation of a laugh. If she married him,
he said, she, so many years younger, could take a young lover and
he would not protest. The psychologist was seventy-nine, but he
allowed himself great expectations of love and other pleasures, and

advised her to do the same. She always mocked herself for dreams, because to dream was to delude herself. She was a waitress and lived in a neighborhood of littered streets, where rusting cars stood unmoved for months. She brought him ten dollars each visit, sometimes more, sometimes less; he asked of her only a fee she could afford. Since she always looked downward in her own surroundings, avoiding the scene that might be all there was to her future, she could not look upward in his surroundings, resisting its dazzling diminishment of her. But out on these walks with him she tried looking up. It was what she had come to see him for—that he might reveal to her how to look up and around.

On their other walks and now, he told her about his life. She had only to ask, and he was off into memory, and memory took on a prophetic sound. His life seemed like a life expected and not yet lived, and it sounded that way because, within the overcoat, was a youth, someone always looking forward. The girl wondered if he were outstripping time, with his long stride and emphatic soles, and if his expectation of love and other pleasures served the same purpose. He was born in Pontefract, in England, a Roman name, meaning broken bridge. He had been a sick child, suffering from rheumatic fever. In his twenties he was a rector, and he and his first wife, emancipated from their time, each had a lover, and some very modern nights went on in the rectory. They traveled to Vienna to see what psychoanalysis was all about. Freud was ill and referred them to Rank, and as soon as introductions were over, his wife and Rank were lovers. "She divorced me," he said, "and had a child by that fellow. But since he wasn't the marrying kind, I gave his son my family name, and they came with me to America. She hallucinates her Otto," he told her. "Otto guides her to wise decisions."

The wife of his youth lived in a small town across the bay, and he often went over to work in her garden. Once, the girl passed her on the path, and the woman, going hastily to her car, stepped shyly aside like a country schoolteacher afraid of a student; and the girl, too, stepped sideways shyly, knowing, without ever having seen her, who she was, even though the woman—tall, broad-hipped, freck-led, a gray braid fuzzed with amber wound around her head—failed to answer the description in the girl's imagination. Some days after, the girl encountered her again, in a dream, as she was years ago: a very slender young woman in a long white skirt, her amber hair to her waist, her pale eyes coal-black with ardor.

On the way home through his neighborhood, he took her hand and tucked it into the crook of his arm, and this gesture, by drawing her up against him, hindered her step and his and slowed them down. His house was Spanish style, common to that vanward sec-tion of San Francisco. Inside, everything was heavily antique—carven furniture and cloisonné vases and thin and dusty Oriental carpets. With him lived the family that was to inherit his estate—friends who had moved in with him when his second wife died; but the atmosphere the family provided seemed, to the girl, a turn-about one, as if he were an adventurous uncle, long away and now come home to them at last, cheerily grateful, bearing a fortune. He had no children, he had no brother, and his only sister, older than he and unmarried, lived in a village in England and was in no need of an inheritance. For several months after the family moved in, the husband, who was an organist in the Episcopal Church, gave piano lessons at home, and the innocent banality of repeated notes sounded from a far room while the psychologist sat in the study with his clients. A month ago the husband left, and everything grew quiet. Occasionally, the son was seen about the house—a high school track star, small and blond like his mother, impassive like his father, his legs usually bare.

The psychologist took off his overcoat and cap, left on his muffler, and went into his study. The girl was offered tea by the mother, and they sat down at the dining table, by sunstruck windows. The woman pushed her sewing aside, and they sat in tête-a-tête position at a corner of the table.

The woman's face was too close. Now that the girl was a companion on his walks, the woman expected a womanly intimacy with her. They were going away for a week, she and her son, and would the girl please stay with the old man and take care of him? He couldn't even boil an egg or make a pot of tea, and two months ago he'd had a spell, he had fainted as he was climbing the stairs to bed. They were going to visit her sister in Kansas. She had composed a song about the loss of her husband's love, and she was taking the song to her sister. Her sister, she said, had a beautiful voice.

The sun over the woman's shoulder was like an accomplice's face, striking down the girl's resistance. And she heard herself confiding—"He asked me to marry him"—knowing that she would not and knowing why she had told the woman. Because to speculate about the possibility was to accept his esteem of her. At times it was necessary to grant the name of love to something less than love.

On the day the woman and her son left, the girl came half an hour before their departure. The woman, already wearing a coat and hat, led the way upstairs and opened, first, the door to the psychologist's bedroom. It seemed a trespass, entering that very small room, its space taken up by a mirrorless bureau and a bed of bird's-eye maple that appeared higher than most and was covered by a faded red quilt. On the bureau was a doilie, a tin box of watercolors, a nautilus shell, and a shallow drawer from a cabinet, in which lay, under glass, several tiny birds' eggs of delicate tints. And pinned to the wallpaper were pages cut from magazines of another decade—

the faces of young and wholesome beauties, girls with short, marcelled hair, cherry-red lips, plump cheeks, and little white collars. She had expected the faces of the mentors of his spirit, of Thoreau, of Gandhi, of the other great men whose words he quoted for her like passwords into the realm of wisdom.

The woman led the way across the hall and into the master bedroom. It was the woman's room and would be the girl's. A large, almost empty room, with a double bed no longer shared by her husband, a spindly dresser, a fireplace never used. It was as if a servant, or someone awaiting a more prosperous time, had moved into a room whose call for elegance she could not yet answer. The woman stood with her back to the narrow glass doors that led onto a balcony, her eyes the same cold blue of the winter sky in the row of panes.

"This house is ours," the woman said. "What's his is ours."

There was a cringe in the woman's body, so slight a cringe it would have gone unnoticed by the girl, but the open coat seemed hung upon a sudden emptiness. The girl was being told that the old man's fantasies were shaking the foundation of the house, of the son's future, and of the woman's own fantasies of an affluent old age. It was an accusation, and she chose not to answer it and not to ease the woman's fears. If she were to assure the woman that her desires had no bearing on anyone living in that house, her denial would seem untrue and go unheard, because the woman saw her now as the man saw her: a figure fortified by her youth and by her appeal and by her future, a time when all that she would want of life might come about.

Alone, she set her suitcase on a chair, refusing the drawer the woman had emptied and left open. The woman and her son were gone, after a flurry of banging doors and goodbyes. Faintly, up through the floor, came the murmur of the two men down in the study. A burst of emotion—the client's voice raised in anger or anguish and the psychologist's voice rising in order to calm. Silence again, the silence of the substantiality of the house and of the triumph of reason.

"We're both so thin," he said when he embraced her and they were alone, by the table set for supper. The remark was a jocular hint of intimacy to come. He poured a sweet blackberry wine, and was sipping the last of his second glass when she began to sip her first glass. "She offered herself to me," he said. "She came into my room not long after her husband left her. She had only her kimono on and it was open to her navel. She said she just wanted to say goodnight, but I knew what was on her mind. But she doesn't attract me. No." How lightly he told it. She felt shame, hearing about the woman's secret dismissal.

After supper he went into his study with a client, and she left a note on the table, telling him she had gone to pick up something she had forgotten to bring. Roaming out into the night to avoid as long as possible the confrontation with the unknown person within his familiar person, she rode a streetcar that went toward the ocean and, at the end of the line, remained in her seat while the motorman drank coffee from a thermos and read a newspaper. From over the sand dunes came the sound of heavy breakers. She gazed out into the dark, avoiding the reflection of her face in the glass, but after a time she turned toward it, because, half-dark and obscure her face seemed to be enticing into itself a future of love and wisdom, like a future beauty.

By the time she returned to his neighborhood the lights were out in most of the houses. The leaves of the birch in his yard shone like gold in the light from his living room window; either he had left the lamps on for her and was upstairs, asleep, or he was in the living room, waiting for the turn of her key. He was lying on the sofa.

He sat up, very erect, curving his long, bony, graceful hands one upon the other on his crossed knees. "Now I know you," he said. "You are cold. You may never be able to love anyone and so you will never be loved."

In terror, trembling, she sat down in a chair distant from him. She believed that he had perceived a fatal flaw, at last. The present moment seemed a lifetime later, and all that she had wanted of herself, of life, had never come about, because of that fatal flaw.

"You can change, however," he said. "There's time enough to change. That's why I prefer to work with the young."

She went up the stairs and into her room, closing the door. She sat on the bed, unable to stop the trembling that became even more severe in the large, humble bedroom, unable to believe that he would resort to trickery, this man who had spent so many years revealing to others the trickery of their minds. She heard him in the hallway and in his room, fussing sounds, discordant with his familiar presence. He knocked, waited a moment, and opened the door.

He had removed his shirt, and the lamp shone on the smooth flesh of his long chest, on flesh made slack by the downward pull of age. He stood in the doorway, silent, awkward, as if preoccupied with more important matters than this muddled seduction.

"We ought at least to say goodnight," he said, and when she complied he remained where he was, and she knew that he wanted her to glance up again at his naked chest to see how young it appeared and how yearning. "My door remains open," he said, and left hers open.

She closed the door, undressed, and lay down, and in the dark the call within herself to respond to him flared up. She imagined herself leaving her bed and lying down beside him. But, lying alone, observing through the narrow panes the clusters of lights atop the dark mountains across the channel, she knew that the longing was not for him but for a life of love and wisdom. There was another way to prove him wrong about her. There was another way to prove that she was a loving woman, that there was no fatal flaw, that she was filled with love, and the other way was to give herself over to expectation, as to a passion.

Rising early, she found a note under her door. His handwriting was of many peaks, the aspiring style of a century ago. He likened her behavior to that of his first wife, way back before they were married, when she had tantalized him so frequently and always fled. It was a humorous, forgiving note, changing her into that other girl of sixty years ago. The weather was fair, he wrote, and he was off by early bus to his mountain across the bay, there to climb his trails, staff in hand and knapsack on his back. *And I still love you.*

That evening he was jovial again. He drank his blackberry wine at supper; sat with her on the sofa and read aloud from his collected essays, *Religion and Science in the Light of Psychoanalysis,* often closing the small, red leather book to repudiate the theories of his youth; gave her, as gifts, Kierkegaard's *Purity of Heart* and three novels of Conrad in leather bindings; and appeared again, briefly, at her door, his chest bare.

She went out again, a few nights later, to visit a friend, and he escorted her graciously to the door. "Come back any time you need to see me," he called after her. Puzzled, she turned on the path. The light from within the house shone around his dark figure in the rectangle of the open door. "But I live here for now," she called back, flapping her coat out on both sides to make herself more evident to him. "Of course! Of course! I forgot!" he laughed, stamping his foot, dismayed with himself. And she knew that her presence was not so intense a presence as they thought. It would not matter to him as the days went by, as the years left to him went by, that she had not come into his bed.

On the last night, before they went upstairs and after switching off the lamps, he stood at a distance from her, gazing down. "I am senile now, I think," he said. "I see signs of it. Landslides go on in there." The declaration in the dark, the shifting feet, the gazing down, all were disclosures of his fear that she might, on this last night, come to him at last.

The girl left the house early, before the woman and her son appeared. She looked for him through the house and found him at a window downstairs, almost obscured at first sight by the swath of morning light in which he stood. With shaving brush in hand and a white linen handtowel around his neck, he was watching a flock of birds in branches close to the pane, birds so tiny she mistook them for fluttering leaves. He told her their name, speaking in a whisper toward the birds, his profile entranced as if by his whole life.

The girl never entered the house again, and she did not see him for a year. In that year she got along by remembering his words of wisdom, lifting her head again and again above deep waters to hear his voice. When she could not hear him anymore, she phoned him and they arranged to meet on the beach below his house. The only difference she could see, watching him from below, was that he descended the long stairs with more care, as if time were now underfoot. Other than that, he seemed the same. But as they talked, seated side by side on a rock, she saw that he had drawn back unto himself his life's expectations. They were way inside, and they required, now, no other person for their fulfilling.

Shoptalk #16
Time and Promise and Luck

The first novelists I've paid the most attention to are those I've known personally at Iowa over the years. . . . They're all fine writers. . . . And damn, I wish they were all here now, in person, so we could sit around and drink and shout and get into wild, violent arguments about fiction, and end up singing songs and telling jokes and acting silly; then when everybody started going home to sober up and get back to work, I'd like very much to shake their hands and to wish them luck. Because plain luck, after all, may be the one thing a good writer needs most. I think it probably *is* the hardest and loneliest profession in the world, this crazy, obsessive business of trying to be a good writer. None of us ever knows how much time he has left, or how well he'll be able to use that time, or whether, even if he does use his time well, his work will ever withstand and survive the terrible, inexorable indifference of time itself.

(Richard Yates, "Interview," vol. 1, no. 3, 1972)

Shoptalk #17
Self-estimation

I think as a writer you constantly rearrange your estimation of yourself and what you've done. . . . We look back on our works and we wish we had done them differently—at least I do. I think it is inevitable because when we look back we're something else, we've altered our perspectives, history itself has formed us, played

with us, caused us to look at life perhaps . . . well, in a
thousand different ways. So therefore we always call
our work into question. Some of it you hope will remain
because it was written out of some ultimate imperative
that has nothing to do with history . . . but I submit this
is quite rare, and we are left with our imperfect offer-
ings and we should, I suppose, just be thankful that
what we have done is acceptable.

(William Styron, "Reflections," vol. 1, no. 3, 1972)

Resources for Writers

ON CONTEMPORARY WRITING CAREERS
AND THE WRITING LIFE

Editing and Publishing and Markets

A Few Good Voices in My Head: Occasional Pieces on Writing, Editing, and Reading My Contemporaries, by Theodore Solotaroff (Harper Perenial Library, 1987). The best writing about the realities of editing and publishing since Maxwell Perkins's letters.

Editor to Author: The Letters of Maxwell Perkins, ed. John Hall Wheelock (Scribers, 1950). A rich, behind-the-scenes glimpse through the letters of the preeminent literary editor into the process of reading, editing, and coaching the writing and publishing careers of F. Scott Fitzgerald, Thomas Wolfe, and Ernest Hemingway, among others.

"What White Publishers Won't Print," by Zora Neale Hurston (from *I Love Myself When I Am Laughing,* 1979; reprinted in *The Story and Its Writer: An Introduction to Short Fiction,* ed. Ann Charters [Bedford St. Martin's, 1999]). Hurston's manifesto for writing the truths of African-American lives: "For various reasons, the average, struggling, non-morbid Negro is the best-kept secret in America."

The Culture and Commerce of the American Short Story, by Andrew Levy (Cambridge University Press, 1994). Studies the "how-to" movement in American fiction writing from the 1920s, the development of the American short story in relation to magazines, and the rise of writing programs. Readable and informative.

"Thinking about Readers," by William B. Goodman (*Daedalus: Journal of the American Academy of Arts and Sciences*, winter, 1983, a special issue on "Reading Old and New"). A former editor at Harcourt Brace Jovanovich, Harvard University Press, and David R. Godine examines the statistical realities of the market for "high culture," then and now, and finds readers both fit and few.

Writers at Work

Mystery and Manners: Occasional Prose, by Flannery O'Connor (Farrar, Straus and Giroux, 1969). O'Connor's essays—such as "Catholic Novelists and Their Readers," "Some Aspects of the Grotesque in the Southern Fiction," and "Novelist and Believer"—attempt to teach the art by which she is to be seen.

One Writer's Beginnings, by Eudora Welty (Harvard University Press, 1995). Memoirs concerning the shaping of the writer's sensibility.

Writing Past Dark: Envy, Fear, Distraction and Other Dilemmas in the Writer's Life, by Bonnie Friedman (Harper Perennial, 1993). Writing about writing that rises to the level of eloquence of literature itself. The chapters on "Envy, the Writer's Disease" and on breaking the taboos of family privacy are particularly apt for younger writers.

A Writer's Time: Making the Time to Write, by Kenneth Aitchity (W. W. Norton, 1995). Suggestions on how to find and better organize time in order to write.

A Writing Life, by Annie Dillard (included in *Three by Annie Dillard,* 1990, Harper Perennial). Meditations on the process of writing, infused with spiritual intensity. "At its best the sensation of writing is that of any unmerited grace."

A Moveable Feast, by Ernest Hemingway (Simon & Schuster, 1996). A classic memoir of Paris in the twenties and the literary and artististic encounters of the young Hemingway with Joyce, Stein, Fitzgerald, Picasso, and others.

Bird By Bird, by Annie Lamont (Pantheon, 1994). As a writer and teacher, Lamont refers to many of the classic books about writing listed here and distills their passion and their tips on craft into her own step-by-step, seasoned guide on how to write and how to manage the writer's life.

Writers at Work: The Paris Review Interviews, ed. George Plimpton (Viking Penguin, 1988). Collected interviews with prominent writers from the literary magazine that all but invented the form; rich with insights into each writer's work, writing process, and career.

The Writers Life: Intimate Thoughts on Work, Love, Inspiration, and Fame from the Diaries of the World's Great Writers, ed. Carol Edgarian and Tom Jenks (Vintage, 1997). Excerpts from famous writers' diaries and journals, ranging from Tolstoy to Virginia Woolf to Gerald Early. "There is delicious surprise and comfort," write the editors, "in discovering that others, even the famous, *especially* the famous, find life just as unwieldy and difficult as the rest of us."

On Writer's Block: Removing the Barriers to Creativity, by Victoria
Nelson (Houghton Mifflin, 1993). Suggestions on how to counter
fear and get free to start writing.

Handbooks, Rhetorics, and Commentaries on Craft

The Art and Craft of Novel Writing, by Oakley Hall (Story Press,
1989). A master teacher and novelist's guide to all aspects of the
craft of storytelling, with particular encouragement for writers to
learn from reading as they write. A new volume, *How Fiction
Works*, is due from Story Press in 2000.

Aspects of the Novel, by E. M. Forster (Harcourt, Brace & Company, 1956). In my view, Forster's is the least pretentious, most
readable and suggestive writing about the mystery of fiction ever
written. Among his influential distinctions is the notion of "aspects" rather than formulaic ingredients or fast rules, and, in his
chapter "People," the notion of "flat" and "round" characters.

Fiction and the Figures of Life, by William Gass (David R. Godine,
1978). Gass is brilliant in his questioning of traditional forms and
his insistence on innovation, in keeping with what critic Richard
Poirier called "the performing self."

On Moral Fiction: The Art of Fiction, by John Gardner (Basic
Books, 1979). A persuasive apologia for the moral imperative of
great fiction, perhaps overstated by Gardner in reaction to the experiments in literary form and theory being championed in the
1970s by critics and writers such as John Barth, Robert Scholes,
Robert Coover, and William Gass.

The Art of the Novel, by Henry James (Scribners, 1934). James's critical prefaces to his own fiction, with an introduction by R. P. Blackmur. The intellectual novelist's difficult discussions of all aspects of fiction, character, plot, setting, including references to novelists from Hawthorne to George Eliot, Dickens, Turgenev, Flaubert, and Robert Louis Stevenson.

The Eye of the Story: Selected Essays and Reviews, by Eudora Welty, ed. Erroll McDonald (Vintage, 1990). Luminous meditations on the art of writing, with comments on the author's own craft, along with penetrating insights into the art of Jane Austen, E. M Forster, Virginia Woolf, and Anton Chekhov.

The Joy of Writing Sex: A Guide for Fiction Writers, by Elizabeth Benedict (Story Press, 1996). Well-written, informed, and cogent focus on sex as one of the universal experiences to be portrayed in fiction, with examples ranging from classical writers to contemporaries.

The Lonely Voice: A Study of the Short Story, by Frank O'Connor, with an introduction by Russell Banks (Harper Colophon Books, 1985). A genial, if subjective view of the medium and message of short fiction, with O'Connor's perceptive reading of the possibilities of different styles. The chapters on Joyce and Hemingway are helpful in questioning the spell of impressionism and its influence on younger writers.

The Rhetoric of Fiction, by Wayne C. Booth (University of Illinois, 1983). An exhaustive, perhaps definitive academic analysis of the form of fiction, with a detailed classification for narrative strategies: outside and inside narrators, reliable and unreliable, re-stricted and omniscient, and so forth. *The Rhetoric of Irony* is a companion work (University of Illinois, 1975).

Introduction to *The Nigger of the Narcissus*, by Joseph Conrad (Ox-ford University Press, 1999). Contains Conrad's literary insistence foremost on making the reader "see."

Writing Fiction: A Guide to Narrative Craft, fifth edition, by Janet Burroway (Addison Wesley Longman, 1999). One of the most widely used guides in writing programs, including stories for new writers to read, tips on craft, assignments, and a section on re-writing.

The Art of Fiction, by David Lodge (Viking Peguin, 1994). Follow-ing the format and spirit of E. M. Forster, Lodge touches on a vari-ety of "aspects" in brief, erudite essays: on the use of the telephone in fiction, for instance, or narration in the teenage slang he labels "skaz." The examples from classical fiction have left some of my students feeling poorly read.

The Writing Room: Keys to the Craft of Fiction and Poetry, by Eve Shelnutt (Longstreet, 1989). In Shelnutt's words, this book "em-phasizes the very hard work that young writers must do in appren-ticeship to form, language, and reading of literature."

Three Genres: The Writing of Poetry, Fiction, and Drama, by Ste-phen Minot (Prentice Hall, 1988). A widely used text, especially for introductory creative writing courses.

What If?: Writing Exercises for Fiction Writers, by Anne Bernays
and Pamela Painter (Harper Collins, 1991). Writing topics and
ideas to prompt beginning writers, along with sample responses
by students.

For a New Novel, by Alain Robbe-Grillet (Northwestern University Press, 1989). One of the influential manifestos for the French
"new novel" of the 1950s, this essay remains provocative in dis-
missing conventional ideas of story, such as the very "aspects" discussed by E. M. Forster. For Robbe-Grillet, the emotion of perception itself is "story."

*The Agony and the Ego: The Art and Strategy of Fiction Writing Ex-
plored,* ed. Claire Boylan (Penguin, 1993). Essays about craft and
the writer's career by Brian Moore, Lorrie Moore, Fay Weldon,
and others. Lorrie Moore's "Better and Sicker" is recommended.

Burning Down the House: Essays on Fiction, by Charles Baxter
(Graywolf Press, 1997). The best recent writing by a contemporary short story writer and novelist on what he considers to be un-
derdiscussed aspects of contemporary fiction and its value. Topics
include "Dysfunctional Narratives," "Rhyming Action," and
"Against Epiphanies."

Informative Websites for Writers

Literary Fiction Home Page, by Carol Edgarian and Tom Jenks
(http://www.narrativemagazine.org/). Novelists Jenks and Edgarian offer workshops and editing services and feature their own
publications, but this site also includes lists of favorite authors and
recent books, and comprehensive literary links.

Web del Sol (http://www.webdelsol.com/). A reader's digest of the best from print literary magazines, including news of the literary world, literary links to featured magazines, and a new electronic magazine feature publishing new work.

Ploughshares (http://www.emerson.edu/ploughshares/). Includes the literary magazine's history, samples and information about recent and upcoming issues, and literary links to recommended literary magazines and other helpful sites.

Mississippi Review (http://sushi.st.usm.edu/mrw/links.html). The most comprehensive list of links to magazines and presses publishing fiction, and to literary and related sites of publishing interest.

PEN New England (http://www.pen-ne.org/). Regional organization of professional poets, writers, and editors, with an events calendar and newsletter.

Council of Literary Magazines and Presses (http://www.litline. org/litline.html/). Listings for small presses, journals, and literary links to additional presses, journals, organizations, and other recommended sites.

Writers' Conferences and Festivals (http://www.litline.org/ wcandf.html/). Links to the major writers' conferences, including Bread Loaf, Squaw Valley, Indiana, Sewanee, and more.

Poets & Writers (http://www.pw.org/). The comprehensive service organization for writers, with publishing advice, contests, news of the writing world, lists of grants and awards, a directory of poets and writers, literary links, and site search engine.

Writers Network (http://www.writers.net). An internet resource for writers, editors, publishers, and agents, including a searchable internet directory of writers and an internet directory of literary agents. It is a free service.

Associated Writing Programs (http://web.gmu.edu/departments/awp/). The central site for information on undergraduate and graduate writing programs; also for services and award competitions available to writers, and publications such the *Writer's Chronicle* (from the Associated Writing Programs, George Mason University).

Agent Research and Evaluation (http://www.agentresearch.com). A for-pay site that seeks to "empower authors by providing them with extensive information about virtually every active literary and dramatic rights agent in the U.S., Canada, and the U. K., then [to] encourage them to use that data to select the agent who is right for them, and convince that agent to take a serious look at their work." Fees are $35 for a newsletter subscription, $45 for a list of agents, and $99 for a search.

Lighthouse Writers Workshops (http://www.lighthousewriters.com). Maintained by writers in the Denver area, this attractive site features an on-line fiction magazine, an events calendar, and valuable literary links, including *Strunk and White* for style.

National Endowment for the Arts (http://arts.endow.gov/). Grants for published writers.

PreviewPort.com (http://www.previewport.com). An international compendium of author-authorized websites, designed to connect authors, publishers, and readers worldwide. PreviewPort launches poets and writers to the growing Internet audience through the online serial release of new work, designs and hosts author websites, coordinates key city literary calendars, and represents new writing of member authors to publishers, agents, and producers.

Cautionary Tales

The Enemies of Promise, by Cyril Connelly (Persea Books, 1983). Suggestive essays, including the long title essay, which explores the temptations that have defeated or limited significant literary careers.

Silences, by Tillie Olsen (Peter Smith, Publisher, 1984). Olsen's impassioned, groundbreaking feminist study of the compromise of talent by patriarchal society as it affected many nineteenth- and twentieth-century women writers.

Advertisements for Myself, by Norman Mailer (Harvard University Press, 1992). Mailer's account of his own creative "self-editing" and the self-promotion of his novel *The Deer Park,* portrayed as the defense of promise against the literary establishment of the 1960s.

The Thirsty Muse: Alcoholism and the American Writer, by Tom Dardis (Tichnor and Fields, 1989). A who's who of major American writers who were alcoholics, along with in-depth studies of alcoholism in the careers of William Faulkner, Ernest Hemingway, Eugene O'Neill, and F. Scott Fitzgerald.

The Crack-Up, by F. Scott Fitzgerald (New Directions, 1956). Essays detailing the writer's midlife breakdown, together with letters and notebook entries, edited by Edmund Wilson.

The Savage God: A Study of Suicide, by A. Alavarez (W. W. Norton, 1990). A literary and philosophical history of suicide, and a study in particular of Sylvia Plath's suicide and the author's own personal issues.

Darkness Visible: A Memoir of Madness, by William Styron (Random House, 1994). An eloquent chronicle of depression at the height of the writer's career, and a testament to the saving effects of drug therapy.

The Adventure

RECOMMENDED LITERARY MAGAZINES FOR SHORT FICTION

General Advice

Before you start sending your work out, you should be confident about its quality, and seek constructive criticism from local writers' groups or workshops, writer friends, and writing conference and program mentors. Read the short fiction award annuals for clues to kindred sensibilities, then look up the magazines where the award-winning works first appeared, as places likely to be receptive to your own work. Be well informed about the magazines you submit work to: read recent issues in addition to checking the magazines' guidelines on the web or in such directories as those listed below. When you are ready to submit a story, look only for a professional yes or no from editors, not instruction. Select up to five magazines, ranging from those with the largest circulations to the smaller and lesser known, whose contents you follow and admire. Be especially alert for magazines just starting up, since they will have the smallest backlog of submissions and will be seeking to develop new contributors.

Keep your cover letter modest and to the point, stating the title of the story. Briefly mention your credentials as a writer, your previous publications (if any), any writing program you are attending (or have attended), and any writers by name who have encouraged you to submit *this* story to *this* magazine. Often an honest mention of a respected writer or writing program in your cover letter will direct your manuscript to a more advanced reader in the screening system.

I would recommend submitting your work simultaneously (unless you choose a magazine that announces it will not consider simultaneous submissions), along with the statement "This is a simultaneous submission and I will withdraw it elsewhere on earliest acceptance."

Always enclose a self-addressed, stamped envelope for return of your manuscript (or, if your work is on computer, instruct the magazine to destroy the printout and let you know by an enclosed postcard if the answer is no). Query the editor(s) by mail about the status of your submission after ninety days, and if you get no response, withdraw your work and submit it elsewhere. Should a simulaneous submission be accepted, be sure to notify the other magazines immediately, as promised, to withdraw it from their consideration. Persist with any work you know is valid. Subscribe to magazines you honor, whether they publish you or not.

At present, to my knowledge, only on-line electronic magazines invite submissions by e-mail. As a rule you should not submit work or correspond to print magazines by e-mail.

Larger Circulation Literary Magazines with Relatively Mainstream Sensibilities

DoubleTake, 55 Davis Square, Somerville, MA 02144

Five Points, English Department, Georgia State University, 33 Gilmer St., SE, Atlanta, GA 30303

Georgia Review, University of Georgia, Athens, GA 30602

Glimmer Train, 710 SW Madison, #504, Portland, OR 97205

Grand Street, 131 Varick St., Rm. 206, New York, NY 10013

Granta, 1755 Broadway, 5th Floor, New York, NY 10019

Kenyon Review, Kenyon College, Gambier, OH 43022

Missouri Review, 1507 Hillcrest Hall, University of Missouri, Columbia, MO 65211

Paris Review, 541 East 72nd St., New York, NY 10021

Ploughshares, Emerson College, 100 Beacon St., Boston, MA 02116

Triquarterly, Northwestern University, 2020 Ridge Ave., Evanston, IL 60208

Vignette, P.O. Box 109, Hollywood, CA 90078

Virginia Quarterly Review, 1 West Range, Charlottesville, VA 22903

Zoetrope: All Story, 126 Fifth Ave., Suite 300, New York, NY 10011

ZYZZYVA, 41 Sutter St., PMB 1400, San Francisco, CA 94104

Other Literary Magazines
with Relatively Mainstream Sensibilities

Agni Review, Boston University, 236 Bay State Rd., Boston, MA 02215

Antioch Review, P.O. Box 148, Yellow Springs, OH 45387

Arkansas Review, Department of English and Philosophy, P.O. Box 1890, Arkansas State University, State University, AR 72467

Berkeley Fiction Review, 703 Eshleman Hall, University of California, Berkeley, CA 94720

Boulevard, 4579 Laclede Ave., #332, St. Louis, MO 63108

Colorado Review, Colorado State University, Ft. Collins, CO 80523

Cottonwood Review, University of Kansas, Box J, 400 Kansas Union, Lawrence, KS 66045

Crazy Horse, English Department, University of Arkansas at Little Rock, 2801 S. University, Little Rock, AR 72204

Epoch, 251 Goldwin Smith Hall, Cornell University, Ithaca, NY 14853

Faultline, University of California, Irvine, P.O. Box 599–4960, Irvine, CA 92716

Iowa Review, 308 EPB, University of Iowa, Iowa City, IA 52242

The MacGuffin, Schoolcraft College, 18600 Haggerty Rd., Liyonia, MI 48152

Marlboro Review, P.O. Box 243, Marlboro, VT 05344

Michigan Quarterly Review, University of Michigan, 3032 Rackham Bldg., Ann Arbor, MI 48109

Nebraska Review, Creative Writing Program, University of Nebraska, Omaha, NE 68182

New England Review, Middlebury College, Middlebury, VT 05753

New Letters, University of Missouri, Kansas City, MO 64110

Nimrod, University of Tulsa, 600 S. College, Tulsa, OK 74104–3189

North American Review, University of Northern Iowa, Cedar Falls, IA 50614

Ontario Review, 9 Honey Brook Dr., Princeton, NJ 08540

Prairie Schooner, P.O. Box 880334, University of Nebraska, Lincoln, NE 68588

Puerto del Sol, Box 3-E, New Mexico State University, Las Cruces, NM 88001

Rosebud, P.O. Box 459, Cambridge, WI 53523

Santa Clara Review, Santa Clara University, Box 3212, Santa Clara, CA 95053–3212

Santa Monica Review, 1900 Pico Blvd., Santa Monica, CA 90405

Sewanee Review, University of the South, Sewanee, TN 37375

Shenandoah, Troubador Theatre, 2nd Floor, Washington and Lee University, Lexington, VA 24450–0303

Southern Review, 43 Allen Hall, Louisiana State University, Baton Rouge, LA 70803-5005

Southwest Review, 307 Fondren Library West, P.O. Box 750374, Southern Methodist University, Dallas, TX 75275-0374

Tampa Review, University of Tampa, 401 W. Kennedy Blvd., Tampa, FL 33606

Third Coast, English Department, West Michigan University, Kalamazoo, MI 49007

Literary Magazines
with Feminist Agendas or Interests

The American Voice (ceasing publication with issue #50, 2000), 1215 Heyburn Bldg., 332 West Broadway, Louisville, KY 40202

Calyx, P.O. Box B, Corvallis, OR 97339

Earth's Daughters, Box 41, Central Park Station, Buffalo, NY 14215

Kalliope, Florida Community College at Jacksonville, 3939 Roosevelt Blvd., Jacksonville, FL 32205

Thirteenth Moon, English Department, SUNY, Albany, NY 12222

Yellow Silk, P.O. Box 6374, Albany, CA 94704

Literary Magazines
with Multcultural/Post-Colonial Agendas

Caribbean Writer, University of the Virgin Islands, RR 02, Box 10,000 Kingshill, St. Croix, VI 00850

Callaloo, Department of English, Bryan Hall, University of Virginia, Charlottesville, VA 22903

Florida Review, Department of English, University of Central Florida, Orlando, FL 32816

Manoa, English Department, University of Hawaii, Honolulu, HI 96822

Literary Magazines
with Avant-Garde Agendas

Another Chicago Magazine, 3709 N. Kenmore, Chicago, IL 60613

Black Ice, English Department, Publications Center, Campus Box 494, Boulder, CO 80309-0494

Chicago Review, University of Chicago, 5801 S. Kenwood, Chicago, IL 60637

Conjunctions, Bard College, Annandale-on-Hudson, NY 12504

Fiction, c/o Department of English, The City College, 138th & Convent Ave., New York, NY 10031

Fiction International, Department of English, San Diego State University, San Diego, CA 92182

Fish Stories, 5412 N. Clark, South Suite, Chicago, IL 60640

Frank, 32 rue Edouard Vaillant, 93100 Montreuil, France

Mississippi Review, Box 5144 USM, Hattiesburg, MS 39406-5144

Sulfur, 210 Washtenaw Ave., Ypsilanti, MI 48197

Literary Magazines with Queer Agendas

Modern Words, 350 Bay Street, No. 100, Box 325, San Francisco, CA 94133

Literary Magazines on the Web (for information, marketing, and sometimes for electronic publication)

Boston Review (http://bostonreview.mit.edu)

Chicago Review (http://humanities.uchicago.edu/humanities/review/)

Creative Nonfiction (http://www.creativenonfiction.org)

DoubleTake (http://www.duke.edu/doubletake/)

Five Points (http://www.gsu.edu/~wwwmag/index2.html)

Fourteen Hills, the SFSU Review (http://mercury.sfsu.edu/'hills/14hills.html)

Literal Latte (http://www.literal-latte.com)

Literary Review (http://www.cais.com/aesir/fiction/tlr/)

Kenyon Review (kenyonreview@kenyon/edu)

Mississippi Review, web edition (http://sushi.st.usm.edu/~barthelm/index.html)

Missouri Review (http://www.missouri.edu/'moreview/)

Nerve (http://www.nervemag.com)

North American Review (http://webdelsol.com/NorthAmReview/NAR/)

Paris Review (http://www.voyagerco.com/PR/)

Ploughshares (http://www.emerson.edu/ploughshares/)

Prairie Schooner (http://www.unl.edu/schooner/psmain.htm)

Santa Clara Review (http://www.sereview@scuacc.scu.edu)

Sewanee Review (http://www.sewanee.edu/serview/Home.html)

Sycamore Review (http://www.sla.purdue.edu/academic/engl/sycamore/)

Third Coast (http://www.wmich.edu/thirdcoast)

Yellow Silk (http://www.enjuew.com.magazines/yellow_silk/current/issue48.toc.html)

You Are Here (http://geog.arizona.edu/~web/youarehere/)

Zoetrope (http://www.zoetrope-stories.com/)

ZYZZYVA (http://www.zyzzyva.org)

Webzines

For the burgeoning universe of *webzines*—not a serious resource for literary writers, in my opinion, but nevertheless a venue of fine madness that interests many students and recalls the "alternative press" days of the mimeograph revolution in the 1960s—search the word "zines" at http://www.yahoo.com/ or other search engines; see also *The Book of Zines,* by Chip Rowe (Owl Books, 1997) and its related website, http://zinebook.com/. Some representative literary zines are:

CrossConnect (http://tech1.dccs.upenn.edu/~xconnect/)

Hawk (http://gate.cruzio.com/~hawk/)

Highbeams (http://stu.beloit.edu/~highbe/index.html)

Grist On-line (http://www.thing.net)

Silence (http://www.altx.com/silence/)

Switched-on Gutenberg (http://weber.u.washington.edu/~jnh/)

Zipzap (http://www.dnai.com/~zipzap)

Sources for Additional Listings and Information

Best American Short Stories (Houghton Mifflin, annual). Provides information on where the prize-winning stories were first published. See also the list of distinctive stories and the list of magazines scanned for "bests" for the collection.

The Pushcart Prize (Pushcart Press, annual). Ditto.

The Beacon Best: Creative Writing by Women and Men of All Colors (Beacon Press, annual). Ditto.

Directory of Literary Magazines (Council of Literary Magazines and Presses/Moyer Bell, annual). Complete information on 500 titles.

Literary Market Place (R. R. Bowker, annual). An expensive tome available in most public libraries, including a section for literary magazines.

Directory of Little Magazines and Small Presses (Dustbooks, annual). Complete information on some 4,000 or more titles and publishers.

Fiction Writer's Market Place (R. R. Bowker, annual). Has a section on literary magazines as well as sections on national cultural magazines and special interest magazines.

Advertisements and announcements in *Poets & Writers Magazine, The Writer's Chronicle,* the *New York Review of Books.*

Credits

Acknowledgments

*Thanks again to my wife, Connie;
to Don Lee at* Ploughshares;
and to my editor, Helene Atwan.